THE 1830 REVOLUTION IN FRANCE

Also by Pamela M. Pilbeam and published by Macmillan and published by Palgrave Macmillan

SAINT-SIMONIANS IN NINETEENTH-CENTURY FRANCE:
From Free Love to Algeria (2014)

THE MIDDLE CLASSES IN EUROPE, 1789–1914:
France, Germany, Italy and Russia

The 1830 Revolution in France

Pamela M. Pilbeam
Reader in Modern European History
Royal Holloway
University of London

palgrave

© Pamela M. Pilbeam 1991

All rights reserved. No reproduction, copy or transmission of this publication may be made without written permission.

No paragraph of this publication may be reproduced, copied or transmitted save with written permission or in accordance with the provisions of the Copyright, Designs and Patents Act 1988, or under the terms of any licence permitting limited copying issued by the Copyright Licensing Agency, 90 Tottenham Court Road, London W1P 9HE.

Any person who does any unauthorised act in relation to this publication may be liable to criminal prosecution and civil claims for damages.

First edition 1991
Reprinted (with minor alterations) 1994

Published by
THE MACMILLAN PRESS LTD
Houndmills, Basingstoke, Hampshire RG21 2XS
and London
Companies and representatives
throughout the world

ISBN 978-0-333-61998-8   ISBN 978-0-230-37686-1 (eBook)
DOI 10.1057/9780230376861

A catalogue record for this book is available
from the British Library.

To Stephen, Ashka, Rhys and Llewellyn

Contents

	Preface	ix
1	Historians and the Revolution	1
2	The Political Crises of the Bourbon Restoration	13
3	The Economic Crisis and the Revolution	37
4	The 'Three Glorious Days'	60
5	The Liberalism of the Orleanist Settlement	80
6	Religion and Revolutionary Politics	99
7	The Bourgeois Revolution	121
8	Une Révolution Escamotée	150
9	Conclusion	187
	Notes	195
	Bibliography	216
	Index	234

Preface

The 1830 revolution is depicted here as more than the Parisian bourgeois victory of the 'Three Glorious Days'. The chronological span of this investigation stretches from the early 1820s to 1835; the geographical span to as extensive a range of departmental archives as purse, family loyalty and professional demands would permit. The approach is thematic, asking how far the revolution can be seen as bourgeois, liberal, artisan or anti-clerical. The exploration of these issues is frequently traced over a broad canvas, relating the situation of the early nineteenth century to that of the 1790s. It is a history of revolution and popular unrest in and around 1830, but it also investigates the significance of revolution in general.

I owe a great debt of gratitude to Professor Alfred Cobban who guided me in my initial PhD foray into 1830 and to all the members of his research seminar at the Institute of Historical Research, London who listened patiently to early drafts of these chapters, posed searching questions and offered wise counsel. On the sage advice of one contemporary, I shall name no names, leaving them the option of receiving the final result with favour. Earlier versions of several chapters have appeared as articles in learned journals. I am delighted to have the opportunity to record my thanks to many patient and helpful archivists: in the *Archives Nationales*, the *Archives de la Guerre* and in departmental and municipal archives too numerous to mention, although I must single out Mlle Odile Colin, formerly *archiviste-en-chef* at Chaumont, Haute-Marne. I am also grateful to librarians, both in the *Bibliothèque Nationale* and many municipal libraries. A very special thank you is due to my undergraduate students, particularly the members of special and optional courses on French history, and also to all those extramural students who enthusiastically shared my preoccupation with early nineteenth-century France. I must thank the University of London, especially the Central Research Fund and the Institute of Historical Research, and the French government, who provided grants and scholarships to support lengthy research in French archives. Above all, it is a privilege to be able to record my heartfelt thanks to my husband, Stephen and our children, Ashka, Rhys and Llewellyn, who unstintingly and with good humour and love shared their lives with this project.

Pamela Pilbeam

1
Historians and the Revolution

The events and significance of the 1830 revolution in France have been largely ignored by academics and social commentators. The most recent account in French was written in the immediate aftermath of the strikes and riots of 1968,[1] while the most comprehensive version in English remains that of David Pinkney, now translated into French.[2] The French are inclined to be somewhat dismissive or even embarrassed when discussing the 1830 revolution. Curiously, despite a generation of intense 'revision' of 1789, from which the middle classes have been almost banished, 1830 is still frequently designated as a 'bourgeois' revolution. French thinking on the 'Three Glorious Days' is dominated by the contrasting views of the modern Catholic historian of the Restoration, Bertier de Sauvigny, for whom the revolution was a brief and unfortunate Parisian aberration, and Karl Marx, for whom it was a stage in the inevitable accession to power of an entrepreneurial bourgeoisie. The revolutions in the rest of Europe in 1830 have also been overlooked, with the exception of one recent pioneering investigation.[3]

The anarchic formlessness of revolutions makes them irresistably fascinating to historians, eager to tidy and organise. But 1830 was apparently a 'controlled' revolution of 'three glorious days' in Paris, whose modest achievements were welcomed by the rest of the country, which perhaps explains the very limited attention it has received from historians. Three major versions of the revolution emerged in the 1830s. The defeated supporters of the Restoration monarchy saw 1830 as the deplorable resurrection and continuation of 1789. The Orleanist victors either regarded the July Days as an unfortunate and embarrassing accident and labelled Charles X the revolutionary or at most expected only modest changes from the revolution. Early socialists and republicans were even more aware than the Orleanists that 1830 had changed little. They described the revolution as 'bourgeois' because they deplored the conservatism and continuity displayed by the new regime. In less than a generation the victors of 1830 were themselves defeated. The short-lived republic that took over was itself replaced by the revival of a Bonapartist empire, under the control of Napoleon's great-nephew. These events inevitably reshaped attitudes to 1830.

In considering the significance of the revolution, it will be valuable to examine these three traditions of revolutionary historiography: the clerico-legitimist, the Orleanist and the republican. To consider first the Restoration royalists, or legitimists as they were called after 1830. The legitimists needed to prepare a convincing account of 1830 with great speed, especially the handful of members of Charles X's last government who were arrested and tried by the Chamber of Peers, accused of causing the revolution. Polignac was the head of Charles X's last government and the main figure in the trial. Accused of causing the July Days, he blamed these events partly on the constitution of 1814, which, he argued, had set up an insoluble conflict between monarchical and democratic principles and which hedged royal power around with too many restrictions.[4] Above all, he asserted, the liberal opposition in parliament had been subversive, and together with liberal newspapers and organisations such as their electoral organisation, *Aide-toi, le ciel t'aidera*, 'a secret and factious power led public opinion astray and threatened royal authority, tending towards the complete disorganisation of society.'[5] Other former ministers went further and suggested that the liberals were actually planning armed resistance to Charles.[6] All were in accord that the four ordinances were justified and entirely within the spirit of article fourteen of the constitution.[7] Interestingly, some convinced royalists, like Martignac, who preceded Polignac and defended him in his trial, condemned the ordinances as 'a brusque invasion made into our laws by royal power.'[8] Some legitimists tried to adopt a defence of ignorance. De Semonville declared that the excitement of the revolution was such that he was quite unable to recall his own role on 29 July. When he composed his memoirs, published in 1894, and presumably recollected in tranquillity, he was more able to give a detailed account of those twenty-four hours.[9]

Although legitimists were at variance in the degree to which they believed that the liberals were entirely responsible for the outbreak of revolution, their general attitudes were representative of a clerico-royalist interpretation of revolutions. All revolution was deplorable and 1830 was a detestable repeat of 1789. 1789 had meant the destruction of an *ancien régime* political order whose dimensions quickly became romanticised in the nineteenth century. The Revolution of 1789 was a challenge to an equally idealised social hierarchy. In short, repeated revolutions precipitated traditional France into chaos and anarchy. Although the legitimist cause was lost in 1830, its adherents cannot be overlooked, for their defeat was limited to the national political arena. They continued to represent a large section of the wealthy notables, predominantly through their landed property, but also through industrial and commercial investment in the case of the most successful. They also retained their local pre-eminence, particularly in western France. This local political, social and economic power was not dented until well into the second half of the nineteenth century, and legitimist criticism of Orleanism as a national political movement was rendered credible by the overthrow of Louis-Philippe himself in 1848. For legitimist writers the July Monarchy was a stage in the political, social, economic and moral collapse of France. The relative decline of the economy of the clerico-legitimist west and the detestable features of the advance of bourgeois capitalist industry in northern France were, for them, all part of the evil consequences of revolution.

The important role played by the legitimist notables in the army officer corps of the Third Republic, the growth of an extreme right-wing nationalist movement with organisations like *Action Française*, ensured that the legitimist view or revolution would not die. Indeed, the development of the fascist-style leagues in inter-war France and the creation of the Vichy regime after defeat in 1940 underlined the resilience of this doom-laden perspective of France's history since 1789. The anti-revolutionary philosophy of the extreme right encapsulated a detestation of all aspects of modernity, which to them was intimately linked with 1789. In it was encompassed all that was evil, ugly and un-French in the modern world. For the extreme right, the Revolution was multi-faceted, with political, social and economic consequences. Every feature of nineteenth-century change they excoriated was born of the Revolution: the decline of catholicism, the growth of lay education, the upsurge of socialism, the excrescence of a burgeoning bureaucracy and the withering of the old provinces, the corruption of democratic politicians, an insidiously expanding

Jewish presence in French culture and society, the shrinking status of France *vis-à-vis* Germany and, above all, the triumph of the bourgeoisie, which to the extreme right was the quintessential feature of the impact of 1789, confirmed in 1830. Drumont had a powerful and sympathetic audience for his claim, 'Thanks to the principles of 1789, so skilfully exploited by the Jews, France was falling into total decay.'[10] However extreme and ludicrous such a compendium of grievances may sound when expounded by writers like Drumont, there can be no doubt that this philosophy is far from dead. Beau de Lomenie's diatribe against bourgeois revolution, written during the Vichy period was re-published in four volumes in the 1960s.[11] The fêted philosophers of the ultraroyalists of the Restoration, Bonald and de Maistre, are still well represented in prominent displays in Parisian bookshops, but publishers would not consider producing editions of leading Orleanist or socialist thinkers of the period. The extreme right has even re-emerged, revitalised by present problems, into the democratic arena of the late 1980s, while celebrations of the bicentenary of 1789 were matched by a 'counter-revolutionary' mirror image.

Orleanist attitudes to 1830 continue to exercise considerable influence on present-day historians, though with a less overt impact than the ideas of the extreme right and left. Those who constituted the liberal opposition and were transposed into victorious Orleanists after the revolution naturally defended themselves against the charge that they had sought the overthrow of Charles X. They argued that it was the king and his supporters who sought change. He departed from established precedent by refusing to select ministers in sympathy with the majority in parliament. Instead the Polignac administration had been diametrically opposed to that majority. Guizot, president of the *Aide-toi* society before the Revolution, claimed that he was both a loyal and a conservative citizen:

> Born a member of the bourgeoisie and a protestant, I am totally devoted to freedom of conscience, to equality before the law, to all these great conquests of our social order. But my confidence in these conquests was full and tranquil, and I did not find myself obliged, to serve their cause, to consider the Bourbon house, the French nobility and the Catholic church as my enemies.[12]

Conservative Orleanists like Guizot stressed the king's obstinacy over Polignac as the main issue in 1830. Refuting the legitimist assertions, all reference to parallels with 1789 were shunned, but comparisons between France in the 1820s and Britain in 1688, popular before the revolution, continued to find favour with Orleanists, including Guizot himself. Guizot became Louis-Philippe's longest-serving minister and when he wrote his memoirs in the late 1850s he was undoubtedly bent on stressing the conservatism of the liberals.

Those who accepted the appointment of Louis-Philippe as king divided, almost before the constitutional revision was finished, into those who wanted the July Days to herald as little change as possible – the *résistance* – and those who wanted a more liberal regime, a broad-based electorate and a less powerful monarch – the *mouvement*. To the left of the *mouvement* a small group of republicans soon concluded that the choice of the duc d'Orléans was a mistake. The division between *mouvement* and *résistance* was entirely based on personal rivalry and competition for office. With the appointment of Casimir Périer as chief minister in March 1831, the *mouvement* sympathisers were permanently condemned to be 'out'. The two groups differed little in their analysis of the origins of 1830. Thiers, one of the editors of the *National* during the July Days and a leading campaigner for the duc d'Orléans (and who was to join the centre-left in the 1830s after holding ministerial office), expressed total satisfaction with the 1814 constitution. Its only fault lay in the assertion in the preamble that it was *octroyée*, granted by royal grace and favour, rather than the product of national sovereignty and the rights of the citizen. In a brief account of the revolution written soon afterwards he remarked, 'No one wanted disturbances, nor revolution; no one wanted to reproduce the violence of '93 or all the theories of '89.'[13] Even *mouvement* Orleanists saw the revolution as a regrettably violent extension of political rivalries.[14]

To contemporaries, the parliamentary conflict was the most obvious 'cause' of the revolution. There can be no absolute definition of a revolution: one person's revolution is another's change of government. Conservative Orleanists who secured power soon after the July Days laid so little emphasis on the revolutionary upheaval that it almost disappeared. Indeed the *résistance* stressed the accidental and avoidable nature of 1830 so much that a reader might reasonably be tempted to wonder if a revolution actually took place. Casimir Périer is famous for his comment that there had been no revolution, merely a change of government. The rapidity of the constitutional revision in August 1830 and the very minor scale of change was a reflection of the desire of those of a *résistance* disposition to show their basic satisfaction with the existing arrangements, but the speed with which an essentially conservative settlement was reached was also a feature of conflict among the victors. Once in control, after March 1831, the conservative element further battened down the hatches on innovation. A powerful incentive was their own nervousness that a regime based on revolutionary upheaval was itself vulnerable. Those who became conservative Orleanists shared many of the attitudes of the more moderate royalists of the Restoration. They disliked and feared revolution in their own streets. Their praise of 1789 was muted and selective. Guizot wrote in his memoirs, 'I always defended liberty against absolute power and I have always defended order against revolutionary spirit.'[15] The conservative Orleanists were responsible for the idea, which was very palatable to equally conservative historians in later years, that the decision to maintain a monarchical system had to be made quickly because of the threat of civil war and foreign invasion.[16] Although Guizot admitted that the idea of a republic had been mooted during discussions at the end of July, his own experience caused him to equate a republic with anarchy. The most timid conservative Orleanists even suggested that the new king be called Philippe VII and declared the rightful heir to Charles.[17] The worsening economic crisis in the second half of 1830, and continued popular unrest, allowed the most conservative supporters of Louis-Philippe to assume permanent control in the spring of 1831 and to construct a moral framework for an increasingly restrictive and intensely elitist political system. The experience of December 1848, when the introduction of manhood suffrage permitted Napoleon I's great-nephew to become president of the new republic that replaced Louis-Philippe, only served to confirm Orleanist beliefs in a limited franchise. Rémusat, a journalist on the liberal newspaper the *Globe* at the time of the July Days, and who, unlike Guizot, believed that there were fundamental social conflicts involved in the genesis of revolution, confided to his memoirs,

The July Monarchy, with all its constitutional consequences, that is British liberty in French society, realised all our ideas, and if we had to play a role of resistance, it was to resist against those who wanted to go further than these ideas and to favour a revolutionary regime in place of one of liberty.[18]

The political experiences of the Second Republic and the Empire only confirmed such views among non-legitimist conservatives.

Those who were called *mouvement* politicians and writers varied between near-conservatives and almost-republicans. Although they generally agreed with the conservatives that there was nothing predetermined about revolution in July and that it was the product of the parliamentary stalemate, most within the *mouvement* favoured using the opportunity of the demise of the Bourbons for a general liberalisation. Thiers wrote,

> The government changed the most obvious symbol, the flag; it also changed something less tangible, the basic principles of government. The *tricolore* became the national flag and the monarchy was founded on the concept of national will.[19]

The revolution, therefore, involved many more than the 90 000 or so voters and their representatives in the Chamber of Deputies. Alexis de Tocqueville, a 'progressive' conservative, asserted in his memoirs that the parliamentary clash was part of a deeper antagonism between the ideas of the *ancien régime*, trying to re-establish themselves after 1815, and those of the 1789 Revolution. The dimensions of the 1830 revolution were not entirely political. De Tocqueville took the view that 1830 was also the product of class conflict between the aristocracy and a new middle class,[20] an interpretation dear to later Marxists.

The experiences of the Second Republic, especially the popular violence of the June Days and the subsequent rapid collapse of the republic and the creation of a dictatorial Bonapartist empire under Louis-Napoleon, made the defeat of the Orleanist monarchy appear a virtuous martyrdom to conservatives. For some writers, the subsequent lawless violence of the Paris Commune in 1871 recalled the horrors of the Terror and the Commune of the 1790s and, as a consequence, the Orleanist regime was remembered with increasing nostalgia. Guizot's account of his own times became widely accepted as reasonable. The early years of the Third Republic saw the publication of a history of the July

Monarchy which has left a permanent imprint on all but the Marxist interpretation of 1830.[21] Fundamentally anti-revolutionary and very sympathetic to Guizot's views, Thureau-Dangin saw the July Days as a mistake made by both sides, both Charles and the liberals failing to see that revolution is never complete, but 'a fatal and sterile circle.'[22] The fear and detestation of revolution felt by conservatives, and the very profound need of politicians of the Third Republic to separate the notion of a republic from revolutionary connotations, led to a bowdlerisation of 1830, in which the element of popular violence was almost eliminated and the July Days became a minor stage in the evolution of moderate bourgeois democracy.

The application of the term 'bourgeois' to the 1830 revolution by contemporary republicans and early socialists was a curse rather than a compliment, not because they believed, as did legitimists, that the revolution encapsulated a regrettable noble–bourgeois conflict,[23] but because, they argued, the middle class held sway before and after July and had successfully resisted all change in pursuit of their own interests. The socialist journalist Louis Blanc, who was to play a role in the 1848 revolution, described the Orleanist regime (in a work published a decade after the 1830 revolution) as a bourgeois monarchy. Bourgeois by accident, not design, for he believed that the bourgeosie had been satisfied with the Restoration.[24] Whereas all contemporaries, including the republicans and socialists, agreed that the middle class gained from the revolution, the republicans alone saw the fundamental conflict as a simple one between rich and poor. The real revolutionaries were the Parisian artisans. Cabet, a convinced republican and socialist, *carbonaro* in the 1820s and opposition journalist and republican deputy in the 1830s, believed that 1830 had been a broad-based, primarily artisan revolt. Opposition to the Bourbons had been widespread. Cabet argued,

> The cause was in all that had passed in forty years; it was the love of liberty, of equality, of independence; it was the memory of our glorious revolution of 1789, the desire to reconquer the immortal principles of our constitution of 1791; it was aversion for despotism, for the nobility, for the emigration – it was hatred for the Bourbons and foreign domination.[25]

For Cabet the July Days were 'une révolution escamotée', an

artisan, popular revolt, smuggled away by the liberal elite in its own interest, leaving the actual fighters with no improvement in their condition. He assumed that Parisian artisans were primarily motivated by political deprivation whereas Blanc, writing several years later when awareness of social and economic problems was more acute (partly as a result of his own writing), stressed basic economic and social grievances and injustice as factors in bringing about revolution.

Socialists were not alone in perceiving the link between economic distress and violent confrontation. Orleanists denied that there was any causal connection, however, and argued that set-backs within the economy were transient and would be self-righting. Evidence of the persistence of grave social injustice within the new economic structures was amassed in the 1830s and 1840s by those whose intentions were sometimes critical of the regime[26] but far from revolutionary.[27] Novelists joined the outcry against the very visible evils of industrial and urban change. All added conviction to the fusion by the socialists of the impact of entrepreneurial capitalism with political grievance. Louis Blanc's moving condemnation of 'competition', first published as a series of articles in his paper, *La Revue du Progrès Social*,[28] concluded that innovative, altruistic and benevolent central government intervention was necessary to overcome the social injustice of capitalism. Etienne Cabet advocated active co-operation between the middle class and workers, but ultimately plumbed for a semi-mystical utopian solution.[29] Both strategies, and those of other contemporary socialists such as Fourier and Proudhon, abhorred violent revolution. It was left to political revolutionaries like Blanqui to press the case for change through violence but his attempted rising in 1839 was a complete disaster. The threat of the violent uprising of the poor seemed real enough, however, given the experience of the 1790s and the early 1830s, the apparent impossibility of regulating periodic economic crises like those of 1817–18 and 1827–32 and the rapidly expanding and volatile 'popular' element in the population of the capital, which doubled in size in the first half of the nineteenth century. The use of troops to suppress popular unrest in the 1830s convinced those on the left that 1830 had installed an entirely self-interested bourgeois regime, which proclaimed more stridently than ever the right of the wealthy to oppress the poor. Leroux, who wrote a striking criticism of the plutocracy of his day, offered a comprehensive definition of the elite of the Orleanist monarchy:

> I name bourgeois all the rich landowners, the seigneurs of our towns, right down to the smallest aristocrats of our villages, the 2000 merchants of Lyons, the 500 merchants of St-Etienne, all of those feudal owners of industry.[30]

Later socialists narrowed this definition of the victors of 1830. Karl Marx wrote,

> Under the Bourbons the big landowners controlled politics, under the Orleanists it was the big financial interests, large-scale industry, big capital and trade. The July Monarchy was simply the political expression of the usurpation of power by the upstart bourgeoisie.[31]

The events of 1830 became a stage in a Marxist theory of revolutionary change, in which economic factors were the principal imperative of political and social change and revolution the prerogative of major social groups. The 1848 revolution, the Paris Commune of 1871 and the Bolshevik Revolution in Russia were all seen as further stages in the struggle by the working classes to wrest power from a selfish and doomed bourgeoisie. A distinctly republican orthodox view of 1830 emerged which, especially after 1917, was intermingled with a socialist interpretation. Early in the twentieth century the influential Charléty exemplified this democratic and republican perspective. He argued that the period was one of the awakening of democratic ideals in the less wealthy, a development as alien to the liberals as to Restoration monarchists.[32] Later, a more specifically Marxist theory became the dogma of the Third Republic's historians in France, unchallenged until the 1950s when the triumph of socialist revolution began to seem less than inevitable.

Even before the shock of the Second World War had caused historians in France to question the optimistic progressive view of history, Sherman Kent observed that the elite of the July Monarchy was not a capitalist bourgeoisie, but was primarily landowning.[33] Revisionist reworkings of 1789, provoked by Alfred Cobban,[34] questioned the whole basis of Marxist theories of that revolution and, by inference, later events. In France, detailed investigations of social groups, often on a regional level, began to uncover the diversity of previously defined 'classes'. Tudesq's monumental analysis of the elite of the July Monarchy adopted the revisionist formula of uniting the wealthy, titled and otherwise, under the label 'notable'.[35] A computer-based assessment of members of parliament stressed the diversity and gradual evolution of an elite, changing not because of a revolution but as a consequence of economic development.[36] David Pinkney, in the most recent account of the July Days to appear in English, roundly rejected any link between the Revolution and social change. The elite was different from that of the Restoration, but the difference was political. Taking up the argument used by Charles Pouthas,[37] Pinkney confirmed that 1830 was an administrative revolution, bringing back to power a Bonapartist elite, excluded from influence by the Restoration.[38] Thomas Beck also traced a Bonapartist legacy, best represented in a new generation of men who had been about to embark upon careers in 1814 when Napoleon was defeated. In a recent and welcome survey of the whole July Monarchy, Hugh Collingham observes a Bonapartist spirit in France during the period, but concluded that one of the major failings of the regime was its inability to capture this flavour.[39]

Guizot's view of the political dimensions of the Revolution seems to prevail, even amongst those whose own politics are very different. Present-day historians are disinclined to believe in the merits of progressive and beneficial change. Stripped of social content, 1830 is seen as a minor political accident. The most recent French chronicler of the July Days, influenced, he claimed, by his own involvement in the events of May 1968 in Paris, stressed the spontaneity, utter confusion and enthusiasm of the revolt.[40] Bertier de Sauvigny, whose ancestor was a fervent ultra (and who is himself a Catholic historian of moderate legitimist sympathies), praised the political compromise worked out in 1814, and blamed the over-logical French character for 1830, resistant as it was to the Anglo-Saxon-style compromise of the constitution.[41] The political and Paris-centred explanation he favours has been modified by subsequent investigations into social and economic problems that underlay popular unrest,[42] not just in France, but throughout Europe, where traditional poorer groups tried to resist the destruction of their way of life. Class antagonism no longer seems the unique motor of historical progress. Those most embroiled in violent protest appear more inclined to fight for a return to a lost ideal than for a future socialist utopia. Their motivation can be analysed empirically, divorced from a Marxist–anti-Marxist slanging match. Thus, the explanation of revolutionary and insurrectionary activity in early nineteenth century France may not be the story of a mere three days, however glorious.

2
The Political Crises of the Bourbon Restoration

Paradoxically, the Bourbon Restoration, with only modest support in France at the outset, developed a stability, making the revolution which overthrew it in 1830 an accident almost as much feared by the victorious liberals as by their royalist opponents. In 1814, and again in 1815 after the emperor's second defeat at Waterloo, it was France's victorious enemies who appointed the guillotined king's brother Louis XVIII. There was only modest and localised support in France for a monarchist restoration, chiefly in the Midi and the west. Napoleon's defeat was followed by the setting up of a constitutional, representative regime in which a tolerable working compromise was reached, combining the imperial framework with the restored Bourbons, harnessed to a two-chamber parliament. Louis agreed to govern within the terms of a constitutional charter, worked out by a group of primarily Bonapartist notables, including the liberal thinker, Benjamin Constant. France retained all but the political institutions of the revolutionary and imperial years. Louis was made hereditary head of the executive, appointed his own ministers and shared legislative power with a parliament consisting of two assemblies, one hereditary and one elected. The franchise was limited to adult males of thirty years of age and over who paid at least 300 francs in direct taxes each year. About 110 000 out of just over thirty million citizens were thus enfranchised. After the upheaval of the revolutionary years, involving prolonged civil war and twenty-two years of foreign war, there was considerable determination among the wealthy to make these new arrangements function effectively. This resolve was strengthened by the presence of an army of occupation in eastern France and the threat of a possible third military intervention by France's enemies if she failed to create a stable regime. That the basis of the system, the constitutional charter of 1814, was an acceptable compromise, was confirmed by the modest changes introduced after the 1830 revolution itself. Why then did the Restoration settlement fail?

There were three episodes of political instability or crisis in these years. Initially the Restoration was challenged by Napoleon's escape from his imprisonment on Elba and his ensuing brief hundred-day rule. After the victory of the allies at Waterloo, Louis XVIII was again returned. The First Restoration had involved genuine compromise and the retention of many of Napoleon's officials. The willingness of a substantial number of these individuals to revert to Napoleon in the Hundred Days*, however, meant that the Second Restoration was accompanied by bitterness and violence – the White Terror – in which supporters of the monarchy took direct vengeance on Bonapartists. This was the first political crisis of the regime, a legacy of imprisonment, summary justice, including murder, and the subsequent exclusion from public office of the Bonapartist partisans of the Hundred Days, robbing the new king of a vast army of experienced officials. Perhaps the compromise of the First Restoration had been an illusion, and it would not have survived. The White Terror ensured that bloody lines of conflict were drawn. It can be no accident that victims of the White Terror were often leaders of both the liberal opposition in the 1820s and the revolution in 1830. Hernoux, mayor of Dijon during the Hundred Days and imprisoned after the Second Restoration, was to be the main liberal politician in his department. In Metz, de Merville, secretary-general of the prefecture in the Hundred Days, was to lead the opposition to the new monarchy during his subsequent prolonged period of unemployment. Thus former Napoleonic officials dismissed in 1815, often lawyers by profession, made up the inner core of an opposition, which may not have been wholly created by the White Terror but was certainly identified with and united by that experience. In Dijon in 1822 these former imperial officials formed a distinct group, called 'jacobin' by the prefect and respected even by their opponents for their abilities and local standing. They exercised a notable influence over less wealthy voters, both in the town and in the surrounding countryside. It would be simplistic, perhaps, to suppose that resentment at the injustices of the White Terror and disappointed ambition alone helped to create a liberal opposition, but it was significant that active, influential men were deprived of their official posts and were in a position to become articulate foci for discontent.

The liberals, or *doctrinaires* as they were sometimes called, were divided among themselves and were far from revolutionary. They were influential in the Decazes government from 1818 and, typically, were outspoken and enthusiastic defenders of the constitution of 1814 against the diatribes of the ultras. They called themselves constitutionalists and insisted that they were suspicious of the arbitrariness of both absolutism and revolution. They considered themselves politically conservative and rejected the more usual label 'left' or 'centre-left'. They admired representative institutions, under the control of a wealthy 'independent' minority, and cherished personal liberty. In certain areas, like Alsace, for instance, they were what later became classically 'liberal', calling for freedom of trade, but many manufacturers sought a more rather than less protectionist commercial policy. Many royalists, except extreme ultras, shared some of these views, and most royalists were aware that, despite revolutionary and Bonapartist antecedents and professional disappointments, liberals did not seek revolution. But the White Terror ensured that such men could not safely be regarded as part of the status quo of a restored monarchy.

The episode also brought divisions among royalists into the open. The White Terror was the work of the extreme right wing of the royalists, the ultras, led in the south by the duc d'Angoulême. The ultras were intensely anti-revolutionary and cherished a romanticised, idealised and totally unhistoric view of the *ancien régime*. They believed that *ancien régime* France had been harmoniously ruled by king, church and nobles. If such a trinity had ever combined to rule, which is more than doubtful, that age was long past. The ultras, many of whom had spent the entire revolutionary period in exile, appeared unaware that their view of history, and the potential for its resurrection, was anachronistic. They expected that the restored monarch, trailing clouds of divine-right glory, as if his brother had never been executed in 1793, would share their faith in romantic mythology. Louis XVIII, conscious of the need to be a constitutional king, was a disappointment to them. Their leader, the comte d'Artois, who succeeded his brother in 1824, gave them more hope. He was crowned in medieval splendour at Rheims cathedral, apparently typifying the fusion of interests of church and state. Much of the support for ultra ideas came from the more Catholic Midi and the west and a number of sympathisers spent the Hundred Days with Angoulême in Spain rather than with the king in Ghent.

The ultras were also at odds with Louis over the issues of centralisation and the role of the church. The king assumed that he ruled a centralised state, that prefects appointed from Paris would do his bidding. The ultras anticipated that the restoration of the monarchy would bring a dilution of Napoleonic centralisation and the assertion of regional, traditional and provincial liberties, quite forgetting, as de Tocqueville was later to remind them, that the *ancien régime* monarchy had also been a highly centralised state. In many respects the anarchic revenge of the White Terror in the south in 1815–16 was the expression of this determination to resurrect the old provinces as autonomous units. The *chambre introuvable*, the first parliament elected after the second Restoration, was resolutely ultra. Convinced that the ultras were dangerously divisive, Louis dissolved the assembly. The first crisis was thus defused by the realism of the king and his immediate advisers. Subsequently, the ultras were never more than a noisy minority within the royalists. The functioning of the new regime convinced many previously sceptical royalists that a constitutional regime was preferable to an absolutist one. It soon became apparent that through the careful exercise of patronage, local notables could use the two chambers to exercise a regional and a national influence undreamt of by the members of *ancien régime* provincial estates. Although royalists detested the Revolution and feared its revival, by 1820 all but the minority ultras were persuaded that the constitutional charter was their best hope for a settled and stable France. Thus, although the episode of the White Terror delineated the lines of potential political conflict, it did not make it inevitable.

The second crisis arose out of a fortuitous incident. This was the murder of the duc de Berri, Louis XVIII's brother's heir, in 1820. The ultras claimed that his murder was a liberal plot. The emotional backlash, although less violent than in the White Terror, allowed the ultra minority to trim the constitution more to their taste. The franchise was restricted, giving the most wealthy quarter of the population a second vote. Thereafter less than 25 000 voters elected 165 deputies in special departmental electoral colleges; they then joined the rest of the electorate to choose the remaining 265 members. This was a specifically ultra measure and well understood by the political community. The richest voters were always landowners because the *cens*, or franchise, was based on tax payments. The *foncière*, or land tax, was by far the most onerous of the four direct taxes on which the *cens* was based, the next largest, the *patente*, being a commercial or industrial tax which was calculated not on profits – the French long resisted a true income tax – but on the value of the property where the business was conducted. It was assumed that France's richest landowners were bound to be monarchists, probably ultraroyalist, and a second vote for such men would ensure a complaisant Chamber of Deputies for the foreseeable future. The liberals were incensed by the law of the double vote, particularly so when the 1824 election left them with only about 40 seats out of 430. Antagonism was all the more profound because immediately after this election parliament passed a *loi septennale*, which changed the system of election. In future the assembly would no longer be re-elected in fifths each year, but in its entirety every seven years. Liberal anger reached a peak when the new chamber also decided that the new law would apply retrospectively to the parliament then in session.

The ultras always depicted liberals as heirs of 1789, committed to the overthrow of the monarchy. Was the intensification of political conflict after de Berri's murder entirely the product of misjudgement by ultras, many of whom, like the comte d'Artois, had spent the revolutionary years as *émigrés* and were predictably ignorant of the ensuing drift in political life? Were there destabilising revolutionary or Bonapartist elements present in Restoration France? The memory of the foreign policy successes of the emperor was a decisive factor in a continuing enthusiasm for the imperial years, particularly, if rather contradictorily, in the eastern departments which were invaded twice during the wars, once in 1792–3 and once during the campaigns of 1814–15. In the Côte-d'Or some cantons were implacably anti-monarchist from the time of the first invasion. The first three years of the Restoration were marked by an expensive foreign military occupation of some 300 000 men, sustained by the occupied eastern departments and the payment of an indemnity to the former enemies of France. The new monarchy, not the old empire, was associated from the beginning with defeat and occupation, even though the occupation was actually beneficial for the economy of the area.[1]

Former imperial officers, retired on half-pay and left by the Restoration with little to do except lead the National Guard battalions and talk about past adventures until the disbandment of the Guard in 1827, provided a nucleus for the glorification of the former regime. After Napoleon's defeat, the reaction of the government, particularly bitter because so many officers and men rejoined Napoleon during the Hundred Days, was to retire as many of the members of his army as possible and to efface imperial military traditions. The number of officers was reduced by 14 000 and the army was cut to 324 000 men. A number of the commanders of the imperial army were arraigned as traitors; Marshal Ney and others were shot.[2] Imperial regiments were replaced by infantry regiments recruited and organised according to departments. The continuity of cavalry, artillery and other regiments was likewise deliberately broken. Military considerations were subsumed, not unnaturally, by political and social dictates. *Emigrés* were promoted. A commission was set up to examine the imperial officer corps; only the smoothest talkers with the most influential patrons survived.[3] Chaos and a possible Bonapartist backlash were only averted by the appointment of Gouvion St Cyr as minister of war in 1817. One of Napoleon's marshals and a known liberal, he introduced a working compromise and a framework of organisation and promotion so successful that it survived until the Third Republic. Many former Bonapartist officers were reintegrated. A surprising 75 per cent of officers were Napoleonic veterans as late as 1824, mostly men from very modest backgrounds promoted from the ranks. Tales were told of the battalion commander who sported an eagle under his fleur-de-lis emblem. An attempt was made to create a professional, national army. Military reformers tried to replace Bonapartist enthusiasm with a monarchist, aristocratic, anti-bourgeois and anti-civilian ethos.[4] They were not entirely successful: an elitist and a popular Bonapartist legend was nutured by frustration and inactivity.

Bonapartism was one ingredient in the ideological mix of opposition to the Restoration, but it was generally accompanied by republican sympathies. Republicanism was a confused and conflicting inheritance in the years after 1814. In 1792 the First Republic had clearly been born in inauspicious circumstances: civil war, invasion and a threat to the capital itself. Subsequently the war was convincingly turned around, but Napoleon kept the credit for himself. Economic disaster also surrounded the republic, with real food shortages and catastrophic price rises leading to the introduction of a maximum price and forcible expropriation of grain. The empire took the credit for industrial recovery where it occurred. The republic was intimately associated with political conflict and confusion, Robespierre, the Jacobins, the Committee of Public Safety, and dictatorship. Social conflict also abounded in the Terror, the witch-hunt against *aristos*, the demands of the *sans culottes* and the programme of de-christianisation; none attracted admiration and repetition in the years after 1814. The history of the republic was not studied in Restoration schools or remembered by those anxious to protect their careers. As Weill commented at the outset of his study of republicanism, 1814 'la république pour les classes élevées, c'était le jacobinisme, c'était la guillotine, c'était 1793.'[5]

Even if their own recollections of the republic were not in accord with the more lurid accounts of the Terror – put about by the Directory in the later 1790s and subsequently by Napoleon, and seized upon as gospel truth by the monarchists – it was in the interests of former republicans to convert to total monarchism if they were politically ambitious after 1814. Lafayette, the already almost mythical republican, demanded Napoleon's abdication after Waterloo. Those who had worked with the revolutionary or Napoleonic governments thought of themselves as professional politicians and administrators and had job continuity as their major preoccupation in 1814. Indeed, Louis XVIII was keen to employ the most able and ambitious among them. Personal and professional ambition aside, they had no coherent political system with which to challenge the restored monarchy. Republican traditions were confused, bloody and dictatorial. No distinct link could be forged with concepts of individual liberty, political freedom, or parliamentary representation. Nor did republicanism offer an alternative set of social and economic beliefs. The most active republicans had served the emperor; republican and Bonapartist ideas had become inextricably fused and for the moment both were associated with invasion, defeat and the presence of an army of occupation. Guizot observed that such men 'had no set of beliefs . . . they had lived through the Revolution with its promises, excesses, defeat, and were fearful. The defeat of Napoleon, in whom they had believed, left them in total disarray.'[6]

During the White Terror some surviving republicans fled to Belgium. The very term 'republican' itself passed out of use during the Restoration and came to have only violent and generalised connotations. It thus suited the ultraroyalists in particular to denigrate the revolutionary period. Its history was not taught in schools. In the 1820s, however, a revival of interest stimulated the writing of the history of the First Republic. The Convention became a cult, Thiers rehabilitated Danton, Robespierre was glorified and by inference the governments of the Restoration were reviled. Family tradition ensured that republicanism would not die. Thus a younger generation of republicans included the Cavaignacs and Carnot, whose father had been a regicide. They were joined later by men concerned with social change, writers influenced by the ideas of Babeuf, as popularised by Buonarotti in 1828,[7] and the writings of St Simon. It was a new generation, with no experience of the previous regime but fired by enthusiasm for notions of republican democracy. It included writers like Destutt de Tracy, the Fabre brothers and Marrast. The last group had been inspired by Guizot's Sorbonne lectures on representative government, a series launched when Guizot, professor at the university since 1812, lost his appointment in the *conseil d'état* after the murder of the duc de Berri. Royer-Collard's lectures on law also aroused interest and student unrest in the period after the introduction of the law of the double vote. University unrest spread to Grenoble, Montpellier, Toulouse and Poitiers. The government's response was to dimiss staff, including Guizot, whose views were judged as liberal and explosive, and to close faculties for prolonged periods.[8] The severity of the official response to the restrained opposition of academics and intellectuals was to provide eloquent spokesmen of opposition in the country at large.

Bonapartism and republicanism were blended together, leavened with a healthy regard for the practical and finally emerged as a vaguely liberal sentiment. The military glories were remembered; the economic disasters put to one side. The constitutional promises of the Hundred Days were recalled, the reality of dictatorship forgotten. A number of the politicians who took a lead in the July Days, notably the lawyer, Mauguin, had loyalties both to the empire and the republic, but ultimately plumped for neither. By 1830 the empire was a romantic memory for many former soldiers; revered, but with no expectation of a rebirth. After Napoleon's death, the most emphatic dampener was surely the absence of a suitable candidate. 'L'aiglon', Napoleon's son, was in his teens, but was both sickly and raised in Vienna in a totally anti-French atmosphere. At this stage the subsequent successful contender, Louis-Napoleon, Napoleon's great-nephew, deferred to the claims of 'l'aiglon' and was employing his talents elsewhere.

There were a number of minor, mostly military based conspiracies in the early 1820s.[9] The motivation for such conspiracies and the sentiments surrounding them were not entirely Bonapartist. There was a republican flavour too. Indeed the two attitudes often merged in a generalised dissatisfaction with the restored monarchy. Bonapartism was primarily nationalist in inspiration, the republican element was idealistic, theoretical and humanitarian, deliberately turning its back on the memory of dictatorship and the Jacobin Terror. Such attitudes crystallised in the *charbonnerie*, an offshoot of the Italian *carbonari*. The *charbonnerie* attracted a wide range of more or less 'left-wing' men critical of the Restoration. The groups were usually led by former Napoleonic officers and officials, but also attracted a new generation, too young to have known the Revolution, mainly young soldiers, and students of law and medicine. It was a secret organisation, divided into tiny cells of twenty or less, to circumvent article 291 of the Penal Code which demanded that societies of more than twenty members obtain official sanction. The *charbonnerie* was organised along masonic lines, borrowing masonic symbolism. Its groups were hierarchically arranged, so that only one man from each *vente* knew the members of the superior one, up to a *vente suprême* located in Paris. At its height it had about 60 000 members in sixty departments, the majority in the east.[10] Its aims were vaguely subversive, stressing the brotherhood and equality of man, and it attracted young idealists as well as republicans and Bonapartists unreconciled to the new regime. In eastern France, in 1822, the *charbonnerie* was the basis for an attempt to raise the army against the regime which was harshly suppressed and in which leading opponents of the government were implicated.[11] Jacques Koechlin, mayor of Mulhouse during the Hundred Days, was imprisoned after the Belfort conspiracy, for which, it was said, he had provided some of the finance. Such liberal notables, like Koechlin and Voyer d'Argenson, the richest individual in the region, seem to have regarded the *charbonnerie* as a sort of insurance policy, to maintain their leadership of radical opinion, while not disassociating them entirely from the legal political game. Members of the *charbonnerie* also took an active interest in the cause of the Spanish liberals, while the French government intervened militarily on the opposite side in 1822. The *charbonnerie* was an outlet for discontent, frustration and idealism, but it did not propose an alternative to the restored monarchy. It was a freemasonry of opposition, whose political sentiments ranged from vague republicanism to a romanticised Bonapartism. Members of the movement later branched out in various radical directions. Leroux and Buchez later followed St Simonist ideas; Cabet turned republican and utopian socialist; others, like Blanqui, became revolutionary republicans. Yet others still, like Dupont de l'Eure and Montalivet, were Orleanists. It was primarily a movement of young men, but it should be noted that it did not attempt to attract a mass membership: like masonry, it was a movement of the elite. The *charbonnerie* used masonic symbols and freemasonry itself was still sometimes considered to be linked with left-wing attitudes.

Masons certainly tended to be anti-clerical. The *Amis de la Verité* lodge in Paris was specifically political, attracting lawyers and both law and medical students. Its members included such young radicals as Buchez, Bazard and Joubert. They organised a procession in protest at the law of the double vote in which one of their number was killed. Prosecution followed. Joubert fled to Naples, bringing the idea of the *charbonnerie* on his return. The *chevaliers de la liberté*, with members in five western departments, including the Vendée, were linked both to a *comité directeur* in Paris and groups in Grenoble, Lyons and other eastern towns. Many masons supported the Belfort conspiracy.[12] Both masons and the *charbonnerie* earned a papal condemnation in 1821. There was, in some eastern departments, a close correlation between the leading members of local lodges and liberals who came to power after the revolution of 1830.[13] Mauguin, for example, a leading radical *avocat* and political activist who played a role in July Days in Paris, was a mason, as indeed was Lafayette. Only ultras, however, believed that masonry and revolution were intimately linked. Many lodges of freemasons gained official authorisation during the Restoration. Grand masters were careful to ensure that their rites were not offensive to the king and Decazes played a leading role in their reorganisation. Active political opposition was organised through other channels.[14]

Conspiracy became the flavour of opposition in the early 1820s, undoubtedly inspired by the concept of the Italian *carbonari* itself. The death of Napoleon in May 1821 released opponents of the regime from thinking in precise Bonapartist terms. There were many different and overlapping oganisations, of which the *charbonnerie* was most famous, perhaps because it best corresponded to the romanticism of the age. The government employed both police agents and independent spies, who often acted as double agents. One is sometimes tempted to wonder whether the rather feeble conspiracies of the period were no more than attempts by the agents to raise their income, as they were paid entirely by results. In 1821, for example, the plan to persuade officers in Belfort to take over the town, proclaim a provisional government and hoist the *tricolore* at midnight, was well known to officials, including the lieutenant-colonel commanding the local regiment. He had the main conspirators arrested when they arrived at a local inn for a meal they had ordered before they embarked on their rising.[15] Elsewhere, local authorities were equally well informed. The Dijon *procureur* sent full details of the local branch of the *chevaliers de la liberté* and of their efforts to gain support within the garrison.[16]

Political criticism and opposition was the product of a wide range of grievances and suspicions. Religion, predictably, after the experiences of the 1790s, was an especially explosive issue. Anti-clerical and liberal attitudes lay deep in the Protestantism of eastern France[17] and in departments such as the Gard, where the large Protestant community, a proportion of which was very prosperous, had welcomed the 1789 Revolution as an opportunity to exercise political influence appropriate to their wealth.[18] Anti-clerical attitudes and legislation were outstanding components of the Revolution in the 1790s. Anti-clerical sentiments had been reinforced by the purchase of church lands. Frederick Hartmann, liberal deputy for Mulhouse in 1830, had bought the Benedictine abbey of Münster and Nicholas Koechlin, another leading local liberal and cotton manufacturer, bought the abbey of Masevaux.[19]

Parliamentary debates in the late twenties often involved acrimonious exchanges on the role of the Catholic Church. The constitution of 1814 declared that catholicism was the official faith, but tolerated others. Liberals were far from being anti-religious but were alarmed by the perceptible increase in the educational, social and political influence of the Catholic Church in these years. A vigorous religious revival, frankly anti-revolutionary and with ultraroyalist political undertones, caused widespread criticism. A new organisation, the *Missions de la France*, embarked on a very active evangelical campaign after 1815 and their habit of erecting their missionary crosses near (but not on) church property became a sensitive issue to those who had bought *biens nationaux* during the 1790s. More pertinent was the increased presence of the church in education. The return of the religious orders, above all of the Jesuits, to unofficial teaching duties caused uproar, as did the appointment in 1822 of Mgr de Fraysinnous as Grand Master of the University of Paris, the bureaucratic heart of the state system of secondary education. The most triumphant symbol of clerical influence, if the least effective, was the law against sacrilege of 1825.[20] Though never enforced, the law helped to confirm liberal suspicions and unite them on an anti-clerical platform. The church seemed to be gaining ground, not just in the religious demesne, which was not much resented, but in society in general, over which it was re-establishing a powerful influence. Worst of all, for those of liberal sympathies, was the increasingly close relationship between the church and politics, epitomised by the presence of ultras in senior posts within the church hierarchy, like Mgr de Quelen, archbishop of Paris, and Cardinal Rohan-Chabot, archbishop of Besançon. In 1829 Baron Belmas, bishop of Cambrai, was made president of the electoral college in Hazebrouck, Nord.[21] Official solicitation of clerical support in elections became more pronounced after the accession of Charles X. The fusion of liberal and anti-clerical sentiments was thus reinforced.

The charter of 1814 guaranteed the permanence of the revolutionary land settlement, but worries remained on both sides. Purchasers of *biens nationaux* were presumed still to have a vested interest in revolutionary principles.[22] While there was no question of the church re-acquiring its former holdings, after 1814 individuals were once more allowed to bequeath property to the church. Unsold *émigré* land, mostly woodland, was returned to its former owners in 1815. *Émigrés* still sought compensation for the land they had lost. This was partially achieved in 1825 by the floating of a state loan. The loan was regarded with a mixture of resentment and suspicion by the new owners of *biens nationaux*, who argued that the legislation called into question the legitimacy of their own titles to property. Opposition to the law of indemnification of the *émigrés* helped to identify and unite liberal opposition to the Villèle government. Thus, early nineteenth-century liberal attitudes emerged gradually out of a multiplicity of components. Half-remembered, half-invented revolutionary ideology, romanticised Bonapartism, disappointed nationalism, anti-clericalism and fears for the land settlement were compounded by frustrated personal ambitions among leading local notables. In the years up to 1827 views thus generated produced a climate of opinion, but did not amount to a doctrine, nor a large, coherent opposition and certainly not a revolutionary movement. Contemporary officials, especially those of ultra tendencies, were convinced of the contrary view. They also argued that the political tensions which grew worse after the accession of Charles X were at root social and that liberalism was a movement of the industrial and commercial bourgeoisie.[23]

In reality, however, political differences predominated, exacerbated by the political naïvety or ignorance of ultras who gained a greater say after the accession of their leader as king. Charles was known to have little sympathy with the written constitution. The ultras appeared to be triumphant, a victory underlined by the two major items of legislation at that time, the law of indemnification and the law against sacrilege. The assembly of 1824 was all that Charles X could have wished on his accession. Apart from the *chambre introuvable*, it was the most royalist assembly during the entire Restoration, including a mere twenty-nine liberals elected in the *arrondissement* constituencies and nine in the double vote departmental electoral colleges. The victory of the ultras, which they claimed it to be, although most of the royalist deputies were not ultra in sympathy, was all the more complete with the passing of the *loi septennale* during the new session. It was suggested that the law could be applied retrospectively, which would leave the royalist assembly in place until 1831. Unfortunately the electoral successes of the Villèle government were not all they seemed. Legislative changes like the law of the double vote and the *loi septennale*, both of which enraged the liberals as infringements of the constitution, were not enough to satisfy nervous royalists. The government started to fudge elections and electoral lists in order to preserve a royalist majority, with remarkable success in 1824. There was no recognised system for checking and revising electoral lists before 1827.[24] The process was left to the departmental prefects who were far from impartial bureaucrats. During the Restoration their main function came to be that of government electoral agent. They left liberal opponents off the lists and included dead and unqualified royalists, with curious consequences for electoral statistics. The number of qualified voters fell from 110 000 in 1817 to 96 525 in 1820 and finally to

79 138 in 1829. In the department of the Ain there were 617 voters in 1820 but only 485 in 1828.²⁵ In the same period the population rose by about 3.5 million and there was no sudden impoverishment of the wealthy to correspond to the shrinking electoral lists. Nor do tax changes account for the embarrassing disappearance of inconvenient voters. Prefects simply excluded them. *Patente* electors were only allowed a few days to prove their electoral qualification and a substantial number of liberals were thus eliminated. With the law of May 1827, prefects were obliged to follow a more regular procedure for revising the lists, but a number of ruses were still perpetrated. In 1829 the prefect in the Haut-Rhin had the list printed in a very small, fine script and displayed it at a great height, with no accessible ladder.²⁶ Another device was to try to exhaust and disenchant liberal voters, with their dual roles as electors and jurymen, by imposing the whole of the jury service on them in the hope that they would then be less solicitous of their constitutional rights. In 1827 the prefect in the Vosges increased the electorate to over 400 by including 91 royalists who were either dead or who paid insufficient tax to qualify. The subsequent election, in which liberal still won four of the five seats, was annulled.²⁷ A great deal of the prefect's energy and time was spent discovering the allegiance of electors, in drawing up complex lists of 'patronage and influence' of leading voters and in trying to convert the undecided. The frequent prefectoral changes, which became more frenzied after 1827, made the task more difficult.

Having compiled the voting list, it was the prefect's job to orchestrate the campaign for those candidates favourable to the government. The concept of political parties was widely regarded as factious, but the Chamber of Deputies consisted of liberal, ministerial and ultra groups, which shaded into each other and had endless and flexible subdivisions. All professed a total commitment to the monarchy, but the extent to which liberals on the left and ultras on the right would support precise government formations varied. Most governments tried to appeal to a broad centre, whose candidates in elections were usually termed 'royalist', and whose principal aim was to seek a compromise between the extreme anti-constitutionalism of the ultras and fervent support for the constitutional charter of the liberals. The ministerial centre was therefore fluid and far less of a party than the groups to the left and right. Governments did not prepare lists of candidates: they normally emerged from the local situation. The prefect acted as intermediary and on the governments behalf studied the influence, attitudes and financial standing of local notables who expressed a willingness to stand for election. In 1824 prefects tried to chivvy known royalists into embryonic committees to select one candidate for whom they would all vote and to agree on tactics, but the prefects found royalists reluctant to form such organisations.[28] The subsequent increased frequency of both prefectoral and ministerial changes made it even more difficult to establish a local consensus. The usual procedure was for the prefect to make it known that the candidate whose opinions seemed most reliable, and who seemed most likely to win, had his support, and to appoint him as president of the electoral college, which put him in a position of considerable influence.

Electoral expenditure soared. From relatively modest totals, like the 2000 francs spent in the Meuse in 1822, prefects began to organise banquets for the whole electoral college on a grand scale. On the eve of the 1827 election the prefect persuaded the minister of the interior to finance such a dinner for 300 electors. The bishop, sub-prefect and mayor were deputed to organise the festivities and were each furnished with 1200 francs to cover costs. The president of the electoral college was also paid a certain sum (the rate was apparently 1000 francs in 1824) if he secured the election of a suitable candidate.[29] In 1827 the new prefect in the Haut-Rhin owed his appointment to his reputation in conducting successful elections. All local officials of all ranks were specifically enjoined on pain of dismissal to follow the prefect's lead. Officials often formed a substantial portion of the electoral college. In 1830, 39 of the 129 members of the departmental college (double vote) in the Doubs were government employees.[30] Since electoral colleges were mostly small and local notables formed a tight group interrelated by friendship, family, marriage and professional ties, a small number of the very wealthy usually controlled the choice of deputy. What is astonishing, given the small size of the electorate and its wealth (and therefore assumed conservatism), plus the irresistible attraction of central government patronage, is that after 1824 increasing numbers of electoral colleges refused to rubber stamp approved ministerial candidates.

By 1827 Villèle was so apprehensive for the survival of his majority, that he advised Charles to call an early election. Religious policies, press censorship and worries over the economy[31] contributed to the government's instability, but the major issue was the management of politics. In 1827 liberals, increasingly aware of the government's manipulation of the electoral system, made their own approach more sophisticated. Two organisations advised voters. The *Société des Amis de la Liberté de la Presse* urged voters to ensure that their names appeared on the electoral lists.[32] Lawyers and journalists, including the editors of the *Globe*, adopted a more formal and thoroughly legalistic approach. Under the chairmanship of Guizot they organised committees in Paris and in the provinces – aptly named *Aide-toi, le ciel t'aidera* – to ensure that all of those entitled to appear in the electoral lists did so. They published a series of pamphlets, widely circulated in France, informing men in a straightforward fashion of their political rights and explaining how to ensure that their names appeared on the final list. *Aide-toi* also published pamphlets explaining how a prefect ought to conduct an election. These very practical and informative leaflets were written in a calm, clear style and the writers stressed that everything they proposed was within the law and was, indeed, designed to enable others to uphold the law.[33] They explained to prospective electors how to take legal action if they were incorrectly left off the lists, or if the election was irregularly conducted. The number of legal actions mushroomed: after the 1827 election twenty-two prefects were accused of improper electoral practice and ten were found guilty to varying degrees. In 1830 the *Aide-toi* committeee in the Nord succeeded in reinstating forty-six liberals and nine royalists in the *cour royale* of Douai whose names had previously been removed by the prefect.[34] In 1827 the electorate of 70 000 was increased to 89 000 as a result of the pressure from *Aide-toi*. Active liberal intervention sometimes added 40 per cent more names to the number of voters in a department. The committees worked with local liberal newspapers and both were ready when Villèle opted for a general election in November 1827. They proposed candidates and organised complaints about prefectoral malpractice. It was rumoured that the committee in the relatively poor department of the Vosges had an electoral budget of 1500 francs.[35]

Thus the electoral campaign of 1827 was unusually lively. Villèle's gamble did not pay off. Instead the new parliament contained 180 liberals, the same number of royalists and 60–80 ultras. The king conformed to traditional practice and accepted Villèle's resignation. A moderate royalist, Martignac, became spokesman for a new royalist government in parliament, and as a concession to the liberals, Royer-Collard was made president of the Chamber of Deputies, which was a great sacrifice for Charles. The king believed that the new government was a genuine compromise, designed to suit the wishes of parliament. The Martignac government was quite ineffectual, however, and opposed by both ultras and liberals, the latter of whom strengthened their position in nearly all the hundred or so by-elections which followed liberal appeals against malpractice in 1827. In this period of deepening economic depression, France was virtually without a government, for the ultra king would not consider the pursuit of a genuine compromise, which would have involved following the convention thus far utilised by constitutional monarchs, adapting the government to suit the chamber.

The results of by-elections changed the balance of the assembly towards the liberals. To stay within established practice and break the stalemate, the king needed to appoint some liberal ministers. His whole background made it impossible for him to do this. Thus, an unnecessarily ineffectual government was preserved by the king out of fear. Debates on the industrial recession and the problems of agriculture only exacerbated the political crisis, for no policy decisions were ever reached.[36] From this point until the July Days, Charles, his ministers and the Chamber of Deputies were in constant conflict, which made government impossible. This third and final crisis was soluble. Martignac made a genuine attempt at compromise, but his efforts merely heightened the tension. The fate of a bill to make local councils elective, an issue dear to both ultras and liberal (albeit for different reasons) illustrates the stalemate. The bill was hotly debated for three months from the opening of the 1829 session. Martignac, in line with the wishes of the ultras, proposed that the electorate be confined to the 25 per cent most wealthy parliamentary electors in order, it was claimed, to exclude extraneous national political issues from matters of purely local concern. The liberals opposed the enfranchisement of only the double vote electors. The essence of the deepening crisis lay in the king's response. Instead of pursuing a solution, the proposal was withdrawn in a summary fashion, having served no purpose except to focus opposition.

Recognising that his government was unworkable, Martignac resigned, tacitly admitting the necessity of parliamentary support for the administration of the day, just as all Restoration governments and both monarchs had done until then. To conform to accepted convention, Charles should have appointed a left-of-centre government that was tolerable to the small liberal majority. On a personal and philosophical level Charles found such a decision repugnant. He argued that the Martignac administration had been his attempt to compromise and it had been destroyed by the liberals. Electoral fraud and a growing polarisation stimulated mistrust and the inability of political rivals realistically to appraise the differences between them. Ultra advisers isolated the king and the liberal newspapers themselves convinced him that liberalism meant revolution. In August 1829 the king made the unprecedented appointment of a group of ultra ministers who were totally unacceptable to parliament, including the king's close friend the prince de Polignac as minister of foreign affairs. Polignac, a former *emigré* and diplomat with no parliamentary or governmental experience, was promoted to the presidency of the council of ministers in November. Such a choice could only render France even more ungovernable. The constitution stated that ministers were 'responsible'. The liberals, cautious heirs of the revolutionary aspects of the charter, assumed that this meant 'responsible to parliament' and that governments had thus to be acceptable to the chambers, which, of course, up to this point, they customarily had been. The ambiguity of the constitution was to contribute to the downfall of the Bourbons in 1830. Liberals argued, through their newspapers and electoral committees, that the appointment of an ultra government was a challenge to parliament, virtually a *coup d'état*.[37] The parliamentary session was postponed until March 1830, which intensified their suspicions. *Aide-toi* organised banquets for liberal deputies.[38] Liberals did all in their power to make electors aware of what they considered to be an unconstitutional and threatening situation.

The liberal press was particularly important because of its unparalleled popularity. In 1826 the liberal Parisian daily papers had 50 000 subscribers, their rivals only 15 000. The *Constitutionnel* was the most popular with 20 000 subscribers. Casimir Périer was both a stockholder and a contributor, and Thiers wrote for it. The *Constitutionnel* was a respected and influential paper, particularly within the business community. In 1828 the *Journal des Débats* had the second largest circulation after the *Constitutionnel* with 11 000. Chateaubriand was one of its founders, but it took a firmly anti-Villèle stance from 1824 when Chateaubrand was dismissed from the government. Guizot, Royer-Collard and Salvandy were among its writers. In 1827 the *Journal* was one of the founders of the *Société des Amis de la Liberté de la Presse* and was one of the staunchest backers of *Aide-toi*. The *Courrier*, with only 6000 subscribers, barely covered its running costs and had little impact on the business world. It attracted some of the most notable liberal writers, however, and some whose views veered towards the republic. Their correspondents included Guizot and Barrot and its senior editors were de Broglie and Benjamin Constant. The *Journal de Commerce*, as its name implies, was designed as a businessman's paper. It was both liberal and anti-clerical but had only 2500 subscribers in 1828. The *Gazette des Tribunaux*, founded in 1825 to serve the liberal legal community, had 3000 subscribers. The *Globe*, later to turn to St Simonism, had a clutch of journalists who were academics dismissed for their liberalism.

Four new papers, founded in 1829, epitomised the growing polarisation of politics. The *Jeune France*, started in June with Marrast as editor, took an idealistic republican stance. The *Tribune des Départements*, also begun in June and run by the Fabre brothers, moved from faith in *Aide-toi* to a theoretical 'patriotic' republicanism. The *Temps* was owned by seventy-four liberal deputies, including Périer. Guizot, de Broglie, Lafayette and Dupont de l'Eure provided articles for its anti-Polignac programme. The *National* was the only Orleanist newcomer. It was financed by Laffitte and Baron Louis. Its three main editors were Thiers, Mignet and Carrel. Among the many periodicals probably the most distinguished was the *Revue Française*, which devoted its monthly editions to literary and historical themes. Its writers included three dismissed professors, Cousin, Jouffroy and Guizot while Carrel, Thiers, Duvergier de Hauranne and Rémusat also provided articles. The liberal press was far from unanimous in its appreciation of contemporary politics, but opposition to Polignac provided the missing cement. The royalist papers never held a common view. Many ultras could never reconcile themselves to Villèle and a section was always suspicious of the clerical influence. The best-seller amongst the royalist papers was the *Gazette de France*. Owned by Villèle and run by Genoude, who was pro-Jesuit, it sold 10 000 copies in 1828. The *Quotidienne*, the second in line, had a circulation of 6000 and took an ultra, anti-Villèle stance. The *Drapeau Blanc*, as its title implies, was the most ultra. It disliked Villèle and condemned Martignac as a Jacobin.

Its circulation was less than 2000. The government offered subsidies to favourable papers.[39]

Total subscription figures are very low by modern standards, but it should be remembered that an annual subscription would cost between seventy-two and eighty francs. However, the Parisian press was buttressed by a network of cheaper local papers. Circulation figures do not give a true picture of readership, since cafés and *cabinets de lectures* subscribed and through them one copy of a paper might reach several hundred readers. Similarly, in times of crisis papers were read aloud in the street. Restrictive press laws[40] and consequent trials in the 1820s gave a boost to the liberals by creating yet another cause around which they could unite and seek popular support. In 1829–30 the press and the *Aide-toi* committees helped to stimulate an unprecedented discussion of political affairs and to convince waverers that the king and Polignac were enemies of the constitutional charter and public liberties. They formed a legislative pressure group and petitions to abolish the *loi septennale* and to demand elected local councils were circulated. A society to oppose payment of taxes not sanctioned by parliament was widely publicised and attracted considerable attention and support. About 500 signed their petition in the Nord and 200 in the Bas-Rhin. Liberal deputies usually headed the lists. At the end of 1829 when the liberal paper in Dijon opened such a list, initiated by Hernoux, the deputy, they informed their readers that the movement was already well established in Brittany, Lorraine, Champagne, Paris and Rouen.[41] Some individuals actually refused to pay their taxes. Prefects were encouraged to employ spies to assess the significance of this protest movement, but the money was ill-spent for liberals gave full publicity to an activity they regarded as a constitutional duty. The twenty francs paid to the spy Bernard in the Meurthe bought only what could have been gleaned from the local paper. In the Nord the prefect underspent his secret fund of 700 francs by 500 francs in 1829 because the liberals saw no need to operate behind closed doors.[42] There was another shuffle of prefects in the autumn of 1829 in the hope of creating a more favourable atmosphere, but the only consequence was to put inexperienced men, totally lacking in local knowledge and contacts, at the head of departments. Prefectoral attempts to prosecute the liberal paper in Boulogne because it published the terms of the association and urged all liberal men and women to unite against the government, 'cette nouvelle tête de Méduse', failed to secure a conviction.[43]

When parliament finally reassembled in March 1830, after a four month delay, the liberal opposition was vociferous and intransigent in its initial reception of the government. The response to the speech from the throne was an unprecedented and outspoken motion of no confidence in the government, supported by a majority of 221 of the deputies present. The vote was unique in the history of the constitutional monarchy. A year earlier the speech from the throne had received an enthusiastic response from all sides. The 1830 response stressed loyalty to the king, but distrust of his government. Charles could have dismissed Polignac and chosen ministers acceptable to the parliamentary majority, or he had the option of a dissolution, followed by another election. For the first time a constitutional king chose to retain his government in defiance of parliament. On 19 March Charles announced the dissolution. In his proclamation, he asserted his affection for the 1814 constitution, complaining,

> This most recent Chamber of Deputies has deliberately misunderstood my intentions. I should be able to rely on its support in order to rule in the interests of my people; the Chamber has refused to support me. As father of my people, my soul was wounded, as king I was offended; the Chamber is thus dissolved.[44]

An election date was not given until May, but campaigning began immediately.

Two distinctive features were present. First, the government used the church as an electoral agent more overtly than ever before. Bishops were urged to support royalist candidates and responded by circulating prayers for electoral success to be used by their subordinates. The bishop of Metz sent a pamphlet on the election to all his *curés*, along with a confidential letter ordering them to explain to their parishioners which parliamentary candidates were worthy of their blessing. The archbishop of Paris, de Quelen, addressed his congregation in Notre-Dame in such stirring and romantic terms that he was quoted by both the *Constitutionnel* and the *Globe*:

> The lily banner, inseparable from the cross, will once more leave the field victorious ... if we never neglect any of the

means which order our duty to obtain monarchical and religious elections. We have reason to be interested in a cause so legitimate to the God of Clotilde and St Louis.[45]

Although the relationship between throne and altar had been growing so close in the last four years that the king was frequently (and somewhat unfairly) cartooned in clerical dress, this was the first election in which the church had campaigned so openly and so systematically.

Second, and even more significant, the king was more personally associated with the fortunes of a specific government than before. In principle the monarch and the government he appointed were separable, and it was possible for both left and right to oppose a government without their loyalty to the monarch being questioned. Indeed, the ultras had not always liked the choices made by Louis XVIII but no one would have suspected their royalism. By choosing and obstinately retaining ministers who echoed his own political thinking and whose ideas were the antithesis of the parliamentary majority, Charles rendered this essential distinction ineffective. Government propaganda posed a stark alternative: monarchy or republic.

By the time of the 1830 election liberal organisation had matured. *Aide-toi* printed a new series of informative pamphlets as soon as it became clear that there was to be an election.[46] The government could not match the network of communication and propaganda which was provided by the liberal press. The main target was the Polignac government. The use of the church in electioneering was a source of antagonism, and a useful riposte was the claim that France was now ruled by its clergy and Rome. The '221' became popular heroes, fêted by supporters in innumerable and well-attended banquets. The local deputy led the revelries of 200 voters in Colmar. Five hundred francs were collected for the poor. Loyal toasts were succeeded by rather seditious melodies. This was a typical convivial social occasion.[47] Thus government candidates faced a well-organised opposition whose enthusiasm and unity had been strengthened by recent events. In traditional liberal areas prefects could give no expectation of reversing the results of 1827.

The elections were held on 23 June in the *arrondissement* colleges and on 3 July in the departmental constituencies. Voting was delayed in twenty departments where disputes over the electoral list had not been settled by the time of the election. Of the 428 elected, 270 were liberals including 202 of the 221. Only 145 convinced 'royalists' were chosen. Liberalism was seen to be much more than the opposition of the commercial and industrial middle class. Despite all the manipulation of electoral laws, lists and processes, Charles's personal political preferences were unacceptable to the tiny, very rich elite. By mid-July the challenge to the Polignac government was incontrovertible. It was still open to the king to appoint ministers in tune with the parliamentary majority. To claim, as did the ultras, that this would have turned the world upside down in terrifying revolution, was nonsense. The liberals wanted constitutional government, admittedly a government in their own image. The personal intervention of the king in the elections made the crisis an acute constitutional one, seen by Charles as a matter of principle, not of mere personalities. He viewed the verdict of the electorate, as he had done the vote on the 221, as an attack on the authority of the ruler. His response was to use the personal legislative power allowed to the king in an emergency, to dispense with existing laws and issue decrees or ordinances.

What did the growth of opposition in Charles X's reign and the political conflict of 1830 signify? Traditional attitudes of sympathy for the ideas and policies of the revolutionary and imperial years and opposition to royal and clerical influence were reinforced in the mid- and late 1820s by the projects of the Villèle government The economic crisis intensified criticism of the government, although it did not unite critics, as Bourbon officials claimed. The crisis of the Restoration monarchy was primarily political. The appointment of Polignac, and the delay in calling the next session of parliament aggravated the situation. Charles and Polignac did much to create liberalism. Those in favour of constitutionalism had needed time to resolve their disagreements, arising from the revolutionary years, and to redefine their aims. Many royalists came to the conclusion that constitutional monarchy was as essential for them as for those to their political left. The ultra stance of Charles X, who refused to separate monarch from government, served as a catalyst in the development of liberal ideas and the division of royalism. The forceful and illegal intervention of the government and administration at all levels in elections gave the liberals a cause around which unity, otherwise unlikely, became possible. Liberals were not revolutionaries. They were the notables of their area, wealthy, respected citizens, with a considerable local following. They did little to inspire popular support; they were as hostile as the ultras towards democracy. In a sense such notables felt their power base threatened by Charles, and especially by the Polignac government. They feared the anti-parliamentary attitudes of the ultras, but did not themselves seek full parliamentary control. Charles X, unwilling to compromise, became the agent rather than the leader of the ultras. The ultras were in a way the real revolutionaries, anxious to return to a hypothetical golden age, when nobility, church and monarch ruled harmoniously over a submissive people. Their final gamble, the four ordinances, worried loyal royalists as well as liberals. Many of the liberal voters of 1827, and those of 1830 even more so, were royalists alarmed by the increased presence of the ultras. It was the onslaught of the ultras on the verdict of the majority of the electors in 1830 that provoked resistance and the overthrow of a king.

*The importance of the Hundred Days in unsettling the Restoration compromise and stimulating the survival of a revolutionary tradition has been observed by Robert Alexander in *Bonapartism and the Revolutionary Tradition in France. The Fédérés of 1815* (Cambridge, 1991) which appeared in the same year as the hardback edition of this book and adds further weight to its central thesis.

3
The Economic Crisis and the Revolution

The 1830 revolution was the product of the coincidence of a political conflict between the fast-growing liberal majority in parliament and the ultraroyalist Polignac government on the one hand, and an economic crisis, which made Paris volatile and disturbed the provinces on the other. Contemporary officials and most subsequent historians assumed that the growth of liberal opposition and popular unrest were linked with the economic depression, but this hypothesis has received little detailed investigation. What part did the economic crisis play in the outbreak of the 1830 revolution? Restoration prefects believed that liberalism was at least as much a socioeconomic as a political phenomenon and that the industrial and commercial middle class was almost exclusively liberal. Karl Marx later developed an influential hypothesis of revolution, in which the bourgeoisie was crucial to both 1830 and 1848.[1] Subsequently it has been assumed, by both his supporters and his critics, that economic disaster is an essential component of any respectable revolution.

In a brief comparative survey of the origins of the revolutions of 1789, 1830 and 1848, first published in 1949, Labrousse concluded that the 1830 depression lasted longer and was in some respects more damaging than that which preceded 1789.[2] A pioneering study of the economic crisis of 1827–32, published a generation ago, emphasised its long duration but noted that the July Days occurred before the depression reached its nadir. Gonnet concluded that the crisis, which persisted until 1832, cannot actually be seen as a catalyst of the 1830 revolution.[3] Historians of 1830 have paid scant attention to economic analysis. Bertier de Sauvigny, in a collection of documents on the revolution, included no evidence outside the chronological span of the year itself and made no reference to economic problems.[4] The most recent scholarly reappraisal of 1830, while accepting revisionist social categorisations of the elite, concentrated on the single year and on Paris. The Parisian artisans are placed centre-stage as revolutionaries while the liberal deputies dominate as beneficiaries of revolution, but the impact of the economic crisis on the liberals is not investigated.[5] A collection of essays on 1830 touched on a range of themes, including Orleanist economic policy, and urged that there should be further study of the significance of provincial unrest, which persisted long after the political crisis had subsided.[6]

This chapter investigates the ubiquitously-assumed link between the growth of liberalism and the economic depression, asks whether popular unrest had a specific political content and considers the relationship between popular and elite grievances. The number of liberal deputies rose during the economic crisis from less than 40 after the election of 1824 to 180 in 1827 and 274 in 1830.[7] Although liberalism embraced all but the most remote and poor departments by 1830, it had most appeal in the main industrial areas, Paris, of course, and the east and the north-east. The Haut-Rhin, Meuse, Bas-Rhin and Vosges were the most liberal departments in 1829.[8] We shall consider the relationship between the economic depression and the opposition of both notables and the less well off with particular, though not exclusive, reference to those departments in northern and eastern France, including the most industrially progressive areas outside Paris. The northern half of the country was depicted by an influential contemporary economist as modernising, educated and innovative, where a new generation sought economic change on a revolutionary scale.[9] It included one of the main areas of the developing factory industry. There was considerable economic and social change: an urban factory cotton industry was to some degree threatening traditional rural and artisan textile crafts while the second major industry, iron, was also experiencing difficulties. In the silk industry of Lyons the traditional structure was being eroded by the deterioration in the status of master weavers as the merchants gained increasing control. Then came an economic crisis between 1827 and 1832 that was partly agricultural and partly industrial. What impact did these various economic problems have on expressions of political discontent and the growth of opposition? Was liberalism itself in part a response to the economic depression? How destabilising was popular unrest? How far was the actual revolution affected by the provincial situation?

Climatic disasters produced periodic subsistence crises in France during the nineteenth century at roughly ten-yearly intervals. Grain shortages were aggravated by expensive and slow transport facilities and the traditional resistance of local people to the concept that grain should be moved from an area of relative prosperity to one of shortage. Between 1827 and 1832 France suffered poor grain harvests while potato and wine production also slumped. In addition, there was a severe commercial, and thus industrial recession.

In good years France could feed itself and the amount of land under cultivation increased, though by less than the optimistic 50 per cent estimate of one contemporary.[10] The population grew only modestly, from 29 million to 32.5 million, between 1815 and 1831. But the excess of production over consumption was slight and when shortages occurred through climatic disaster the cost of food exceeded the purchasing power of the poor, for whom bread or potatoes, even in good years, used up well over half a weekly wage.[11] More fertile arable departments usually produced a surplus and there was a substantial and well-established internal traffic in grain by road, river and canal to serve Paris, the Midi and the more mountainous and remote departments which customarily bought up to 50 per cent of their grain needs from elsewhere. The Ile de France was rapidly developing a market economy based on large-scale grain production, concentrated on substantial, mostly tenanted, arable holdings. Elsewhere big estates were often mainly forested and cereal production came third after timber and wine. Unique in Europe were the large and growing number of peasant-owned farms, but contemporary concern revealed that, apart from in the poorer and mostly southern departments, an increase in the number of holdings was usually the result of subdivision rather than a growth in the amount of land owned by peasants. In the Nord, as elsewhere, subdivision was blamed for widespread rural indigence.[12] Holdings of three hectares or less were common, insufficient to support a family and much too poor to implement technical improvements. In eastern France medium-sized leasehold farms were usual and these offered more potential.

The commercial policy of the Restoration was made by and for the large-scale producer, not the consumer, with tariffs to protect his profits. In the famine years of 1816–17, free import of grain had been permitted on a temporary basis, but a subsequent swift price fall had caused landowners successfully to demand protective tariffs, and a sliding scale was introduced, similar to that in operation in Great Britain. Tax regulations, instituted in 1819, forbade foreign grain imports when the price of top quality French grain fell to twenty francs a *quintal* (100 kilos). In 1820 prices stayed low and producer pressure strengthened the tariff to exclude all grain imports until French grain had reached twenty-four francs and to allow free import at twenty-six francs. After an abundant harvest in 1825 the law was rigorously applied until the 1830 revolution, with imports severely restricted, with an especially sharp impact in 1828 as prices rose.[13]

In the years 1827–32 France suffered an unusually long run of consistently bad harvests, more sustained even than the crisis that preceded the 1789 Revolution.[14] In some areas the 1827 harvest was a third or more below the norm. Price rises and fears of dearth added to anxieties surrounding the election at the end of the year. Low yields continued in 1828 and the spring and early summer of 1829 were universally bleak. In the Moselle, which usually produced a surplus, prices rose suddenly in May from nineteen francs, to twenty-five francs per hectolitre of wheat.

Near-panic-buying for Paris was blamed for the sudden and dramatic price increases in Burgundy.[15] Although the wheat harvest of 1829 proved fair, that of other grains such as rye and oats, used in the making of the poorer quality bread, was seriously reduced. Unusually heavy rain in the autumn made it necessary to sow between a quarter and a third more than in an average year,[16] thus diminishing saleable stocks, and the very harsh winter of 1829–30 made the prospects for 1830 bleak. Potatoes froze and grain that had already been sown was ruined. In stark contrast to 1820–25, the years 1826–30 saw food supplies become precarious and expensive: in eastern France wheat prices rose from an average of 16 fr. 75 per hectolitre in 1826, to 21 fr. 13 in 1830. The rise was not uniform, and prices could vary markedly even between neighbouring markets.[17] The more remote departments, which often were those most in need of supplementary grain supplies, experienced the biggest price rises. In the spring of 1829, when problems were particularly acute, the prefect in the Eure demanded an increase in the local garrison to protect grain routes into Brittany.[18] Panic could arise even where there was no actual shortage. The succession of poor harvests led to fears of dearth and price rises, even when supplies for the whole country may have been adequate. National statistics do not illuminate the question of distribution, and in this pre-railway age the transport of grain either by cart or barge was slow, expensive, irregular and likely to lead to grumbles and violence from the poor in bad years. One statistic is revealing, however: there were ninety separate markets, each setting different prices. This was a major factor in creating panic, confusion and constant suspicion of merchants.[19]

The escalation of basic food prices made the income of many inadequate. How did the local population react to such problems? Bands of roaming beggars, mostly women and children became a common sight, particularly in the north, causing panic among landowners.[20] Although internal free trade had been practised theoretically for over forty years, the poor believed that it was merely part of the armoury of sharp practice of merchants moving grain elsewhere to force up the price. They clung fiercely to the idea that grain should be sold locally at a 'fair' price. Cart-loads of grain in transit would be stopped by crowds and sold; merchants at the market would be intimidated into selling at a lower price than that set for the day.[21] Such unrest, sometimes accompanied by violence, became common in 1829–30. In April 1829 an army of 200 angry women in Châtillon, Côte-d'Or, forced merchants to sell at nearly a sixth below the agreed price.[22] In the same month in the Nord there were three days of rioting in which over 200 women and children threatened merchants and attacked their homes. Most of the demonstrators were textile workers and unrest was only quelled through severe repression by the authorities, threats from employers that operatives who participated would be sacked and the implementation of food requisitions for the needy.[23] By now imported grain was entering France through the northern ports, but suspicion and resistance to the movement of this grain led to a number of incidents.

Potatoes were also scarce. Between 1825 and 1830 the yield was too negligible to be assessed. The failure was important, for the potato was the basic food of the poor in the north, and of industrial workers especially. Potato riots were common. In 1829 women and children forcibly opposed the transport of sacks bought for a neighbouring commune. Some were stolen, which was fairly unusual, and the rest sold at a 'fair' price. Fourteen rioters were arrested.[24] Such episodes normally involved mainly women and children: women were less likely to be arrested because of their responsibility to provide for their families. Bread and grain riots were most numerous in areas of the greatest concentrations of unemployment, like the Nord, but in the spring and early summer of 1829 rioting became endemic and seemed to occur spontaneously in response to the sudden substantial price rises.[25] Occasionally makeshift posters indicated underlying political grievances of a general nature. In May a poster was found in one of the poorest areas of Metz which urged the hungry, 'Brave people of Metz. The time has come to fight for the revolution! Take up your weapons!' People were urged to march on local bakeries.[26] About the same time a poster in Douai declared roundly,

> Down with Charles X – he's a fool! Down with the nobles – they're scum! Down with the rabble of grain speculators who put up the price of our food! Long live the revolution![27]

Such direct political invocations were rare, however. The poor normally confined themselves to demonstrations that followed a traditional pattern, attempting to force an abnormal situation back into the perceived norm. Grain and bread riots were rarely violent and seldom involved theft, but tried to assert age-old conventions. High bread prices affected everyone, but particularly the urban artisan bereft of a rural base, and above all the Parisian worker.

The wealthy, whatever their politics, totally discouraged such behaviour. Mayors, prefects and ultimately the commander of the local garrison worked in close liaison to bring riots under control, but widespread unrest put strains upon limited manpower. Troops were only called out as a last resort after the mayor had tried to calm tempers and mediate. Municipal and private charity collections were seen as the solution. In April 1829 each commune in the Pas-de-Calais was ordered to set up a *bureau de bienfaisance* to distribute bread and other food – but not money – to the poor and to organise navvying work on local roads for the unemployed.[28] In Calavados the *bureau* had a budget of 12 000 francs. The prefect commented that the gratitude of the indigent was such that popular unrest had ceased.[29] Occasionally officials seemed almost overcome by the visible suffering of the poor.[30] Liberal politicians were as apprehensive of grain riots as royalists: their rationale queried the whole basis of capitalist agriculture, in which landowners of all political persuasions could well have an interest. In the provinces, however, such rioting was no more than an irritant. Such manifestations of grievance were small-scale, sporadic, worrying for local property owners but sufficiently isolated to be quite easily contained.

Disquiet over food supplies was aggravated by difficulties in other branches of agriculture. Throughout the Restoration there was sharp criticism of the government monopoly of the production of tobacco in departments (such as the Meurthe, Nord and Rhenish departments) and pressure for the reintroduction of private initiative. More serious in the years after 1827, however, was the crisis in the wine-producing industry, a very important source of wealth for France. The grievances of viticulturalists came nearer to uniting elite and popular discontent than any other aspect of the economic crisis, for the production of wine involved both wealthy firms supplying a national and even international market and small peasant farmers selling their mediocre produce locally. Despite enormous disparities of income, both tended to envisage their problems in political, not just climatic dimensions. The amount of land under the vine had expanded fast during the Empire and continued to grow, for the grape was regarded as a good investment. Land used for viticulture was reckoned to be worth, on average, 2400 francs per hectare, while arable land was rated at 600 francs.[31] In 1789 about 1.5 million hectares were under vines and this had risen to 2 million by 1829, partly at the expense of arable land. The average yield had also risen from 17.23 hectolitres in 1786–88 to 21.93 in 1826–28.[32] Farms, which were usually cultivated by the family with no outside help, were very small, averaging 20 *ares* (1 *are* = 100 square metres) in Alsace, where there were over 75 000 viticulturalists,[33] working in an open-field strip system. In Burgundy, where most farms were leasehold, the short leases of six to nine years, normal since the Empire, added to the difficulties unleashed by periodic climatic disasters.

During the Empire French viticulturalists were able to dominate the European market; the former Austrian Netherlands and the Confederation of the Rhine had been excellent customers. The Treaty of Paris ended this favourable situation and French wine soon encountered hostile tariffs. The Low Countries put a 100 per cent duty on French wine.[34] Wine exports from Alsace to Baden, Württemberg and Switzerland, previously her best customers, consuming twice as much Alsatian wine as the rest of France, dropped alarmingly. Wintzenheim, which before 1822 had exported one-third of its harvest abroad, could barely dispose of one-ninth of a much reduced harvest in 1829.[35] Viticulturalists pressed the Chamber of Deputies to open discussions with other nations on comparative tariffs.[36] Official statistics do not wholly confirm the viticulturalists' impression of total devastation, although there was a distinct falling-off in the export trade – those areas served by eastern France, for example, notably the German states, whose imports fell from 11 million litres in 1821 to 1.3 million in 1824.[37] Prices collapsed. In 1828 the selling price in Colmar was only just over half that of 1789, when prices had been lower than usual, following a serious slump.

The full explanation for the crisis in the wine industry lies in a myriad of factors, but most were seen to have national political implications. High indirect taxes caused much resentment. Restoration governments continued Napoleonic policies and five indirect wine taxes were retained (of which the most substantial was the *droit d'entrée*, a tax on wine entering a commune, which varied according to the size of the commune). These duties resembled old and long-detested taxes revived after a short break during the Revolution. They were levied on quantity, not quality, and could almost quadruple the price of wine.[38] In Strasbourg in 1821 the *droit d'entrée* tax alone was more than the value of the wine itself. In addition, ironically, the abundance of the harvests in the mid-twenties caused prices to fall catastrophically and built up a huge unsaleable surplus, for most wine would not keep longer than three years[39] and would not travel outside the region.

The Martignac government took the whole economic crisis seriously and held parliamentary enquiries and debates into the wine industry and other major industries (mainly metallurgical and textile). They sought and received evidence from manufacturers and officials. Parliamentary coverage was unprecedented. In the spring of 1829 the Chamber of Deputies held a special debate on the wine industry. Seventy-two petitions, with over 60 000 signatures, were sent from all wine-growing areas of the country. A petition from the Bas-Rhin stressed that in 1828 total production costs for one hectare, including land tax and wine taxes, were 753 francs, whereas the wine itself was only worth 428 fr. 40. Over 3000 *vignerons* in Arbois, Burgundy, vigorously condemned the army of parasitical, thieving tax-collectors.[40] But the wine taxes remained unaltered and the problem was made more acute by the harvest of 1829, poor in both quantity and quality.[41] In the Moselle the yield dropped from nearly half a million hectolitres to a mere 165 000.[42] In the Doubs some left the grapes to rot, judging the costs of processing and taxation not worth the effort of picking.[43] The bitter winter of 1829–30 ruined the 1830 harvest throughout the nation. Only 15 million hectolitres of wine were produced compared with nearly 38 million in 1828.[44] Even local officials took the view that the wine taxes needed revision[45] but nothing was done.

Their concern was far from altruistic. The plight of the viticulturalists had become a lively political issue. The petitions of 1829 had been drawn up and presented to the chamber by liberal deputies and the drafting committees, usually identical with the *Aide-toi* liberal electoral committees, often remained in existence to continue the campaign. Liberal newspapers, like the *Impartial* in the Doubs, vigorously criticised the wine taxes. The failure of the government to respond provoked a more violent reaction. In October 1829 groups of viticulturalists marched on the town hall of Besançon to press for an immediate tax cut. Troops had to be called out to break up this typical demonstration.[46] Tax offices were often wrecked and the files and tax registers burned. There were numerous incidents of this kind. Persistent rioting came to a climax after the July revolution, for wine producers hoped in vain that a new regime would grant immediate redress for their grievances.[47] The problems of this large and vocal group (comprising both very small-scale and wealthy producers) linked the liberal parliamentary opposition with popular discontent, gave a specific content to liberalism and led to a high level of violent popular political activity. Their activity was far more politicised and organised than that of other small farmers, perhaps because in some areas they farmed in a communal-type enterprise, but perhaps also because rich and poor shared common grievances against the government of the day, whatever its political complexion, while *droits réunis* and protectionist tariff policies remained.

Harvest failure and resulting problems made the small towns of this area centres of demonstrations and riots, in which the sufferers – small farmers, their employees, artisans and some factory workers – sometimes gained the sympathy and leadership of the wealthy liberals. To aggravate both the misery and the violence of the response, France also experienced an industrial depression in the late 1820s, produced in part by international circumstances, and which had a marked impact. A financial crisis in Great Britain in 1826 led to a tightening of credit resources in France by October. The number of bankruptcies in France rose from 1095 in 1825 to 1757 in 1828 and the amount of capital involved doubled to over 100 million francs. In the Haut-Rhin the number rose from four in 1825 to nineteen in 1828 and did not begin to fall until 1832. Bankruptcies had a snowball effect, undermining many small tradesmen, and were disastrous for the economy of poorer districts. In Mirecourt, Vosges, the disappearance of a banker in 1828 left 120 000 francs to be accounted for, mostly in the small town itself. A large number of local families were ruined, for all lost at least 60 per cent and many their whole savings. In this period all business enterprise involved considerable risk. Even large Parisian concerns crumbled in 1830.[48] Bankers, merchants and industrialists were all vulnerable, and the fragility of the credit structure had a decisive impact on both production and orders, not to mention investment itself.

During the Empire the demands of war, and even more the effects of the Continental System, had stimulated some local industries for a time, particularly the metallurgical and textile trades, although for many it had been a time of set-backs. Of the twenty-five most distinguished firms in Alsace nine were set up between 1795 and 1805, including two of the most wealthy cotton manufacturers in the region, Dollfus-Mieg and Koechlin.[49] While industry remained on the whole small-scale and artisan, with family organisations, small workshops and rural industry of great variety, using local raw materials in an almost subsistence economy in some instances, the developing cotton industry, concentrated around Mulhouse, Haut-Rhin, but also to some extent around St-Die and Chatillon, introduced large-scale manufacture. The peace of 1815 saw the return of less commercially advantageous circumstances. Orders for war materials fell, foreign outlets dried up and were often closed completely by prohibitive tariffs. The renewed availability of American cotton and export potential outside Europe was insufficient compensation for the rude shock of British competition. During the war France had imposed only a 10 per cent duty on foreign iron, but in 1814 the sudden influx of much cheaper, British-produced iron, lowered prices by 40 per cent.[50] The cotton industry suffered too. In 1814 the number of workers employed in Alsace fell fom 44 000 to 17 400. British imports were blamed.[51] Pressure for the imposition of protective tariffs grew and local views were forcefully expressed in the departmental general councils composed of wealthy notables. Restoration governments responded and a highly protectionist system evolved between 1815 and 1826. The tariff on imported iron was raised to 50 per cent, from 4 fr. 50 to 16 fr. 50 on 100 kilos, and by 1822 duties on imported coal-smelted iron stood at 120 per cent. By 1826 duties on raw wool amounted to the prohibition of foreign imports. Certain ranges of manufactured textiles, particularly cotton goods, were banned in 1816.[52] Thus, unlike the wine producers, manufacturers and merchants were successful in gaining governmental sanction to protect their commercial ambitions and in 1827–32 their problems lay elsewhere.

There was a sharp increase in the demand for smelted iron in the 1820s as the introduction of new techniques in cotton production, for instance, stimulated the manufacture of new machines. The amount of iron used nearly doubled between 1820 and 1824[53] and producers benefitted. The industry was in an equivocal position, however, for although it was long established, and had a quality product, manufacturing costs were high. Mines and forges, scattered through large forested estates (the Haute-Marne was France's biggest producer), were often isolated and small, their location determined by the source of iron ore. Until the 1820s charcoal from local timber was used almost exclusively for smelting and refining, and one of the fundamental problems of the industry was the soaring price of timber as well-located sources became exhausted. Systematic replanting of forests only began in the 1820s. Some forge-owners could supply their own needs, but those who had to buy timber were in difficulties. In the Champagne area the price of wood rose (from 3–3 fr. 50 per corde in 1819–21, to 9–10 francs in 1824) and continued to increase.[54] Charcoal prices more than doubled between 1822 and 1828.[55]

Ultimately the shortage led to technical change; in 1821 the first English-style coal-run blast furnaces were introduced in France, mainly in the Saône-et-Loire, Moselle and Meuse. Geology did not smile on this development, however; in France usable supplies of iron and coal rarely coincided. Coal could be transported by river or canal, but France's canal network was still incomplete and insufficient for this purpose; transport costs by the existing waterways were high. It was reckoned that a load of St-Etienne coal of 2770 hectolitres, which cost 2475 francs at the pit-head, would fetch 13 425 fr. 25 in Paris. Tax doubled the original price, navigation tolls accounted for 600 francs and the rest of it was made up by general transport costs.[56] As coal-smelting used nearly three times as much fuel as charcoal-smelting, it was only practicable where the coal and iron existed naturally in close proximity. Thus by 1825, only seven coal-fired blast furnaces were operational,[57] but twenty forges refining smelted iron were running on coal and Franche-Comté charcoal-smelted iron was transported to St-Etienne for refining and the production of bar iron.[58] The difference in production costs was striking. It cost 88 francs to produce a ton of coal-smelted iron, but 300 francs for a ton of charcoal-smelted.[59] In the short term, however, transport costs, increased demand and prohibitive duties on foreign iron meant that iron prices soared.[60] St-Etienne bar iron rose from 49 francs per 100 kilograms in 1821 to 65 francs in 1825.[61] The circumstances allowed an uneconomic growth of the traditionally organised industry. Numerous small forges were set up in the 1820s in the Champagne area and Franche-Comté, adding to the rise in timber prices.[62] Eventually ironmasters combined to close certain forges periodically and compensate the owners.[63]

The Martignac government organised a detailed and critical investigation into the industry. Manufacturers were unfavourably compared with their British counterparts for their lack of technical innovation and high prices. In 1830 French bar iron varied between 420 and 500 francs per 1000 kilos at the place of manufacture. British iron cost 167 fr. 50 at the port of entry. A tariff of 275 francs and high transport costs pushed it to a comparable price. Only the lack of investment and poor transport facilities held the government back from lowering tariffs. Manufacturers were appalled by the tone and implications of the enquiry. They had all contributed to the detailed evidence studied by the government, clearly had fairly close relations with each other and were united in the conviction that their problems were of the government's making. They argued that the timber shortage was artificially sustained by the government itself, for the state was the single largest forest owner and controlled the size and price of the annual timber sale.[64] Thus, not for the first or last time, a debate on economic affairs turned into a political wrangle.

The short-term crisis certainly damaged the industry. Production was down by one-third, but producers hid like ostriches under the tariffs for which they had lobbied, and the resulting exorbitant cost of iron in France was damaging to all other industries dependent upon it. Did the problems of the iron industry provoke a concerted political response at the popular as well as at the elite level? The structure of the industry, with numerous small, scattered forges, meant that contact between the relatively tiny groups of workers was minimal and worker unrest slight. It was a rural industry, whose workers were involved in agriculture for part of the year, which perhaps gave them some protection from the effects of the recession. Their employers, who constituted a powerful liberal pressure group, were vocal in their criticism of the failure of governments to help them. It is hard to see what any government could have done. It was inconceivable that tariffs could go any higher. Many of the ironmasters were wealthy landowners and they had combined during the Restoration to push successive governments to raise tariffs rather than make their product genuinely competitive. The Martignac government knew that the restructuring and investment needed to convert to coal-smelting was not in their hands. For the first time in the Restoration a government recognised that high tariffs were damaging and uneconomic. However, it was another thirty years before substantial tariff cuts were attempted. The short-term crisis at the end of the twenties afforded the opportunity to discuss the industry, but the rich ironmasters were too influential for a weak government like that of Martignac to challenge them and consequently the national enquiry contributed little but opprobrium for Charles X and his governments.

The relatively newly established cotton industry suffered specifically as a result of the short-term crisis. The Norman industry, centred on Rouen, was very different in structure and markets from that of Alsace. In the early nineteenth century, there were 3000 mills in Normandy, many started by local foremen or clerks. The structure of the industry was thus more traditional and artisan than the larger-scale, more factory-based industry of Mulhouse. Cotton in Normandy was dominated by two main groups, however: ten Protestant families from Bolbec who entered the industry in 1750 and a group of merchants and bankers from Rouen. They either put up the money for mills established by English experts in the 1780s or set up their own firms after the French Revolution of 1789. By the 1840s the ten largest of these firms employed over 60 per cent of all workers and their hold gradually increased with the escalating cost and complexity of new machinery. The 'artisan' industry was principally a 'putting-out' exercise.[65]

The Alsatian industry had begun in the middle of the eighteenth century and the Mulhouse area was famous for high-quality printed cottons. The first spinning machines were introduced in 1806,[66] and steam engines in 1812, which meant spinning, weaving and printing could all be done in one factory. During the Empire, supplies of raw cotton were scarce, but the period was one of rapid technical progress. Until the mid-1820s, however, cotton was normally spun mechanically in a factory and then put out to rural weavers in the surrounding area (or even as far away as the Vosges and Haute-Saône). By 1829 four firms had introduced weaving machines, some imported from Great Britain, some made locally. The rural side of the industry was thus being rapidly eroded in these years.[67] The total number of workers rose to 59 800 by 1831.[68] Despite contemporary eulogistic reports of its progress,[69] the industry did experience some set-backs. It had grown fast, with many new factories opening with a slender credit margin,[70] and the drive to expand somtimes outran both credit and outlets.

The Norman and Alsatian industries served different markets, the former concentrating on cheaper goods and competing at home with wool and abroad with British cotton, the latter cultivating the luxury trade in direct competition with silk. Markets at home were promising, but not secure, and the potential of foreign markets was limited both by tariffs and the lower prices of British and Belgian cotton goods. After 1815 manufacturers wooed non-European customers and had some success in Persia, India, China, Turkey and the New World. The financial crisis of 1826 brought new problems. In 1826 exports fell by 10 million francs and, after a slight recovery in 1827, by 2 million in 1828.[71] The Mulhouse manufacturers began an intensive marketing campaign in Europe[72] but despite their efforts bankruptcies increased and unemployment grew. Several expedients were resorted to: early in 1827 wages were cut,[73] then a shift system of three days off and three days on was adopted. By January 1828 10 000 were idle, even though many of the foreign workers had been sent home.[74] Similar tactics were tried in the Nord where rates of pay no longer covered basic subsistence.[75] Previously the relationship between employer and worker had been reasonably harmonious, apparently, with housing and technical education classes provided,[76] but during the crisis employers forced their operatives to work for lower rates by bringing in the troops, which seriously reduced mutual trust.

There were no formal organisations of workers, although on rare occasions they did band together to achieve a temporary respite. Women operatives in the Aisne refused to work after a reduction in their daily rate until it was restored to its former level and work guaranteed. Their brief success was not due to their strength, however, but to a riot a few days earlier when 200 youths, brought from poor houses in Brittany and Normandy to work at the factory, had protested at their ill-treatment, refused to work and wrecked the workshop. The women were presumably judged a better bet. As a large proportion of operatives were women and children, the appearance of troops was usually enough to persuade them of the wisdom of accepting a wage cut and shorter hours. When their economic position became totally untenable, they simply left. In May 1827 100 of the employees of a leading manufacturer in Mulhouse went back to their small family plots of land in desperation, rather than work for starvation wages. By April 1828 most operatives had followed suit, leaving only foreign workers employed. The foreigners were detested by native operatives, as were local Jewish money-lenders, to whom the urban and rural poor were often in debt. The factory workers' links with the countryside had not been severed, but because of the accompanying harvest failure, the land owned by their families could not provide sufficient sustenance and misery, begging and stealing increased sharply. At the beginning of 1830 free distribution of bread became the norm. In Sedan, Ardennes, where many of the cloth manufacturers had reduced hours and wages, posters appeared in the town at the beginning of 1829, threatening employers and inciting workers:

> You workers sound tough, but your hearts' not in a fight! If you were as brave as your words you'd say, as Napoleon did, "Conquer or die in the attempt!" The time has come to decide whether to go on working, or shut down the worshops![77]

In this instance, however, the workers failed to answer the call. Although such posters were carefully copied, with all their errors in official reports, there was apparently no investigation into their source, perhaps because they were so exceptional. Indeed, there is far more evidence of worker unrest after the July Days than before the revolution.

The crisis in the factory system had a direct effect on rural industry for much of the weaving was still done on a domestic basis. There is, however, no evidence of organised or violent protest against cut-backs from the handloom weavers. Combining agricultural labouring or small-scale agriculture with weaving, this group had experienced a brief period of prosperity, as technical improvements in spinning preceded the development and use of weaving machines in the factories. But by the late twenties their wages were plummeting, never to recover. In 1832 a handloom weaver averaged seventy-three centîmes a day,[78] less than half the wage of a machine operator. Between the mid-1820s and the mid-1840s when the average wage of workers varied little, a survey of wages and living costs calculated that a minimum subsistence wage was 1 fr. 25. Unless a handloom weaver could substantially supplement his income through agriculture, therefore, he would be constantly dependent on charity.[79]

It will be apparent that the manufacturers themselves, for all their 'charity', were ruthless in the running of their businesses. They were highly critical of official policy, and of the Polignac government in particular. They argued that tariffs, which protected other textiles, kept their costs high and markets limited, leading to a crisis of over-production. Whereas manufacturers elsewhere in France, particularly where production techniques were less modern, favoured the maintenance of prohibitive tariffs on British cotton (which was cheaper than French cotton although wages were double) some leading manufacturers in Alsace argued that the tariffs kept them out of the foreign market[80] and caused them to pay dear for coal and machinery. Concentrating on the luxury end of the trade, they were, of course, less in direct competition with the British than the cotton industry of Normandy. The crisis intensified the already lively and almost total opposition of the Alsatian manufacturers to Restoration governments, but the roots of their opposition were unquestionably more complex, and indeed, many disagreed with Nicholas Koechlin's view that the abolition of the prohibitive tariff would benefit them. Thus, although major Alsatian entrepreneurs formd the core of local liberal opposition, it was an opposition that had its genesis well before the crisis of 1827–32, which simply provided a new stick to lay about the government (or, rather, several small sticks, for the liberals were in open disagreement on how the government could help to resolve the crisis). Their workers, many of whom were foreigners, women or children, were in no position to sustain a coherent protest. The illusion that employers were genuinely concerned with the moral and physical well-being of their operatives, although dented in this crisis, survived into the July Monarchy and some working men actually joined the opposition societies of the early 1830s.

The problems of the second major textile industry that was producing for more than a local market, the silk industry of Lyons, were only partially related to the crisis of the late 1820s.[81] The industry, which dominated France's second city, was long established and had a traditional craft structure, with independent masters working their own looms, employing their own family and a limited number of journeymen and others, and producing cloth for a merchant, or *fabricant*, as he was rather misleadingly called.[82] The industry had expanded rapidly since the end of the eighteenth century. In 1786 there were 15 000 looms. The number fell during the Revolution, then picked up and increased during the Empire, encouraged by the virtual monopoly of the Continental System. By 1827 there were over 30 000 looms, two-thirds in Lyons, the rest in the outskirts and the surrounding villages.[83] The industry had become increasingly urban since the introduction of a weaving machine by Jacquard in 1805: it required a high capital outlay and began to alter the character of production, tending to make the formerly independent master more reliant on the merchant, often borrowing from him to buy a machine.[84] The protectionist system of the Restoration was blamed for the failure to increase silk exports, but in fact high quality cottons and foreign silk were redoubtable rivals. The crisis of the late twenties thus hit a far from contented city. Temporarily the main export markets of Great Britain and the United States were partially lost and exports fell by 25 per cent in 1826.[85] Cut-backs in the silk industry affected other trades and in September 1826 many workers in a variety of trades were unemployed and surviving by begging.[86] By the end of the year one-third of the weaving machines were idle.[87] Some blamed over-expansion and high production costs, especially wages. Lyons' silk was over twice as expensive as its British equivalent – 1 fr. 20 to 1 fr. 25 per ell (45 inches) compared with forty centîmes – but wages do not seem to have been outrageously high, even at the best of times. A master could expect to make about three francs a day, out of which he had to pay his assistants. Such rates were far from princely when the lowest quality bread was twenty-five centîmes per half-kilo[88] and when the nature of the industry meant that work and orders were precarious.

Following the crisis of 1826 wages fell well below the basic level of subsistence.[89] Craftsmen tried to band together to protect their livelihood. *Compagnonnages*, traditional journeymens' associations, provided a nucleus. Societies, like the masters' *Devoir Mutuel* tried to provide for needy members. However, as the membership fee was three francs with a monthly subscription of one franc, only the better off could participate.[90] Local officials, nervous because of the well-known Bonapartist sympathies of workers, were quick to act.[91] In May–June 1830 a ten-day strike was held by workers in various trades, including carpentry, to protest against low wages. Up to 1200 took part in a number of hostile demonstrations and sixty people were arrested. At the end of June, when sentences of between three and five months were passed on the men, their colleagues tried to release them by force.[92] Thus in Lyons the combination of the deterioration in the status of the weavers and the economic crisis crystallised the development of worker co-operation and action. Realising the seriousness of the problem, the prefect tried to organise navvying work for the unemployed at 1–1 fr. 50 a day and set up a poor relief committee, financed by private charity subscriptions. By April 1829 the committee had raised 82 000 francs and was supporting 3156 families.[93] The prefect appealed for central government help, particularly for the carpentry trades, and in June a temporary workhouse was set up. The urban poor were both afraid and suspicious of the new institution and shunned it. Only fifty people applied for help; the government rapidly concluded that there was no real problem,[94] but the crisis was far from resolved. The sophisticated and vigorous worker protest had barely begun, as the governments of Louis-Philippe found to their cost.

Other textile industries faced similar problems of competition with cotton and adjustment to new techniques and structures. Machines brought lower prices and the decay of rural trades made redundant by factory-produced alternatives. The rural textile trade were based on locally grown products. Sheep were kept for their wool and in many areas there was a traditional, small-scale woollen industry operating in close conjunction with agriculture and producing for a very local market.[95] The quadrupling of the tariff on foreign wool between 1820 and 1826 led to a 10 per cent price increase in raw wool and the virtual exclusion of imported wool. This may have helped large-scale producers, but did little to restore the price of spun wool which, with the fall in demand, had collapsed by 1826 from forty-two francs per 140 pounds, to just over twenty-six francs.[96] Other trades suffered the same type of double assault, including the spinning and weaving of flax and hemp, the production of cambric, lace-making, stocking manufacture and so on. The 11 600 workers in lace and linen crafts in the Pas-de-Calais could scrape together a mere sixty centimes for a day's work.[97] Because such trades were based on local agriculture, their slow decline had repercussions elsewhere, creating a long-term problem of poverty and adjustment to new jobs. In the summer of 1828, when unemployment should have been at its lowest point in the year, the relief committee in Lille had a record 31 000 unemployed on its books.[98] Craft workers in the towns tended to suffer more than those in the countryside, where workers were prepared to accept the lowest rates and thus continued to find work.[99] The leather industry of the Haute-Marne which concentrated on gloves for a luxury market was suffering, as were small-scale metallurgical crafts, like cutlery-making, which traditionally provided work for 5500 in a hundred communes around Nogent and Langres entirely on a 'putting-out' system. In Besançon clock-making was well established, but in 1827 some 3000 Swiss clock-makers were forced to return home through lack of orders. Those employed in paper manufacture, especially in the Vosges, experienced widespread unemployment in 1828, but in this case it was not the short-term crisis, but a new machine for production which engendered lively protests.[100] The slackness of the craft industries was of crucial importance for both agriculture and industry, particularly as this coincided with harvest failures, because a high proportion of the local population depended on a combination of farming and cottage industry work to survive.

Another element in the delicate balance of the economy of the poor was also under threat in these years. Since the Revolution, aspects of communal traditions had been eroded and legislation in 1827 authorised the sale of communally owned forests. Traditionally, wood gathered from these forests had been a vital ingredient in the programme of survival for the poorer members of the commune. Now those who persisted in the practice were hounded by troops and charged with theft. One such 'thief' who was caught was in such a miserable state that he hanged himself.[101] Thus, the dilution of the communal system, accelerated by revolutionary legislation in the 1790s, added markedly to artisan and peasant distress. More commercial and competitive methods in both agriculture and manufacturing stimulated peasant protest, which smouldered throughout the century, although the impact varied according to the importance of communal land and traditions in different regions. As both French and British researchers have shown, peasant and artisan resistance to rural 'modernisation' and the introduction of more capitalist practices became increasingly politicised in some areas. Of relatively modest significance in these years, it was to reach greater proportions in the 1840s and 1850s. The defenders of communal rights were uniformly poor, whether peasant or peasant–artisan, and their preferences were derided as anachronistic by modernisers.[102]

The economic problems of these years were real enough. In 1828 the prefect of the Nord reckoned that one-sixth of the population of just under a million were being kept alive through charity contributions, and that in Lille half of the town was entirely dependent on the charity of the other half.[103] Popular unrest became almost the norm. Grain and bread riots, forced sales of grain, rebellions by viticulturalists, minor strikes and industrial unrest were daily occurrences. Only in Lyons and Paris did coherent and sustained protest develop, however. Most industries lacked sufficient concentration, and the workers were without the experience to defy existing punitive legislation and the rapid use of troops against them. On the whole, popular protests against unemployment, technical innovation or rural misery tended to be sporadic, spontaneous and out of the mainstream of national and parliamentary life.

It was a different matter for the wealthy liberal electors. Universally those electors whose vote depended at least in part on their payment of a tax on industrial or commercial property were considered by successive Restoration governments and their prefects a group hostile to the regime, working through elections, electoral committees and the Chamber of Deputies to criticise the government. Many historians have concluded that there thus existed a bourgeois, capitalist opposition to the Restoration.[104] It is true that whole groups of industrialists were liberal, like the cotton magnates of Mulhouse, for example, but so were the majority of electors throughout France in 1830, and most of these were landowners. In other respects, too, government officials misjudged the liberals. They complained that liberal electoral agents tried to stir up the urban and rural poor against the regime. In fact, the links between the opposition of the elite and the discontent of the poor were slight. Liberal deputies were involved in the protests of viticulturalists but in a legal, parliamentary fashion. There is no evidence of liberals encouraging violent resistance or criticism. The parliamentary liberals did not attempt to make political capital out of the impact of the economic crisis on the less well off by appealing for mass support. The liberals contributed to charity organisations in the same fashion as did ultra and government supporters.

Liberals were, on the whole, happy with the Restoration settlement as they understood it. Bonapartist sentiments were prevalent particularly in Alsace, but they were romantic memories, not a practical political programme. Although liberals sometimes took up the cause of the poor, it was generally in a patronising, patriarchal spirit. Neither they nor the government wished to democratise politics. The liberals were reasonably content with a 300 franc franchise. Although they were critical of the law of the double vote and the *loi septennale*, they worked within these new parameters, reserving their legalistic wrath for governmental cheating in elections and in the compiling of electoral lists. They feared that mass action could lead to a recurrence of the civil war of the early 1790s. There was total separation between popular unrest and the activities of the liberal notables. The liberals did not differ markedly from Restoration governments in their economic thinking. Few were free traders; many were in the van of pressure groups for higher tariffs. This investigation of the economic crisis, the Martignac commissions particularly, shows that, far from concentrating the minds of liberals in opposition to the regime, it tended to split them. Their views on the depression, its causes and possible solutions, were dictated by regional considerations and by the type of industry in which they were involved. Grain producers favoured tariffs, whereas wine-growers detested them as albatrosses, imposed on them by the grain and iron lobbies. Iron and textile manufacturers clung to the highest tariff they could obtain, although some of the most wealthy cotton kings resented the impact of tariffs on the cost of their machines.

On the other hand, they appeared more in unison in their opposition to government intervention in the workings of the internal economy of France, particulary over *droits réunis*. Liberals could agree in condemning the electoral deceptions of Charles' governments, in their hostility to the increasing influence of the church, in their opposition to press censorship and in their suspicious jealousy of the indemnification of the *emigrés*, but economic policy was another matter. On the vital question of commercial policy, the economic crisis of 1827–32 revealed deep divisions among liberals. Their concerns were personal, local and regional, light-years away from any agreed economic theory, particularly a recognisably liberal one. Their quarrel with Polignac was political. They opposed his appointment in order to win back what had become the traditional influence of the parliamentary majority over political and economic decisions, not because their own solutions were radically different.

Liberals were elected throughout France in 1830, not just in the industrialised departments, although it is true that Paris, the most industrialised area, was 100 per cent liberal and that some of the poorest and most remote departments, like the Var, Finistère and the Hautes-Alpes and Basses-Alpes, remained royalist. But this is insufficient proof that liberalism can be equated with a modernising, industrial France, as has been suggested,[105] because some of the most industrialised departments, like the Nord and the Pas-de-Calais, elected liberals only from 1827. In no sense did the liberals of 1830 simply represent capitalist, bourgeois France at odds with a regime of right-wing, noble landowners.

At the popular level, the economic crisis clearly added a dimension of popular unrest and disturbance in rural and urban areas, but it was only significantly destabilising in large cities like Paris and Lyons. Popular unrest was ubiquitous, not limited to areas where liberals were particularly successful in elections. It was only in Paris, however, that the less well off changed the course of events. Paris was the fastest-growing industrial centre in France. Unprecedented immigration from the provinces, not simply the traditional temporary and seasonal, but increasingly semi-permanent and permanent settlement of working people pushed by the poverty of their native regions, doubled the population of the metropolis to 1.5 million by the middle of the century. They were crowded into the traditional artisan districts of central Paris, physically uncomfortable and deprived of resources at times of economic crisis.[106] In Paris, as elsewhere in Europe, the crisis of 1827–32 was threefold. A financial and banking crisis of confidence developed from the beginning of 1827 and had a knock-on effect on Parisian industry. The building trade was badly hit, along with luxury crafts such as furniture, precious metal and luxury textile goods. The crisis was thus geographically concentrated in central Paris, especially on the right bank of the Seine between the Tuileries and the Hôtel de Ville, which was also the heart of both government and the influential newspaper industry. The artisan workshops were small, often encompassing a master, his family and a small number of journeymen and/or apprentices. They were without reserves in a crisis. Paris was also beginning to experience the impact of the introduction of new machines, both the physical presence and the psychological threat. Printing workers in particular were much exercised on this issue around 1830. The harvest failures, food shortages and consequent rise in prices aggravated an already tense situation. From 1827 there were repeated demonstrations, marches and riots. The artisans were also affected by the political crisis. Although they were not part of the *pays légal*, high rates of literacy and a tradition of political involvement meant that they were not indifferent to the parliamentary situation. In the capital, the centre of government and industry, the crises in the economy and in politics coincided, which brought an unexpected opportunity in July 1830 with the issuing of the four ordinances. The July Days may be seen as an escalation of the impact of the artisan crisis, overlaid by the intensification of the parliamentary duel, and fuelled by the activities of the liberal journalists and their workers.

The notables, whether ultra, royalist or liberal, were committed to the repression of all popular violence. Had the dimensions of the economic crisis produced artisan demonstrations on a revolutionary scale earlier, the Restoration liberals might well have tried to work with the Polignac government and even within a political system reconstructed in accordance with the king's four ordinances. The economic crisis was a catalyst of revolution only for the artisans of Paris. The unrest engendered by the depression actually made the liberals more conservative, convincing them of the urgent need for order and stability.

4
The 'Three Glorious Days'

The parliamentary crisis precipitated by the liberal electoral victory in the summer of 1830 was turned into a revolutionary situation by two factors: the response of the liberal press to the ordinances of St-Cloud and the volatility of the artisans of Paris faced with both the political crisis and continuing deprivation resulting from the economic depression. Following the overwhelming liberal triumph, which he interpreted as the first step towards his own revolutionary overthrow, and after much hesitation, Charles determined to seize the initiative. Emboldened by the victory of the French troops in Algeria, and overestimating the patriotic enthusiasm thus aroused, Charles was persuaded by some of his ultra ministers that the liberals were so dangerous that he was justified in invoking the emergency decree powers given to him in article fourteen of the constitutional charter. He hoped that the ordinances he signed at St-Cloud on 25 July would end the emergency, which he believed had been created by the election, and restore his own position. The liberal press was blamed for the absence of a stable government, accused of dominating parliament, depressing the army and subverting religion. The first ordinance therefore suspended the liberty of the press and decreed that any paper of less than twenty-five pages needed royal authorisation, which had to be renewed through the prefecture every three months and which could be revoked at any time. The second ordinance dissolved the new chamber before it could meet, on the grounds of unspecified electoral malpractice. The electoral laws were revolutionised. The Chamber of Deputies was almost halved in size to 238, and only the quarter most wealthy electors, the members of the special departmental electoral colleges, were to vote for deputies. The old *arrondissement* colleges were merely to select candidates for consideration by their more wealthy colleagues. The right to vote was to depend solely on the land tax (*foncière*), thus excluding those who had formerly qualified wholly or partly through other direct taxes, principally the tax on industrial property (*patente*).[1] The electorate was thus cut to 23 000. The final ordinance called a new election for 6 and 13 September.

The publication of these decrees on 26 July in the *Moniteur* was the catalyst for three days of street fighting in Paris. Opposition journalists were the first overtly and publicly to resist the ordinances. On that first afternoon forty-four journalists signed a protest, which they subsequently published. They were not united in their defiance, however. On 27 July the two largest papers, the *Constitutionnel* and the *Journal de Débats* did not appear and the printer of the *Tribune* refused to bring out an edition, fearful that his presses might be destroyed if the new law was enforced. The main papers to appear were those inclined to Orleanism, the *National*, the *Globe* and the *Temps*. Mangin, the prefect of police, tried in vain to arrest their editors. He made an attempt to enforce the ordinance against the press and also to close the *cabinets de lecture* where many Parisians read the newspapers. Gendarmes were sent to seize the presses of the *National* and the *Temps*. They were intimidated by their staff who declared that their action was illegal. The presses were partially dismantled as angry crowds milled around.[2] The *Globe*, in its edition of 27 July, commented, 'legal government has come to an end; force has taken its place.'[3] Artisan street demonstrations and protests, endemic in the capital as a consequence of high food prices and lack of work, gathered a new momentum. Sporadic street fighting grew on 27 July involving newspaper workers, long-established artisans and relatively new migrant workers, who threw up barricades to defend their districts in central right-bank Paris, which was also the seat of government. Fighting was concentrated around the Louvre, the Tuileries and the Palais Royal, centres of government and newspaper offices and as far east as the Hôtel de Ville, including the main artisan communities of the heart of the capital. The first barricades appeared in the early hours of the morning of 28 July near the Palais Royal, a *tricolore* soon flew from Notre-Dame and the Hôtel de Ville was seized.

The insurgents fought to defend their own districts and had an intimate knowledge of the narrow streets and interconnecting alleys and courtyards. They had weapons retained since the dissolution of the National Guard in 1827, although there was no participation of former guardsmen in uniform. Being close to home, they could snatch some rest and food. The majority of those who took part in revolutionary unrest in Paris as well as in provincial France (as far as one can ascertain in the provinces where material is more impressionistic) were artisans. As with the provinces, statistical analyses are limited for Paris too. About 2000 people were killed in the fighting, 200 soldiers and 1800 insurgents. In addition there were 800 injured within the army and 4500 in the ranks of the opposition.[4] Specific evidence on the revolutionaries exists only for the minority who applied for compensation. The vast majority of these 'blessés de juillet' were working men. Two-thirds of the 1500 or so who claimed compensation for injuries incurred during the revolution in Paris (including the families of the 211 killed) were artisans. Their numbers reflected the occupational structure of the working population of the central districts of Paris: 126 belonged to the carpentry or allied trades, 118 were stonemasons, 94 were shoemakers, and so on.[5] The revolution was primarily the work of artisans, as claimed by contemporary left-wing Orleanists like Odilon Barrot[6] and socialists and republicans like Louis Blanc and Etienne Cabet. Delacroix was perhaps part of the later conspiracy to hide this embarrassing truth when he painted the top-hatted young bourgeois, the impressive lady and eager young boy prominently on his barricade, or maybe he was simply using poetic license. The lady has certainly made her contribution to the popularity of the painting, although some historians prefer to exclude her. No women were killed in the fighting, although two bystanders died and only fifty-two applied for compensation for injuries. Women figured prominently in building barricades and in the more traditional roles of feeding and tending the combatants. Only eighty-five members of the professions applied for compensation. There were no bankers, no lawyers, no deputies and interestingly, considering the major role the ultras assigned them, only twenty-eight journalists. Delacroix's bourgeois was very young. To a certain extent there was a generation gap within the propertied classes, the familiar contrast between more radical youth and cautious age,[7] but attempts by historians to trace the inception of a 'new' revolutionary generation in the 1830s proved somewhat abortive.[8] Some of the fighters were students from the *École Polytechnique*; there were also some law and medical students. Their involvement was predictable, given both the traditional attitudes of such students and the repressive censorship inflicted by the Bourbons on institutions of higher learning. Four boys were killed and nineteen were injured, including one of fourteen who was awarded a medal for his contribution. If 1830 was an artisan revolt, it included both established, settled Parisian artisans as well as more recent migrants. In a sense the fighters represented a younger generation of men who had no personal knowledge of the 1790s. Of the dead and wounded, 54 per cent were between twenty and thirty-five years of age.

While the composition of the crowd thus seems clear, and right-wing allegations that the revolutionaries were vagrants and criminals cannot be sustained, the motivation of the revolutionaries is far less easy to decipher. The men interviewed who were claiming compensation spoke of their wish to support the cause of 'liberté' (76 per cent), 'la nation' (29 per cent) or both. They were given scant opportunity to enlarge on these concepts. Those who did sometimes described their motivation in a manner quite disagreeable to the new regime. For printing workers 'liberté' might include the chance of applying Luddite measures against the new mechanical printing presses.[9] Writers like Blanc and Cabet assumed that the combatants were primarily motivated by economic deprivation accompanied by political hostility to the Polignac government. Contemporary liberals were inclined to stress the impact of the economic crisis. With their own fear of popular unrest, they could not accept that the less well off could be motivated by political issues. The day the ordinances were issued, Monday 26 July, was a holiday for many workers. It has been suggested that those who formed the revolutionary crowds were holiday strollers in the Palais Royal, the area where the main opposition papers were printed, and that their involvement was quite accidental.[10] The 5000 printing workers extended their holiday to the Tuesday, specifically to try to stir up others against the ordinances, the first of which would be disastrous for their own jobs.[11] The liberal journalists were in an excellent position to stress their own role after the event and no ultra commentator would have been inclined to contradict them. If the contribution of their workers to the fighting was so great, however, where were they when the *Commission de Récompenses* garnered its statistics and presented grateful awards? Surely they were not too modest to apply?

Paris had experienced repeated marches and demonstrations of artisans complaining of high food prices and shortage of work since the onset of the depression. Artisans blamed the government for their economic difficulties, especially when the Martignac administration encouraged discussion of the economic crisis but offered no solution, and when the Polignac government was also ineffectual. Economic motivation was undoubtedly very important, as revealed by the subsequent artisan expectations and the demands made of the new regime. After the July Days the new prefect of police for Paris, Girod de l'Ain, was petitioned by different groups of workers for higher wages and shorter hours.[12] It is surely not unreasonable to suppose that the disposition of far from uneducated and unpoliticised artisans of central Paris was already hostile to the Polignac government and that the ordinances added to this sense of grievance. Men do not usually die fighting for a cause in which they become accidentally ensnared on their day off, especially as the revolution was not all over on that one day. There is very little hard evidence for artisan motivation, but the experience of the 1790s in Paris, and the terrified reaction of the elite to opposition in the early 1830s, might lead one to suppose that the Parisian artisans were exercising a positive political choice in July 1830 in the only way available to them at that time.

Their opponents were regular troops, put under the command of Marmont, the duc de Raguse, unpopular because his defection to the Bourbons in 1814 had led directly to the allied capture of Paris. 'Ragusard' had entered popular usage as a synonym for traitor. Theoretically Marmont had 12 000 troops,[13] but only about 7000 could be used at any one time. Troops were traditionally quartered outside central Paris. It was as if the soldiers were moving into alien territory in more senses than one. They were obliged to fight in full uniform in exceptionally hot July weather. No plans had been laid to provide them with ammunition, food or drink. They were reluctant to attack the barricades, defended by women and children as well as men very much like themselves in background and social position. They began to desert.

The liberal deputies living in the capital, alarmed at the escalating violence, began to meet in each other's houses, notably in those of Casimir Périer and Jacques Laffitte, to voice their disquiet. They also lived in the streets surrounding government buildings and were appalled to witness popular violence so close to their own homes. Only on the third morning of the 'Three Glorious Days' did they agree to issue a public protestation against the ordinances, and even then only forty-one of the seventy-three present signed the final document. The liberal deputies were merely fearful spectators of revolution. In Paris the troops had given up, the reorganising of the National Guard was well under way, symbolically headed by Lafayette, hero of the 1789 Revolution. Guardsmen were used in patrols, to protect property and to maintain order when Marmont withdrew his remaining troops.[14] On 29 July, when the king's writ no longer ran in the capital and Charles ineffectively tried to save himself by dismissing Polignac, some deputies joined in the proclamation of a provisional municipal administration for Paris at the Hôtel de Ville. This included moderates like Casimir Périer and the comte de Lobau, friends of the duc d'Orléans, like Jacques Laffitte, and others of a more republican or even Bonapartist disposition, like Mauguin, deputy for Dijon, de Schonen and Audry de Puyraveau. On 31 July the committee proclaimed

> The whole nation is on its feet, adorned in the national flag won by the shedding of its own blood; the nation wants a government and laws worthy of it ... We share your desires and principles; instead of a government imposed by foreign troops, you will have one which owes its power to you alone; all social classes are equally worthy; all have the same rights which are forever sacrosanct.[15]

Given the physical and chronological nearness of the artisan revolt, they could be forgiven such rhetoric, but such a group of men could never have agreed on a way forward and do not seem to have thought of themselves as any more than a holding operation.

On the initiative of a small group of liberal journalists, in which Thiers of the *National* took a lead on 30 July, the candidature of Louis-Philippe, until then mainly favoured by his banker Laffitte, was presented as a solution to the problem of a vacant throne in a country where a republic was unthinkable. A rump of the liberal deputies, in public grateful to the insurgent artisans, but determined to contain popular violence and all talk of a republic, declared the throne vacant on 3 August. Charles had fled. Louis-Philippe, duc d'Orléans and, of course, the king's cousin, was made lieutenant-general of the kingdom, a fairly conservative choice; if the heir to the throne, the young Henri, had succeeded Charles in normal circumstances (Charles himself died in 1836), Louis-Philippe might well have been regent. 'His lack of both popularity and power was to our advantage, leaving him with no bargaining powers.'[16] On 7 August the assembled parliament proposed that the throne be offered to the portly and pedestrian son of the regicide Philippe-Egalité. Of the 430 members of the Chamber of Deputies, only 252 were present; 219 voted the necessary constitutional revision, 33 opposed. On 9 August Louis-Philippe was installed as king of the French. The revolutionary crisis was relatively long, not because of the strength of Bourbon resistance (fewer than 2000 died in the fighting in Paris) but because of conflicting interests within the elite, and because of the need to assemble parliament. The 'Three Glorious Days' had really been fourteen, with much hesitation, reluctance, circumspection and calculation. Revolutionary *élan* had been visible only among the artisans on the barricades, and they were not Orleanists. The confusion and potential conflict between fighters and the liberal elite was made evident in the popular title of the new regime, 'la meilleure des républiques', and of the king, 'le roi des barricades'. For the moment, however, there was patriotic enthusiasm and naïve optimism in Paris, with much energy devoted to the setting up of a subscription to provide for the 'blessés de juillet'.

The Parisian revolution, although it has received far less attention than other French revolutions, has attracted the attention of historians within the last generation.[17] Far less has been written about the situation outside the capital.[18] After the dramatic telegraphs of 26 July carrying news of the ordinances, though sometimes no specific details, the provinces had no official account of what was happening in Paris until well into the first week of August. Confusion, rumour and speculation were rife. Revolutions do not yield official correspondence; most of our knowledge of the July Days comes from memoirs, which have been used extensively in a modern collection of documents on the revolution.[19] Unfortunately, old men often remember what it suits them to recall and often poach each other's published memories. Private diaries of men far from the centre of power, kept for the vanity of the individual and not for an admiring reader in the future, can convey the extent of confusion at the end of July in a manner which is far more illuminating and convincing than the tidy and self-glorifying memoirs of former leading figures.[20]

There was already a struggle for power in many departments between the successful liberals and their electoral committees and the electorally and morally defeated prefects. During the prolonged period when there was no official news from Paris, prefects were often accused of deliberately withholding news. The prefect at Lons-le-Saulnier deemed it wise to conceal news of the ordinances until after the duchesse d'Angoulême had left the town on an eventful journey from Vichy to Paris.[21] Undignified scrambles for prefectoral correspondence were often followed by angry scenes at the prefecture, until officials capitulated and agreed to read out all letters in public. In Metz the prefect read aloud his correspondence surrounded by the liberal electoral committee.[22] Private correspondence with the capital dried up and newspapers also failed to reach many departments. The absence of the liberal national dailies caused speculation that the ordinances were being enforced.[23] The regular coach services failed to function, leaving the provinces virtually cut off. Any travellers from Paris were eagerly questioned. On the night of 27–28 July two young workmen from the capital, rumoured to be emissaries from a liberal government, were interrogated closely by the prefect and *procureur du roi* in Chaumont.[24] The liberal electoral committee of Metz sent representatives to find out what was happening in Paris,[25] while several of the deputies of the Haut-Rhin set off themselves. Many expected that the ordinances would produce trouble for Charles.[26] Wild rumours of bloodshed and terror were combined with a total official silence.

The departments became, in the words of a contemporary *juge de paix*, little separate republics, ruled by their prefects.[27] How did prefects cope with this sudden elevation and liberation from centralised control? Some were on leave. Some were still away, having returned to their own area to vote in the special departmental college elections. The prefectoral changes of April and May 1830 meant that a number of prefects were still fairly ignorant of their new departments. In departments where liberals had been successful in the elections (the majority), prefects were under threat of demotion, having failed in their prime task. Thus the self-confidence of the prefectoral corps was at a very low ebb. Some prefects, directly or through their subordinates, tried to publicise the ordinances and begin to carry out their requirements. By 27 July liberals in Lyons were already discussing how to cope with the new electoral law, but were defying the first ordinance by continuing to publish their newspaper.[28] On 28 July the officials of the prefecture in Dijon suspended the liberty of the press, but the proclamation was ignored and the liberal newspaper appeared.[29] In Besançon placards displaying copies of the ordinances had to be erected without the authority of the prefect or the mayor, for both were on leave. The absence of so many prefects, an entirely predictable electoral and seasonal absence, which the central government ought to have considered, meant that the initiative was lost. There was conflict among local officials concerning the legality of the decrees. The *procureur du roi* in Besançon declared them illegal,[30] and other members of the judiciary took the view that they needed parliamentary approval. Thus the initial attempt to maintain royal authority was hindered within the administration itself by the absence of some officials and the opposition of others.

The hesitation and lack of unity and authority in the local administration at the end of July contributed to outbreaks of severe rioting in many towns. They also gave the opportunity to the liberal opposition to seize control. Faced with growing hostility, and without orders, most prefects deemed it wiser to abdicate. In the Puy-de-Dôme the prefect more or less gracefully handed over responsibility to a provisional committee in an elegant if ambiguous proclamation tastefully embellished with fleurs-de-lis.[31] In the Haute-Marne the prefect authorised a provisional municipal administration and the revival of the National Guard,[32] only to be chased from the department by a contingent of the latter a few days later. The recently appointed prefect of the neighbouring Doubs attempted to return to his post on 4 August, only to meet the same fate.[33] Several prefects decided to stay on leave, or hasten to Paris to try to preserve their careers. Administrative revolutions could be times of great opportunity for the prudent. Occasionally, as in the Vosges and the Bas-Rhin, the prefect remained in nominal control. In the latter department he was sending reports to Guizot until 24 August.[34] Prefects were at the head of highly centralised departmental structures, having authority over all local officials, from immediate subordinates like sub-prefects, to local postmasters (a job carrying specific political responsibility, as Stendhal demonstrated in *Lucien Leuwen*). They were all appointed on his recommendation and were answerable to him in all their official activities. Sub-prefects received orders directly from the prefect and transmitted them to mayors. The formal machinery for the consultation of local opinion was negligible, for the prefect also determined appointments to consultative departmental, *arrondissement* and municipal councils. With the collapse of prefectoral authority, the officials of this centralised structure were without orders. Predictably, none took any independent initiative or action. Some continued to write to their former chief, others withdrew without resigning.

What of the other foci of government authority in the provinces, the judiciary and the army? The contribution of the judiciary to the maintenance of the authority of the restored Bourbons was negligible once the prefect was gone. The opposition of some members of the judiciary to the ordinances themselves is interesting. Several refused to hold their courts at the beginning of August on the grounds that they did not know in whose name to give judgement. In Bar-sur-Aube the *procureur* removed the visible trappings of the Bourbon regime from the court-room (a bust of Charles and a portrait of Louis XVIII) and an enormous *tricolore* was draped over the fleur-de-lis wallpaper. The response of the army was varied. In Paris the victory of the rebels was assured by the demoralisation and desertion of the men. It was rumoured in eastern France that the insurgents were being decimated by troops loyal to the king, and in Bar-sur-Aube there were clashes between soldiers and local people.[35] In the frontier departments the army had a dual function: to keep order at home and to defend France from foreign attack. During the revolution rumours of a possible invasion to maintain the Bourbons multiplied and in Strasbourg the army was put on a war footing.[36] Elsewhere troops were ordered to fulfil their usual peacetime role of breaking up riots and demonstrations, which made them unpopular with local people. In Dijon on 29 July the troops were forced to withdraw from a violent struggle with civilians because of the injuries inflicted on them by the irate crowd.[37] In Besançon troops were also used in an attempt to contain the local revolt, but with similar diminishing success. Here, as in Paris, and in Metz too, the soldiers were divided. On 1 August large numbers threw down their arms and fraternised with the rioters. Four days later, after the proclamation of Louis-Philippe as lieutenant-general, the section of the garrison loyal to Charles X mutinied, encouraged, it was said, by the prefect before his own hasty departure. Their rising was suppressed with some violence by the other troops. In Metz the soldiers of the sixth regiment revolted and deposed their colonel. Local people, in concert with the troops, sacked the house where he lodged, causing 30 000 francs' worth of damage.[38]

It would be wrong to imagine that all army units were in ferment, however. The military commander in Nantes tried to use his troops to stir up a Bourbon rising in the Vendée, but the soldiers deserted him and the local people remained passive. The commanders of the thirty-third infantry and the fifth hussars stationed in Thionville, Alsace, suggested that they should fraternise with any invading foreign army in order to restore Charles. They received no active support, but later a large proportion of the officers in the hussars resigned rather than serve Louis-Philippe.[39] Some commanders and officers were more circumspect, though whether this was out of sympathy for a change of regime or because they could not afford to lose their jobs it is impossible to judge. In Clermont-Ferrand, after a slight hesitation, the revolutionary *tricolore* was flown from the garrison.[40] In Lyons the military commander made himself temporary head of the revolution, confirming changes of civilian personnel.[41] It was very unusual for a military commander to lead rather than follow in political matters and almost unique in the July Days for an officer to cross the divide and become involved in non-military appointments. No commanders seem to have made any sustained effort to maintain the Bourbons, perhaps not surprisingly, given the flight of Charles X.

The most awkward problems for the army surrounded its firefighting role. Local people, with a grievance that drove them into physical protest, traditionally resented troops being used against them. Physical confrontation was not wholly inspired by high politics. Soldiers and civilians quarrelled over many more personal matters and revolutions provided the opportunity to settle old scores under the excuse of political argument. In the regions, as in Paris during the July Days, soldiers sometimes refused to put down popular demonstrations. Their commanders tagged along behind the revolution, fearful of the dangers of domestic unrest and the threat of foreign invasion to uphold the settlement of 1815.

The provinces did not wait passively for news from Paris. There was a positive reaction against Bourbon rule, particularly marked in eastern departments. This took two forms. There were noisy street demonstrations, which often became violent, with attacks on property and threats against individuals. These were particularly pronounced at the end of July before the full story of the fighting in Paris was known. The violence either coincided with, or was followed by, local liberals seizing power and forming provisional administrations. The rioters and the liberal elite shared some antipathies, but their methods were different and in practice the only links between them were their common reverence for two revolutionary symbols, the *tricolore* and the National Guard. Even before the four ordinances there was extensive opposition to Polignac's government. Criticism was only muted in traditionally Catholic, monarchist departments, such as those of the west. In eastern France hostility to ultraroyalism was laced with a distinct undercurrent of Bonapartist sentiment and republican sympathies. The journey of the duchesse d'Angoulême from Vichy to Paris coincided with the publication of the ordinances. Her visit to the theatre in Dijon had to be curtailed and she was chased back to the prefecture by an angry crowd shouting 'Vive la Charte! Vive les 221! Vive la liberté de la presse! Vive la liberté!'[42] When the news of Parisian resistance to the decrees became known in the town the slogans of the crowds (who roamed the streets day and night at the end of July and the beginning of August) became more specifically anti-Bourbon. A local notable recorded with horror the cries of crowds armed with *tricolores* and singing 'La Marseillaise': 'A bas les rats! A bas les royalistes! Vive l'Empereur! Vive Napoleon II! Vive la République!'[43] It is interesting to note that the duc d'Orléans had no popular following, but that republican and Bonapartist sentiments were common among the less well off.[44]

Anti-Bourbon feelings were not confined to words. One of the worst days of rioting in Besançon reached a climax with the destruction of a statue of Pichegru, a locally born republican general turned royalist conspirator, whose portrait hung in the palace of St-Cloud. Hatred for Pichegru, whose statue had been erected in Besançon in 1828, was such that the statue was not only smashed to pieces, but the head was subsequently paraded through the streets and finally pitched into the river.[45] Such destructive expressions of hostility to the Bourbons were publicly deplored by the liberal elite, although some shared the basic sentiments. The provisional administration in Besançon, composed of wealthy citizens, sent a petition to Paris at the beginning of August urging the establishment of a republic.[46] One of the Côte-d'Orien deputies was Mauguin, a member of the provisional commission in Paris and well known for his republican views. In Arbois the republicans took total control of the commune.[47] The majority of the provisional committee in Strasbourg were for a republic,[48] as were many other liberals in Alsace. In Metz a placard was erected outside the *hôtel de ville* on the morning of 29 July which stated that Charles X was king by virtue of the charter and had violated his oath. People were urged to withhold tax payments and the poster ended 'Vive la Nation!'[49] In Alsace a strong affection for the Empire remained, particularly among industrialists. Such sentiments – by 1830 historical and sentimental more than pratical – pervade the private diary kept by Nicholas Lebert, a close associate of local industrialists and deputies. Many of the members of the revolutionary provisional administrations were former Bonapartist officials, some of whom had joined the *charbonnerie* in the early 1820s and even more of whom had helped to organise *Aide-toi* committees since 1827. Retired army officers, who had rarely been involved in *Aide-toi*, were represented in these provisional local governments. Thus republican and Bonapartist traditions to some extent linked the attitudes of rich and poor, particularly in eastern France.

Such views merged into an almost classless patriotic nationalism, in part, presumably, a product of France's conscript army. From the end of July there was an enthusiastic rejection of the Bourbon fleur-de-lis flag in favour of the *tricolore*, with its revolutionary associations, both old and new. The flags and *cocardes*, dug out of cupboards where they had lain since the Hundred Days, were worn with enthusiasm.[50] They were sometimes inscribed 'vive la liberté!' and more usually 'vive la charte!' By the first few days of August they could be seen on *hôtels de ville*, prefectures, garrisons and churches. Crowds obliged everyone to fly the revolutionary flag, sometimes, presumably, with a touch of devilment, knowing how much such an imposition would be resented. The flags could certainly arouse real passion. In Bourbon-Vendée, as might have been expected, there were riots when the *tricolore* was hoisted. Lest the eager historian should detect a whiff of active royalism, it should be noted that in July 1815 the white flag of the Bourbons had been ripped from the *hôtel de ville* and burned.[51] There was a considerable eagerness to revive the National Guard, with its democratic membership and elected officers, many of whom had served in Napoleonic armies. Local people did not wait for Paris to give a lead. In Lyons National Guard formations were organising patrols on 28 July.[52] By 31 July few departments were without a battalion; in Metz membership had reached 3000.[53] Liberal deputies and former National Guard officers naturally took a lead. Weapons were a problem: most members had retained theirs when Charles X had ordered the dissolution of the Guard in 1827, but few companies were armed outside the main communes.⁵⁴ Initially the Guard accepted all volunteers and the reorganisation had the enthusiastic support of the local population. It was seen as the proud symbol of revolution and patriotism, but for the liberal elite it was most important, as it had been for the revolutionary leaders in the 1790s, as an additional police force. In Lyons, Metz and other centres it was immediately employed to maintain order. In addition there was growing apprehension in August that France's enemies might invade to restore Charles X and that the Guard would be needed for national defence.

The church was often the target for revolutionary violence. The close connection between clerics and ultraroyalist politics, and the very open use of the clergy as electoral agents in 1830, made such demonstrations almost inevitable except in areas where the church had successfully established a dominant role, such as in the western departments. The visible symbols of the religious revivial of the 1820s, the missionary crosses, were particular targets during the revolution and for nearly a year after the July Days. The crosses had been erected on communal rather than church land and the indignant crowds who gathered around them during the revolution were usually willing, once they had felled the offending object, to see it re-erected within the church. The provisional municipal government of Nancy petitioned for the removal of a cross, erected by the bishop, to prevent its demolition by force.⁵⁵ Individual *curés* were threatened by crowds and forced to fly *tricolore* from their churches. In Arbois the republican revolutionary committee chased the *curé* from the commune.⁵⁶ Both sides often over-reacted, remembering old grudges that often had nothing to do with high politics. Personality clashes were sometimes blown up out of all proportion, being given more apparent justification in a revolutionary setting.

The ultraroyalists' politicisation of the church caused most dissension. The most disturbed departments were those blessed with an ultra senior churchman. The two cities in eastern France where anti-clerical sentiments caused most violence were Besançon and Nancy, where the archbishop and bishop respectively were deeply involved in ultraroyalist politics. In Nancy both the cathedral and the seminary were attacked. On the night of 30–31 July the seminary was pillaged and the furniture set on fire by an excited crowd of artisans.[57] Popular hostility to the Catholic Church was easily aroused in the crisis and the attitude of some of the clergy did not help. Some *curés* showed a marked reluctance to bless National Guard *tricolores* and to holding special services of blessing for the Guard, perhaps not an entirely surprising response. The clergy did not want to offer prayers for the new king as they had done for the old. Indeed, the bishop of Dijon, ignoring his own Bonapartist past, was said to have described the revolution as the punishment of the Lord.[58] There were numerous reports and rumours about priests meeting secretly, of priests in disguise being seen in local inns and travelling to spread tales of disaster and destruction. In the west the situation was made more tense because of the higher profile of the church in the Vendée and surrounding regions; in the east the presence of the archbishop of Besançon in exile in nearby Fribourg added to worries. Problems were exacerbated by the revival of old Catholic–Protestant rivalries in areas like Alsace, Montbéliard and the department of the Gard. Protestant elites welcomed the revolution warmly. The new minister of the interior, Guizot, was a Protestant and a Protestant pastor headed the provisional municipal committee in Nancy.

Patriotic, republican, Bonapartist and anti-clerical sentiments were thus shared by many of the participants in the revolution. But those who formed the crowds, on one side, and the provisional administrative committees running the departments, on the other, were very different. Artisans and peasants, notably wine producers, were at the centre of violent upheaval. On 2 August winegrowers from the area around Besançon besieged the tax offices[59] and in Arbois and Dijon they were also prominent in the crowds. Wood-stealing incidents were reported.[60] The presence of craftsmen in the crowds of rioters was noted by many observers. The impact of short-time working and reduced rates of pay during the economic recession has already been noted. During the revolutionary period many workshops were closed to protect their fabric rather than because of economic uncertainty. For artisans the revolution was an opportunity to bring their problems to the notice of the politicians. In Chaumont unemployed glove-makers were prominent in the unrest[61] and 1000 francs from municipal funds was used by the provisional administration as an emergency fund to help artisans and their families.[62] In Lyons, where joiners had led four days of riots a month earlier, the *hôtel de ville* was invaded by crowds and there was a mutiny at the local prison.[63] In Mulhouse the cotton factories were closed during the revolution and troops were used to keep order amongst the workers.[64] In Nancy, after the attack on the seminary, twenty people were arrested, all, except for one woman, craftsmen in the clothing, shoe-making or printing trades. Their social superiors made no attempt to consider their desperate economic plight or political attitudes. Drink was always seen as the motive for any disturbance of the peace, large and small.[65] We have no direct record of their actual motives, of course, but as in the case of Paris, it seems reasonable to suppose a level of hostility to the Polignac government, stimulated in part by the unprecedented intensity of the liberals' own campaign against him.

The self-appointed provisional local governments were very different in composition from the rioting crowds, as was the provisional commission of the *hôtel de ville* in Paris. In 1830 no one bothered to consider including even a token artisan. The leaders were wealthy men of property. In the Nancy committee there were six *marchands* and *négociants*, six lawyers, mainly *avocats*, three *propriétaires*, two bankers and a sprinkling of other members of the liberal professions.[66] This was typical. In the Puy-de-Dôme seven of the fifteen were lawyers;[67] in Dijon, of thirty-two co-opted members of an enlarged municipal council, thirteen were lawyers and ten *négociants* or *manufacturiers*; in Besançon the editor of the liberal newspaper was elected onto the municipal committee; in Dijon Proudhon, the doyen of the faculty of law, well known for his liberalism, was brought in. The committees represented a wealthy elite, as the prefect on the Puy-de-Dôme remarked in his parting proclamation, 'les propriétaires les plus honorables'.[68] Young people may have been present in the riots and formed a high proportion of those who applied for compensation after the July Days, but many retired notables figured on the self-appointed committees. There were no nobles but the committees represented a fair cross-section of bourgeois occupations and wealth. Many of these temporary administrators were well advanced in their careers, sometimes begun under Napoleon. They were an older generation than the men who manned the barricades. All were united in their opposition to Polignac, but even more by their desire to prevent further local unrest and rebellion.

A number of towns were, according to wealthy observers, totally out of control for several days as a result of popular unrest, but such activity seemed to have been uncoordinated and relatively anonymous. Local liberal notables took advantage of the fact that no one knew what was happening in Paris to establish their own power and their own version of law and order. It has been seen that they shared many of the political and anti-clerical attitudes of the crowds. They were eager to destroy the Bourbon administration and to take over jobs themselves. The July Days in Paris were their opportunity. In public later they honoured the sacrifice of the people of Paris, but they feared the potential of revolution: future disturbances might threaten their own political or economic dominance. Politically ambitious, nearly all were socially conservative. The motive adopted by the Orleanists later – 'Liberty and Order' – aptly conveyed the feelings of many liberal notables. The ways to power varied. Dijon was apparently saved from anarchy by the forceful action of its liberal deputy. The municipal council persuaded the prefect to authorise it to co-opt thirty members to run the department. In Besançon a popular revolt was succeeded, after the hurried departure of prefect and mayor, by a hundred-strong assembly of notables. This was a more radical experience than that of Dijon, for they called themselves the sovereign people before electing a committee of twelve to run the city and the department. Such almost Jacobin overtones were not found elsewhere. In Metz after popular unrest and fighting the old liberal electoral committee constituted itself into a provisional administration with no pretence of election. Sometimes the prefect remained as a figurehead, as in Strasbourg, with real local control in the hands of the committee. In the Puy-de-Dôme a 'commission spontanée de paix et de sureté publique' of fifteen members created a comprehensive network of subordinate bodies. The idea of these provisional committees owed something to the example of 1792, perhaps, and something also to the Parisian committee established on 29 July, but the initiative was local. The departmental organisations were spontaneous foundations formed in response to local and not Parisian conditions.

What were the aims of these departmental revolutions? Weiss commented tartly that the Besançon group, representing the ideas of the extreme left in the Chamber of Deputies, would lead to nothing but disorder, but the members proved him wrong. They showed great consistency in their emphasis on public order. Citizens were counselled moderation and wisdom; excesses of violence were to be shunned. The organisers of the Puy-de-Dôme committee wrote to its members that their aim was to keep the peace, to protect persons and property and to ensure that the triumph of the national cause in the area did not lead to disorder. In a proclamation of 7 August they stressed first the patriotic duty of prompt tax payments, and second, the need to obey the law. The people of Paris, having risked their lives for constitutional principles, were now, they assured the local population, paying their taxes obediently.[69] The committee sought, and obtained, the backing of the local garrison, although troops were used against rioters more cautiously than a few days earlier. The rapid formation of a National Guard was regarded as a prime necessity for law and order and in Lyons, as elsewhere, it was used in preference to troops to keep order.[70] The provisional committee was aware of the gravity of local economic problems. In the Haute-Marne 1000 francs were distributed to unemployed artisans in Chaumont. The state of industry was a cause of concern to the provisional council in Metz and in the Puy-de-Dôme the poor were assured that the new government would reduce taxes.

The main preoccupations of these provisional committees were in the area of national rather than local politics. They assumed the role of the prefect and took over the machinery of government. On 3 August the Puy-de-Dôme committee informed all local officials that they were in command of the department and where the replies they received were tepid, new appointments were made. In the Moselle delegates were sent out into the communes to investigate the worthiness and patriotism of officials and to secure support for the new regime.[71] The Lyons committee replaced all seven *commissaires de police*.[72] By the end of August the Clermont committee had thoroughly purged even the municipal councils. The new government in Paris accepted most of the decisions thus reached and confirmed the appointments. Guizot even accepted the appointment of a new prefect by the Metz committee. The Elbeuf committee organised a rousing welcome for the new prefect. Public buildings were illuminated and there was dancing in the streets.[73] Thus the effective revolution at the provincial level lay not in the success of popular riots and demonstrations – the commitees were anxious to crush these – but in the swift and total transfer of power within the localities to the liberal elite.

Liberal deputies left their electoral committees to reorganise the localities while they hastened to Paris, on the news of violent upheaval, to try to take control of events from the provisional committee that had established itself in the capital. The more radical members of the committee were persuaded that any attempt to try to turn France into a republic would bring foreign intervention and civil war. The cousin of Charles X was thus offered the throne. The departments showered the Chamber of Deputies and the duc d'Orléans himself with petitions welcoming this arrangement in the days and weeks after 5 August, but it would be a mistake to interpret this cascade of good will as a reflection of popular emotion. In the first week of August the provisional government in Paris distributed models of patriotic petitions. A project for a spontaneous address from Bar-sur-Aube arrived from Paris via Troyes in the luggage of the local deputy. The provisional committees and the new prefects were urged to give full publicity to the merits of Louis-Philippe, who was little known, having spent the revolutionary years in exile. They often drummed up congratulatory addresses covered with signatures from communes. Despite their complete lack of spontaneity, the petitions give some idea of the acceptability of the regime. The municipal council of Epinal paid homage to Louis-Philippe for keeping the peace. One petition from the Vosges urged that he be proclaimed king by the Chamber of Deputies in the name of the sovereign people.[74] There were mass petitions and select ones from official organisations. Liberal deputies rushed them to Paris. Some communes waited prudently until the new regime seemed secure before welcoming it and some were eager to list the difficulties the government would encounter.[75] National Guards were particularly prolific with their loyal welcomes and frequently sent delegations to Paris to present them to the king. Occasionally one appreciates that Louis-Philippe was received less with joy than with resignation. In Bar-sur-Aube the public proclamation of the new monarchy was preceded by an announcement of the date of the next market and was written in the same flat tone.

The local liberal newspapers, taking their tune from their Parisian brethren like the *Globe* and the *National*, welcomed both the revolution and the new monarchy. On 1 August the *Spectateur* of Dijon proclaimed that the people had recovered their freedom and two days later began a collection for those injured in the fighting and for the families of the dead. The *Journal de la Côte-d'Or*, which had been more outspoken in its opposition to the Bourbons, was lyrical in its description of the triumphs of the people over the ordinances, by which the former regime had tried to rob them of their rights. The attitude of the papers quickly became more sober, like the *Impartial* in Besançon when riots there had persisted for a whole week, but all papers welcomed Louis-Philippe as a king who would rule according to a charter determined by parliament. Newspapers that had supported the deposed king offered neither resistance nor criticism, but stressed the need to support the government as the only practical alternative to anarchy.

Thus the new government was accepted with little immediate resistance, perhaps inevitably in view of the flight of Charles X and the arrest of his ministers. In every case the practical appeal of the new arrangement was emphasised, compared with the threat of civil war if other political experiments were attempted. After a week or so of independence, the departments accepted the decision of the liberal deputies on the organisation and nature of the new central government. It, in turn, accepted the administrative revolution effected by the local notables. The dichotomy of a highly centralised system, in which local notables actually exercised considerable power and initiative in the regions, was to persist into the July Monarchy and beyond. Prefects only maintained the semblance of centralised control by acting in concert with the most important liberal families in their department. 1830 was indeed a Parisian revolution in that Parisian liberal journalists orchestrated the protest against the ordinances and newspaper workers and other artisans fought successfully against royal troops. But it was the liberal members of parliament from the whole of France who made the political decision to appoint the duc d'Orléans, and who, in their regions, through their electoral committees, directed the local administrative take-over. The events of 1830 were satisfactory to the local notables because they were able to assert control after the artisan revolt and were able to ensure that subsequent decisions were theirs. Artisan and peasant unrest did not abate, however. For the less well off the July Days, despite the hopes of rather out-of-touch theoreticians like Blanc and Cabet, proved to be merely an interlude in a continuing struggle against established authority, whether Napoleonic, Bourbon, Orleanist or indeed, later, republican.

5

The Liberalism of the Orleanist Settlement[1]

The idea of political parties was considered factious, even traitorous, in early nineteenth-century France. Yet the term 'liberal' was (and still is) applied to the opposition majority in the Chamber of Deputies towards the end of the reign of Charles X and to the Orleanist regime and its political elite. It is common to associate liberalism with revolutionary and nationalist ideas in the years up to 1848 and France is always seen as their inspiration. This chapter seeks to investigate these assumptions with reference to the regime that was established after the revolution of July 1830. Is it possible to define a common set of liberal beliefs and an indentifiable group of men? Liberalism was as much the will-o'-the-wisp of nineteenth-century politics as it is in our own day. Liberal beliefs had their far from unique origins in enlightened concepts of the eighteenth century, looking forward to a more rational organisation of the state and the elimination of irrelevant and damaging traditional privileges. The Revolution of 1789 was central to the thinking of French liberals, though they would have been unable, in 1830, to agree on the exact contribution the Revolution made to the way in which they looked at the world. While exalting certain philosophical and institutional triumphs of 1789, they were appalled both by the memory and the prospect of mass violence.

The term 'liberal' was (and is) used to describe a disparate section of the Restoration political elite, which was loosely united in criticism of most Bourbon governments. They were, severally or together, also called 'left', 'centre-left', 'constitutional royalist' or 'doctrinaire'.[2] Nearly all accepted the restored monarchy, although the 'doctrinaires', as they were rather derisively called, were more committed to the 1814 charter than the person of the king. Some retained a profound attachment to the Napoleonic era, but this was fast becoming a romantic myth, while others held vaguely republican preferences. Some joined the *charbonnerie* of the early 1820s. Nearly all feared the potential anarchy of violent revolution. In the later years of the Restoration, especially after the appointment of Polignac, liberal opposition newspapers and pamphlets repeatedly drew parallels between the French monarchs, Louis XVIII and Charles X, and those of England, Charles II and James II respectively, indicating Louis-Philippe as a worthy William of Orange.[3] The vigorous liberal daily, *Le National*, financed by one of the few active Orleanists, the banker, Laffitte, was particularly forceful in pressing these comparisons. The duc d'Orléans was no subversive, however. He always showed proper deference for his poorer royal cousins because, like them, he was anxious above all to avoid a second exile, particularly when, in 1825. he and his sister were the chief beneficiaries of the state loan raised to indemnify *émigrés* whose land had been confiscated during the Revolution. The liberals were positively not united behind an Orleanist alternative to the Bourbons, although their literary efforts may have given that impression.

Liberalism was not a political programme, but a tendency or attitude of mind which crystallized in response to Restoration government policies, such as attempts to restrict the electorate by legislation or administrative fraud, the law to indemnify *émigrés*, the sacrilege law and legislative restrictions on press freedom. By 1828 their stand on these issues, particularly fraudulent electoral lists and elections, gave them a majority in the Chamber of Deputies. Their vigorous campaign against Polignac and the other ultra ministers appointed in August 1829 galvanised them into a semblance of unity. They always wanted to influence Charles X, not to remove him.[4]

There was a disturbed, but not a revolutionary situation in Paris before the publication of the ordinances. Charles failed to take into account the popularity of the liberal newspapers and the unsettled state of Paris after three years of harvest failure, expensive food and commercial and industrial crises. The ensuing 'Three Glorious Days' of fighting represented a modest struggle for the control of the governmental, and coincidentally, but disastrously for Charles, the depressed artisan centres of right-bank Paris. The 'Three Glorious Days' were relatively economical with human life: about 2000 deaths on both sides, the majority among the insurgents, fighting to defend their homes and workshops.[5] Charles apparently preferred political suicide to a liberal government, which places some blame for the revolution on the uncompromising verbal opposition of the liberals.

The Parisian provisional commission seemed to offer sweeping changes of a democratic nature. But despite the theatrical embrace of Louis-Philippe and Lafayette at the Hôtel de Ville, the commission claimed no more than a transient, ephemeral existence, deferring to the larger parliamentary assembly, to which several of its members belonged, as soon as parliament could be called together. Apprehensive after the street fighting of the 'Three Glorious Days', they took control of a revolution they had never sought. A few days later the Chamber of Deputies was hastily convened by the liberal deputies present in the capital and a few quickly improvised minor constitutional revisions were passed. For the liberals revolution meant a potentially dangerous vacuum, resonant with terrifying myths and memories, to be quickly and conveniently filled.

Already in possession of a comfortable parliamentary majority, the members of the liberal elite wanted little more than the re-establishment of public order under their own direction. They were organised, in parliament itself, in the press and in unofficial groups like *Aide-toi, le ciel t'aidera*, and had the coherence, experience, status and power to assert their control. They were not in accord, however. A minority wanted a more open political framework and the Orleanists, as the liberals were predictably dubbed, split into *résistance* and *mouvement* tendencies almost instantly. Their differences were of degree only, not substance or principle, as the titles by which they were known indicate. In many respects they were mainly squabbling over the division of the political cake, which ultimately became a feast for those of the *résistance*. Outside Paris local issues and rivalries played a major role in the delineation of such groups.

The circumstances in which they created a new regime were significant. Charles X fled and was allowed to leave the country unchecked. The economic crisis worsened and popular unrest continued spasmodically for several years. Liberal deputies were thus easily convinced that the restoration of the status quo was vital to avoid a repetition of the civil war of the 1790s and also, possibly, to forestall a third attempt by the Great Powers to restore the Bourbons. Many were lawyers or academics and their perception of their own role was legalistic. They always sought to clothe the naked and violent source of their power in garments of necessity and legality. They were anxious to disprove the allegation of Charles X that their opposition had been subversive, to the extent that, after the revolution, four of his ex-ministers were themselves tried on a charge of having caused the July Days and suffered a brief jail sentence. It has been suggested that Bonapartist sentiments underpinned the thinking of many notables and it has been demonstrated that many of those who succeeded in the rush for official appointments after July were long-dispossessed Bonapartists,[6] but there was no suitable adult Bonapartist candidate: Napoleon was dead, his son was being raised in Austria and his great-nephew had not yet made his mark. Although a number of those who took part in the municipal commission revered the memory of the republic, the spectre of the Terror excluded this option. Nearly thirty years later Guizot, one of the liberal leaders during the Restoration and the longest serving of Louis-Philippe's ministers, wrote,

> The necessity of choosing between a new king and anarchy was for honest men in 1830 the basic cause of the change of dynasty ... only a king could have saved France from disaster.[7]

Charles was thus replaced by his cousin, Louis-Philippe, duc d'Orléans, who would have propbably served as regent if Charles X had died, for his actual heir was a young child. The deputies made Louis-Philippe king for the same reason that the restoration of the Bourbons had been accepted by all notables in 1814 and 1815. They believe that a monarchy was the safest and most expeditious way of protecting their own interests, property and political power. Louis-Philippe was simply offered a vacant post by a large section of Charles X's parliament. The new king was given an hereditary tenancy, but as king of the French people, no longer as king of France. Some of the liberal elite subsequently claimed that these alterations amounted to nothing more than a rather violent change of government, that what mattered was not the decision of parliament to nominate a king, but that Louis-Philippe was the head of the younger branch of the Bourbon family and had some vestige of hereditary right.

The July revolution was no Orleanist plot. Louis-Philippe fled Paris for his country house at Neuilly when fighting broke out around the Palais Royal and returned when relative calm had been restored only on the insistence of Thiers and his sister, Mme Adelaide. In a poster widely distributed in Paris on the final day of the conflagration, 30 July, Thiers, a leading journalist on *Le National*, claimed 'A republic would divide us disastrously; it would lead us into conflict with the rest of Europe.' Louis-Philippe, son of the regicide, self-styled Philippe-Egalité, was depicted as a friend of the revolutionary and national cause. Thiers recalled that he had fought during the revolutionary wars at Jemappes, but forgot that, subsequently, he had joined the royal family in exile. Patriotic claims were hollow excuses for convenience, as was the often mentioned embrace of Lafayette and Louis-Philippe on a balcony of the Hôtel de Ville and Lafayette's description of the new regime as the 'best of republics'. Louis-Philippe may not have been made king 'parceque Bourbon', (because he was a Bourbon), as the most conservative of Orleanists like to claim,[8] but he was certainly not raised up 'quoique Bourbon' (despite the fact that he was a Bourbon), as some *mouvement* supporters suggested. There were limits to the most conservative hankering after continuity. De Broglie was in a minority when he proposed the title of Philippe VII to emphasise dynastic associations.[9] But Duvergier de Hauranne went too far for most deputies when he described the new regime as 'in reality a republic with an hereditary president.'[10]

Louis-Philippe was a chameleon king. Contemporaries defined his role to suit their own political preferences. To Louis Blanc, the socialist, he was a 'king of the barricades',[11] to others a 'republican' king or a 'bourgeois' monarch. He certainly became king because of the barricades, but the more long-term shelter offered to him by the liberal notables encouraged him to forget the transitory embarassment of his revolutionary origins. He bought Delacroix's, *Liberty leading the People*, but, after the exhibition of 1831, quickly consigned it to the basement of the Louvre. But the point should not be laboured. Presumably, after the event, the terms 'monarchie républicaine', and even more 'roi citoyen', were used chiefly with bitter and sardonic irony.[12]

It should not be forgotten, in the mists of ultras' romantic dreams, that the Restoration monarchy had also been an affair of compromise and contract, masked only by a contentious royalist preamble to the constitution and a suitably devout and medieval-sounding oath. In 1825 Charles X swore,

> Before God I promise my people that I will honour and protect our holy religion, as befits a most Christian king, the elder son

of the church, to dispense justice to my people; finally, to govern in accordance with the laws of the kingdom and the constitutional charter, which I promise to observe faithfully. God and the holy saints will succour me in this task.[13]

Louis-Philippe, heartily relieved that he did not have to emigrate once more, began his oath in August 1830 in a rather circumspect manner:

I have read the declaration of the Chamber of Deputies and Peers with great care. I have weighed and considered the whole. I accept, whole-heartedly, and without reservation the declaration and the title of king of the French people. . . . In the presence of God I swear faithfully to observe the constitutional charter, as modified in the declaration; to govern with and by the law; to dispense justice to all, according to their rights, and in all things to have as my sole guide the interests, well-being and glory of the French people.[14]

To further underline the difference between 1830 and 1825, when Charles had been crowned at leisure, several months after his accession, in romantic (medieval) splendour in Reims cathedral, Louis-Philippe took his oath with unprecedented haste on 9 August before the assembled peers and deputies in a parliament chamber crammed with members of the National Guard and draped with *tricolores*. On his side the duc d'Orléans accepted the contractual offer of a throne made vacant by the flight of his cousin and agreed to withdraw the anachronistic, face-saving preamble which had been inserted in 1814 the constitution and which had declared that the 'charter' was *octroyée*, a grant of royal grace and favour in an invented tradition of supposed pre-revolutionary constitutional royal benevolence.[15] On 14 August the revised document, still rather curiously referred to as a 'charter', was published.[16]

The political crisis of 1830 had centred around whether the king could appoint ministers with no parliamentary following and whether he could then break the inevitable stalemate by making laws without consulting the assembly. This was apparently a serious issue. How did the definition of royal authority change after the revolution? As in the 1814 constitution the king was to be the executive and share legislative power with parliament. The constitution of 1814 had stated that the king was to propose legislation, which would then be put 'au gré du roi' to parliament. After the 1830 revolution, the constitution stated, 'The right to propose laws belongs to the king, peers and deputies. However all tax changes must first be voted on by the deputies.' In 1814 the king had been given much broader legislative authority, not only to initiate laws, but also to suspend and dispense with existing legislation. In an emergency, 'The king issues decrees vital to maintain the rule of law and the security of the state.' Charles had used this article of the 1814 charter to justify the four ordinances he issued from St-Cloud in July 1830. Hence the liberals were careful in their constitutional revision to state that the king could not make laws without consulting parliament (article thirteen): 'the king can never suspend laws nor dispense with their execution.' One source of potential conflict was thus eliminated, but no attempt was made at this time to remove the ambiguity of the 1814 constitution on the issue of ministerial responsibility, perhaps because only Charles X and the ultras had considered that the phrase, 'les ministres sont responsables' meant that they were responsible to him and not to parliament. Discussion of this point was deferred, but oddly, in view of its significance in the political crisis of the Restoration, no specific constitutional change was ever made. Finally, the new constitution was entrusted into the safe keeping of 'all national guardsmen and French citizens'. There was no longer the pretence of divine will and divine right mentioned in the 1814 document.

Thus the main immediate alteration to France's system of government after the 1830 revolution was the unavoidable necessity of the appointment of a new head of state. Surprisingly, in view of the number of subsequent attempts to assassinate him (more than any other nineteenth-century ruler endured and survived), the decision to make Louis-Philippe king was generally popular. Those with republican tendencies, like Cabet, Blanc and the founders of clubs such as the *Amis du Peuple*, did not oppose the choice of a king. Their quarrel lay with the failure of the liberals to organise elections for a constituent assembly, which, they believed, would have transformed the political and social system of France, by introducing more radical political and social measures. The new charter promised other changes: juries were to be used more extensively in political and press trials; members

of parliament who accepted an official post were to be required to seek re-election; the National Guard and local councils were to be reorganised. There was to be legislation on the freedom of education, the abolition of the law of the double vote and a new electoral law.

The vast majority of parliamentary liberals were determined to complete these changes in the life of the exisiting parliament, which was consistent with their general satisfaction with the Restoration system itself. By a vote of 246 to 12 the assembly decided that it was empowered to complete the process of revolutionary change. In the July Days the parliamentary liberals had, somewhat tardily, united in public criticism of Charles X's four ordinances. What happened to this majority after the revolution? Only 99 of the deputies refused to take the oath of allegiance to Louis-Philippe and resigned. In total, 110 by-elections were needed, including vacancies created by death and promotions. These were held in October 1830 before a new electoral law had been devised, but after the abolition of the law of the double vote. Electoral participation was low: 60 per cent compared with over 90 per cent in June and July before the revolution. Legitimists who refused the oath to the new king were not entitled to vote. The liberals had already begun to disagree about how revolutionary the consequence of July ought to be and 20 per cent of the new deputies were sympathetic to the *mouvement*. The rest of the new men, whose views would have been judged to be leaning left a few months earlier, were now on the right of the chamber. Some had been out of politics since the fall of Napoleon, but the vast majority, nearly 80 per cent, were new to the chamber.

Liberals had been reasonably content with the principles of the Restoration electoral system. In the crisis of 1827–30 they had been the defenders of the charter. Not surprisingly, in view of their own success at the polls, most wanted few changes after the revolution. The experience of popular revolt placed the wealthy minority in a comfortable but beleaguered citadel. They justified the retention of a small electorate – judged to be vital to 'public order' – and thus their supremacy, on the grounds that wealth indicated respect for social and political order and guaranteed political independence and incorruptibility. The belief that wealth equalled political conservatism and that a democratic vote would bring political anarchy and social chaos was fairly universal among property owners. That republicans demanded a broader based suffrage, albeit ambiguous at first,[17] was sufficient to convince the *résistance* liberals that it was not in their interests to enlarge the electorate. The more radical *mouvement* pressed for a lower *cens*, the tax one had to pay in order to vote, believing that they would gain. The new law of 19 April 1831 governing parliamentary elections was a triumph for the *résistance*. The electorate was increased from 90 000 to 166 000 by reducing the *cens* from 300 to 200 francs per year. Certain *capacités*, such as members of the Academy, could qualify if they paid 50 per cent of the required tax contribution. The minimum voting age was lowered from thirty to twenty-five. In future 5 in every 1000 Frenchmen could vote, compared with 32 per 1000 in Great Britain after 1832.[18] The tax qualification for candidates was halved to 500 francs and the minimum age lowered from forty to thirty.[19] The body of potential candidates was thus increased from 15 000 in 1830 to 57 000 by 1840. Elections were held under the new law in the summer of 1831, and produced a parliament similar in social composition to that of the Restoration. The new electorate was not noticeably different in socioeconomic terms. It was still predominantly a landowning elite which included tradesmen, manufacturers and professional men in the towns. It was still small and compact enough for elections to be dominated, as before 1830, by a small number of very wealthy local notables.

Thus the *pays légal* battened down the hatches on even modest change and Orleanist parliaments lacked real political argument. Many ultraroyalists withdrew from national politics temporarily in the early 1830s, until the remoteness of a legitimist challenge to Louis-Philippe convinced them of the expediency of taking the new oath of allegiance. Most parliamentary candidates claimed to be moderate royalists, just as had those of the previous regime. There was a very brief radical honeymoon in 1831, which had faded by the elections of 1834. Cabet, republican in the early years of the reign and later a utopian socialist, was elected for Dijon in 1831 and again in 1834, but this was exceptional. The lack of pay for deputies in addition to the high tax qualification required of them guaranteed that most would be supporters of the status quo.

The most outstanding transformation in the structure of parliament was in the Chamber of Peers. The principle of hereditary succession to the chamber was replaced by life peerages in 1831.[20] Even this seems more novel in principle than in reality. The 1789

Revolution had become a bloody witch-hunt in its attack on hereditary rights but Napoleon not only welcomed those *émigré* peers who returned to France and were prepared to work for him, he added new honours to an already complex array. Although the Restoration paraded the virtues of an hereditary caste, a title was only one component of power and distinction. The electoral system sanctified the supreme importance of wealth for the aspiring politician. After the legislation of 1831, the Chamber of Peers continued to provide a fair proportion of Louis-Philippe's ministers. On the other hand, it could be said that the law reduced the status of the upper chamber without affecting the social prestige of a title, even an invented one. A certain negligent attitude to the upper house emerged. In 1834 the prefect in the Côte-d'Or remarked on the unwillingness of ambitious politicians to accept 'elevation' until their political career was over.[21] Did the Chamber of Deputies adopt a dominant political role? Orleanist France was no more of a parliamentary monarchy than the Bourbon regime. The deputies never came into conflict with the monarch of their choice as had the Restoration parliaments, perhaps because of Louis-Philippe's political knowledge and skill. Royal power and influence remained considerable. Elections were managed by successive governments with increasing professionalism. The use of official appointments to sweeten deputies was so extensive that in the 1840s nearly 40 per cent of the chamber were placemen. What is surprising is that there was a similar proportion of *fonctionnaires* before 1830, when conflict between king and parliament became so acrimonious. The difference was not the triumph of parliament itself, but that of the notables in their localities, where they were wooed and conciliated by an effective prefectoral corps.

The Orleanist liberals were criticised by the new radical clubs after the July Days for the minor revisions they made to the 1814 constitution. But their critics were a small, if energetic, minority, mainly of Paris-based professional writers. The almost imperceptible revisions of 1830–1 seemed in tune with the *pays légal*, and at the time, no one else could make their wishes heard. Although those with *mouvement* sympathies were quite successful in the national elections in 1831, they were far less so in 1834 and the departmental councils were even more conservative than those appointed by Louis-Philippe. Within the *mouvement*, some would have liked a lower qualification for voters, but support for universal suffrage was almost non-existent. The electoral reform movement of the 1840s – the 'banquet' campaign – concerned itself with the proliferation of placemen and the over-representation of rural areas, as much as with the tax qualification for voting, which reformers would have still retained but at a reduced level, probably 100 francs. Few 'banqueteers' were democrats. Thus the liberal majority met no serious challenge to their determination to avoid change and to nullify the disturbing implications of the 'Three Glorious Days'. They were conservatives, they believed, not through pusillanimity, but conviction. Their victory ensured that Orleanist liberalism was quickly and permanently associated with the *résistance* wing of the former opponents of Polignac.

When the term liberal was used by contemporaries, it was often associated with 'patriot'. Nationalism was thought to be a safe outlet for democratic sentiments. Even Charles X was persuaded to gamble on the acceptability of the four ordinances on the strength of the army's very recent success in Algeria. In the 1790s the revolutionaries had waged war on the monarchies of Europe in the name of freedom and a rerun of this performance was anticipated by some in 1830. Revolutions in Poland, Belgium and the Italian and German states strengthened the hopes of the radicals and the fears of the more cautious.[22] Volunteers to fight for foreign revolutions gathered in Lyons and on the Belgian border and their numbers grew as disappointment with the conservatism of the Orleanist regime mounted. Popular nationalism (manifest in 1831 in the formation by *mouvement* notables in the border departments of 'National Associations' to defend France in case her former enemies tried to enforce the 1815 settlement) was no doubt often genuine, but it was also an attempt to threaten the Périer government by those who had lost the power struggle to control the regime.[23] The conservative Orleanists preferred passive, symbolic nationalism. They were aware of the benefits of being seen as the champion of the nation. The *tricolore* of the 1790s replaced the fleur-de-lis during the July Days and was officially proclaimed as the national flag in the constitution. Trees of liberty, patriotic headgear, badges and hastily erected statues, not to mention paintings and other symbols of revolutionary fervour, abounded. The enthusiasm was short-lived. Within a few months trees of liberty were embarrassing, even threatening, to the Périer government, especially when mayors and prefects continued to bless their planting.

The most significant symbol of the nation-at-arms of the 1790s, the National Guard, was spontaneously reborn in the July Days in innumerable provincial towns as well as in the capital. The almost mythical revolutionary Lafayette put himself at its head in July. On 31 July plans were made for creating twenty regiments of a volunteer mobile guard, open to all and offering a small daily wage. By October 1 300 000 men had enrolled as members of the National Guard, of whom half a million were armed and 320 000 possessed uniform and equipment.[24] The Guard was democratic in composition and form and distinctly radical, often republican, in sentiment. Its ethos was always ambiguous, however, in the period of the constitutional monarchy as in the 1790s, for many of its middle-class members saw it as the only potential for maintaining public order. In the July revolution the liberal notables hastened to gain control of the Guard to contain popular unrest. Subsequently its policing role was increasingly resented by many volunteers. In popular disturbances after the revolution its members were often either among the rioters[25] or refused to turn out. Imprisonment and prosecution of offenders was counter-productive: juries almost always acquitted them.[26] It became a nuisance to an increasingly conservative regime eager for public order and stability. The Parisian Guard was particularly vociferous in its criticism of the modest punishments meted out to Charles X's former ministers in December 1830. Lafayette was forced out of command at that time and the Périer government, formed shortly thereafter, urged prefects not to be too pressing in the reorganisation of battalions and to try tactfully to recover weapons that had been issued by the local barracks. But the National Guard was precious as a revolutionary symbol and its reconstruction had to be placed on a permanent footing. The law of March 1831 made all tax-paying adult males between the ages of twenty and sixty eligible for service.[27] Battalions were to elect their own officers, although the king was to select the colonels from lists provided by senior officers. National Guard elections were the nearest thing to democracy in the period, but most people were very apathetic. The Guard continued to function only in towns and the elections were always disturbing to the regime because only local radicals, particularly republicans, bothered to stand and so they controlled it.[28] The patriotic heritage of 1789 was a doubtful blessing for the Orleanist elite.

Liberal thinkers like Benjamin Constant were primarily

concerned, before 1830, with the individual liberties of worship, of association and of speech. They were the self-conscious heirs of a revolutionary tradition of anti-clericalism, a sentiment often enhanced by ownership of former church land bought in the 1790s as *biens nationaux*. Anti-clerical attitudes were revived in the 1820s by the overtly anti-revolutionary evangelical campaign, the attempts of the church to enlarge its influence over education, legislation making sacrilege a capital offence and the close association between church and government, especially the Polignac government, which turned the pulpit into an electoral platform for the ultras. A number of senior members of the church hierarchy were outspoken ultras, including the archbishop of Paris, Mgr de Quelen, and went into exile with Charles X. In addition, a number of senior liberals were Protestant, and religious conflict was a feature of the July Days and subsequent unrest in areas with a sizeable Protestant community.

The Orleanist liberals might, therefore, be expected to manifest overt hostility to the church. In August 1830 the revised charter reduced the status of catholicism from the religion of the state to the religion of the majority and article five of the constitution guaranteed religious freedom and the payment of clerical salaries by the state. The months following the 1830 revolution were punctated by repeated popular anti-clerical outbursts.[29] Evidence presented at the trial of Charles X's ministers underlined the role played by the church in Restoration politics. Some local officials appointed after the revolution openly sympathised with popular demonstrators, but those in central government became increasingly circumspect. Concerted resistance to the new regime by the church was half-expected, but not forthcoming, even in the west. On the other hand fear of left-wing demonstrations convinced many Orleanists that it would be expedient to win at least the tolerance of those most committed to the church, the legitimist supporters of the previous regime. Hence after March 1831 there was an attempt to re-establish relations on a more favourable footing. In addition, Orleanists were always worried that their right- and left-wing opponents might ally. The 1833 Guizot law on education gave the church a cause, however, 'freedom of education', the significance of which grew as did the number of primary schools run by communes. Education kept anti-clericalism a live issue, despite the value to the regime of a conservative church.

What of the two liberties apparently most prized by liberals before the revolution: the right of association and press freedom? According to the Napoleonic Code, inherited by Louis XVIII, only associations of twenty members or less could be formed without prefectoral approval, otherwise full membership lists and statutes had to be provided for official scrutiny. Political associations either remained underground and, like the *charbonnerie*, effectively split the society into groups of twenty or, like *Aide-toi*, subsisted as *ad hoc* small committees that came together for specific, short-term goals. Immediately after the revolution there was little check on political societies. *Aide-toi* flourished alongside the *Société pour la liberté de la Presse* and new radical formations including the *Amis du Peuple*. Initially, totally ignoring the law, the latter held 1000-strong rallies. Fairly numerous riots and demonstrations led first to a law against unlawful meetings (*attroupements*) in April 1831, and repeated prosecutions of leaders of opposition societies. Concerted repression followed, the Orleanists pursuing a policy of surveillance, prosecution and ultimately changes in the law on associations which made the new liberal regime even less tolerant than the Restoration. By 1834 even societies of less than twenty were subject to official scrutiny and required authorisation.

Freedom of the press suffered a similar fate. Idealised, like freedom of association, in the Declaration of the Rights of Man of 1789 (and equally abused subsequently), the Restoration had made an ambiguous declaration in favour of its liberty. Article eight of the Restoration constitution said 'all Frenchmen have the right to publish and have printed their views, in accordance with laws designed to check the abuse of this liberty.' Such laws cascaded forth, trying to destroy the proliferation and popularity of liberal newspapers. Restrictions on press freedom followed in 1814, 1815, 1817, three pieces of legislation in 1819, two in 1822, and finally the first of four ordinances of July 1830, which tried to silence opposition papers completely. Most of this legislation permitted the administration to apply a muzzle. All newspapers had to be registered at the prefecture. An editor had to pay a prescribed sum in caution money, which would be forfeit if the paper was accused of infringing the law. Resulting trials often failed to secure prosecutions and trials themselves were excellent, if costly, publicity for the newspapers.[30] The 1830 constitution was unambiguous. Article seven read, as before, 'All Frenchmen have the right to publish and have printed their views in conformity with the law' but added, 'Censorship will never be reestablished.' The most popular newspapers in the provinces as well as in the capital did not support the conservative tone of Orleanism set by Périer, however, and the government took refuge in the means of silencing the press that had proved so disastrous for Charles X. Censorship was rapidly reintroduced in October, November and December 1830, April 1831, February 1834 and finally in the laws of September 1835, which even banned political caricature and the use of words like 'republic' in the press.[31]

The tortuous shifts of policy of the Orleanist liberals when faced with opposition demonstrate the essential dichotomy between the ideal of the liberty of the individual and the perceived concept of a liberal state. The problems of industrialisation and urbanisation appeared to threaten the consensus vital to the Orleanist liberals' notion of *juste milieu*. Memories of the violence of the 1790s, sometimes personal and increasingly historic, coupled with an acute awareness of the disorder of the 1830 revolution and subsequent years, caused Orleanists to over-react to opposition. The great 'conspiracy' of April 1834 was little more than the invention of police agents who were paid by results.[32]

Liberals were most criticised as hypocrites by contemporary socialists and social reformers for their attitudes to social and economic questions and their lack of sympathy for the urban and rural poor, whose difficulties were easily dismissed as the consequence of drink, idleness or the flagrant disregard of the Almighty. Liberals in the Côte-d'Or and other wine-producing departments, thought it quite reasonable to organise petitions against the wine tax in the late 1820s, but were discomforted when wine producers attacked the offices of the tax-collectors and burned their records after the July Days.[33] Those officials who remained openly sympathetic to the wine producers were rapidly dismissed when the Périer government took over in 1831. Overt supporters of progress, liberals underwrote the erosion of communal rights. The last major attempts of artisans to preserve traditional rights and organisations in the 1830s and 1840s met with the consistent opposition of the elite. The full force of the Orleanist state was used against silk weavers in Lyons, struggling to maintain their traditional independence against merchants who were developing into embryonic entrepreneurs.[34] Liberal ideas on the role of government in the national economy swung with the pendulum of their own material well-being and perceived economic wisdom and were indistinguishable from the opinions of many other reasonably well-off citizens. *Laissez-faire* clearly did not mean opposition to the development of the role of the state and recent commentaries note the acceleration in interventionist legislation in the 1840s.[35]

During the Second Empire liberalism was associated with free-trade policies but this was a radical departure. Restoration liberals were divided in their attitudes to tariffs, depending on their own economic interests and the area they represented. With the important exceptions of wine producers and some cotton manufacturers, however, most believed in protectionism. Governments before and after the 1830 revolution reflected the views of the powerful producer pressure groups in parliament. Typical was the legislation on the importing of grain, which prohibited both import and export on sliding scales and which effectively kept out all imports of wheat except for one month, February 1828, despite the 50 per cent increase in price. Legislation in April 1832, as the food crisis showed no sign of abating, brought minor reductions in the price levels at which grain could be imported. But a good harvest that year brought vociferous and successful objections from producers. Iron manufacturers had their way in the Restoration, with duties on imported iron which by 1822 added 120 per cent to the price of imported iron. After 1822, despite the persistent crisis, domestic manufacturers defended a tariff that made iron prohibitively expensive.[36] Only in 1836 were some reductions in duties made, and then only on coal-smelted iron, little of which was produced in France.

Liberals put their faith in an effective monarchical executive authority combined with elected institutions. They assumed that monarchy would be based on rational and utilitarian principles. The interests of the individual would be protected by the existence of elected representative assemblies, in which both voters and candidiates were obliged to qualify by paying a substantial amount in direct tax, primarily on land. It was argued that a tax-payers' franchise was egalitarian since, by hard work, anyone could qualify. Liberals saw no essential conflict between a strong executive and an elected assembly. They appear to have seen no sinister contradiction between the growth of the power of the state and elected assemblies stuffed with men holding official appointments. The demise of intermediary bodies, which liberals promoted in the name of efficiency and rationality, served to increase the role of the state in administering justice and running local affairs. Liberals were keen to expand the bureaucratic machinery, not just to feather their own nests, but because they believed that an effective state was crucial to a civilised and settled society. Press censorship, the banning of 'unsuitable' political groups and the use of the army in industrial disputes expanded the role of the state as the protector of the property owner. Thus, after the fright of the July Days, liberal ideas became more overtly conservative, with respect to political and social issues, and liberalism became indistinguishable from *résistance* Orleanism. Propelled by the potent fear of Jacobinism, the determination to control unrest in their own day and the difficulties they encountered in doing so, they narrowed their spectrum of permissible criticism, pushing former allies to the *mouvement*, or socialist or republican ideas.

One can chart the fragmentation of Restoration liberalism by looking, not at the big names, but at a group of liberals elected in and after 1830 for a department, chosen, not for any assumed 'typicality', but simply as an example. In the wine-producing department of the Côte-d'Or in 1830, before the revolution, three liberals were elected, plus two moderate legitimists, selected by the double vote constituencies. The liberals were all *Aide-toi* organisers hostile to the Polignac government. Hernoux, *avocat*, *négociant* and one of the richest local landowners,[37] had been mayor of Dijon in the Hundred Days and imprisoned during the White Terror. Like his father, who had been a representative of the third estate in 1789 and a member of the *conseil des anciens*, he was a deputy in both the Restoration and the July Monarchy. Although he was an active organiser of the July Days in Dijon, he quickly became an opponent of the Périer government.[38] Mauguin, also elected in 1830, was a Parisian *avocat*, an active member of the Parisian municipal commission in July, and politically to the left of Hernoux.[39] Variously described as republican and Bonapartist, he was summed up by Guizot as 'an elegant and daring orator, pretentious, vain and wholly lacking in both judgement and scruples.'[40] Louis-Bazile, the third liberal, a wealthy local landowner and forge owner, was also an opponent of Périer, but was described as 'voyant bien, mais ne parlant pas.'[41] All that really seemed to unite them was their dislike of Polignac. Unfortunately for simple political definition, the two moderate legitimists elected at the same time were also hostile to Polignac and would also have voted the *adresse* of the 221 if Saunac's amendment had been accepted.

To make the characterisation even more problematical, in 1831, the two legitimists were replaced by two more 'liberals'. Cabet, a former *carbonaro*, was a fighter in the July Days and *procureur-général* in Corsica after the revolution.[42] He was not only to become an opponent of Périer, dismissed from his post in March 1831, but also an active republican and socialist. The fifth deputy in 1831, replacing the other legitimist, was Vatout, the king's librarian,[43] member of the *conseil d'état* and the author of a number of timorous liberal allegories in the 1820s,[44] a man almost at the opposite end of the political spectrum to Cabet. In 1837 Cabet was replaced by Saunac, the moderate legitimist, now very well thought of by the Orleanist prefect.

Why did such fissures develop within the Restoration liberal group? In part, of course, the explanation lies in the tenuous nature of pre-1830 unity and in part in the achievement, or not, of personal career ambitions after 1830. The staunchest patrons of the *mouvement* were often those who had served Napoleon, like Hernoux, not only during the Empire, but also during the Hundred Days. The division of the liberals reflected the fragmentation produced by the political upheaval of the revolutionary and Napoleonic years, which left no single tradition but a number of overlapping and conflicting tendencies. These differences were subsumed in the campaign against the ultraroylists in the late 1820s, for the latter seemed to posit a right-wing revolutionary challenge to the compromise of 1814. It is also clear, when one begins to look at individuals, that the gap between moderate supporters of the Bourbons, like Saunac, and Orleanists was fairly narrow. A preference for a measure of individual liberty, combined with an ordered and defined state structure, government by and for a restricted landowning elite and the preservation of a conservative church, were concepts shared, not only by Orleanist *résistance* liberals, but by many to their right and even to their left. Much has been written about the disastrous consequences for France of the fragmentation of her elite after 1789. Events were dominated by the crippling fear of popular intervention in politics, manifest equally by royalists before 1830 and Orleanists afterwards. Notables, Bourbon and Orleanist, shared these apprehensions, but because the former detested 1789 above all and the latter represented themselves as the heirs of the Revolution, they never appreciated the degree of common ground they shared. Few royalists wanted a return to the *ancien régime*; no liberals could stomach the Jacobin phase of the Revolution.

Liberalism was in many respects a flag of negotiation, compromise and convenience, evolved by those with some power and influence to retain their position in changing times. There could be no single liberal doctrine or set of policies, for liberalism represented a *juste milieu* between the perceived injustices of 'traditional' societies and the projected evils of mass power. Liberalism was a compound of a belief that society should be based on moral, rational foundations, respect for wealth and private property and horror of uncontrolled popular violence or other forms of extremism. The tensions resulting from the interrelated economic developments and urban growth meant that a liberal *juste milieu* would be subject to constant modification. But, ironically, a set of ideas supposedly designed to accommodate change manifested self-destructive rigidity when challenged. The liberals of 1830 many have been heirs to 1789, but they were primarily concerned with defusing revolution in their own day. Orleanist liberalism may have been appropriate in 1830, but eighteen years later it seemed to many far from a 'middle way'.

6
Religion and Revolutionary Politics

Revolutions were anathema to the Catholic Church in the nineteenth century; anti-clericalism had been a powerful and, ultimately, a very self-destructive element in revolutionary thinking and policy in the 1790s. The revolutionaries, influenced in part by the ideas of the mid-eighteenth-century *philosophes*, had been determined to destroy the church as one of the most powerful privileged corporations in the country. The church was the first of the three estates into which *ancien régime* society was divided. It was one of the largest and richest landowners, its senior posts were dominated by old noble families and it exercised a major political role, not always in sympathy with the monarchy. In the eighteenth century the estates of Languedoc, in which the clerical first estate was a powerful force, fought to preserve their autonomy from royal interference.[1] Arguably it was a colossal block to innovation in ideas, institutions and behaviour.

The year 1789 brought the sale of all church lands, 1790 the abolition of the right to collect a tithe and the obligation on all ecclesiastics to take an oath of allegiance to the revolutionary government or forgo their living and their right to a salary from the state. Only a minority were willing to become constitutional priests, the rest were forced underground. A ten-day week replaced the Christian seven-day one. The domestic ceremonies of the church were declared redundant. Civil registration of birth, marriage and death was introduced. Divorce was permitted. Religious orders were closed and their charitable, nursing and educational functions taken over, if very imperfectly, by the state. In particular, aware of the importance of education, the revolutionaries struggled, with insufficient cash, to establish a lay system of education. Napoleon gave up the fight with regard to primary schooling, but had confirmed the creation of a lay system of secondary and tertiary education under the control of the University of Paris. For a time in 1793 and 1794 a new religion of the Supreme Being was practised in former churches; others were sold and turned into commercial ventures like fish markets. The anti-clericalism of the revolutionaries provoked an equally violent counter-revolution, however, bringing civil war to France and thenceforward merging Catholic and monarchist loyalties in an indissoluble union unknown in the *ancien régime*.[2] In the later 1790s, and conclusively under Napoleon, a compromise had to be reached, given the pressure of foreign and civil war, the latter fuelled by resistance to anti-clerical policies. But the church was always aware that Napoleon's *concordat* of 1801 and the Organic Articles were a matter of expediency and calculation. Napoleon showed scant respect for the pope in Rome or the church in his Empire.

In 1814, although on the road to recovery after the vicissitudes of the revolutionary period, the church was still divided and seriously understaffed. Fourteen of the fifty dioceses were vacant, including Paris. Four bishops were still refractory clergy, who had refused the revolutionary oath of the clergy to the civil constitution, while eleven were constitutional priests. Among the clergy in general there were over 13 000 unfilled posts in 1814, including 3654 for *curés*. Women's orders had been tolerated for their important practical role, but otherwise Napoleon had been hostile to the regular clergy, although the Jesuits and others had managed to maintain a hold.

Thus in 1814 the church welcomed the return of the Bourbons. It was restored as the state church of France and the totality of the embrace was such that many doubted the genuineness of the accompanying declaration of toleration for other religions. The *concordat* of 1801 and the Napoleonic Organic Articles were maintained. Clerical stipends remained the responsibility of the state and the constitution made it clear that the revolutionary sale of church lands was sacrosanct, although unsold land was returned. In 1817 the church was permitted to accept legacies of land, although these were never received on a scale to rival its landed wealth in the *ancien régime*. State expenditure on the church almost trebled during the Restoration, from twelve million francs to thirty-three million. The number of bishoprics was increased to eighty in 1821 after a battle with the papacy. Clerical salaries were increased. One thousand scholarships were instituted for those wishing to enter a seminary. In 1814 there were fifty-two seminaries in France, run by orders like the *Frères des Écoles Chrétiennes*. Recruitment improved noticeably during the Restoration; the number of seminarists doubled to over 13 000. Religious orders re-emerged, including twenty non-recognised ones. Schools run by teaching orders proliferated, including *petits séminaires*, supposedly run solely for the education of potential priests, which expanded rapidly. The Jesuits, though not authorised, began to run boarding schools, which attracted an aristocratic clientele.

The church also worked to broaden its control of education as a whole, a matter of passionate concern to both sides. In 1821 bishops were given a supervisory role over secondary education. Churchmen could be made heads of *lycées*. A year later Mgr de Fraysinnous, a senior cleric, was made Grand Master of the University of Paris. Two years later he became head of the joint ministry of ecclesiastical affairs and education. The battle of earlier revolutionaries for a lay system of education seemed lost.

The church was encouraged to reassert its influence over a divided and increasingly de-Christianised or indifferent nation. A vigorous evangelical campaign, launched in 1816, in which young, post-revolutionary and rather intransigent priests made week-long visits each year in town and country, created an unprecedented religious revivial. To mark their passage the missionaries erected crosses, normally on municipally owned land in the centre of communes. The priests were devout and energetic and the reinvigorated Catholics, many of them women, were undoubtedly also fired by religious zeal. But there was a not insubstantial element of concern over the destructive force of the revolutionary years. As the climax of their visit, the missionaries organised ceremonies of atonement for the crimes of the Revolution. The evangelists were linked to the politically motivated *congrégation*, founded in 1801 to work for the monarchist cause.[3] Evangelism and ultraroyalism were two sides of a coin. Newspapers could be prosecuted for insulting religion and in 1825 a general law against sacrilege made profanation of the host punishable by death. The new law was more of a marker for the extent of church influence in parliament than a piece of legislation to be actively employed.[4] The ultraroyalist leader, the duc d'Artois, was king by now, and the close association of royal and clerical authority was emphasised in his coronation oath.

It was clear that clerical ambitions reached well beyond the minds of the young and faithful to the political fabric of the nation. The relationship between the church and state in the Restoration was based increasingly on an elaborate, romantic, ultraroyalist myth. This alignment of senior clerics with one section of the royalists was emphasised in the pronounced social elitism in clerical appointments themselves. The episcopate was almost entirely renewed during the Restoration, with 110 appointments being made. The major qualifications for a bishopric in the period were nobility (the older and more senior the better), to have served during the *ancien régime* and to have opposed the Revolution. At the outset twenty-six *ancien régime* bishops were reappointed. Between 1821 and 1823 twenty-one *ancien régime* priests of the revolutionary period gained promotion to bishoprics as opposed to only one constitutional priest.[5] A specifically royalist, and even ultraroyalist, episcopate was built up. The ultras were keen to employ such ubiquitous emissaries to further their political ambitions. In the elections of 1824, 1827 and 1830 the clergy were strictly enjoined by the government, via their bishops, to work for the election of royalist (effectively ultraroyalist) candidates. A number of senior churchmen, including the archbishop of Paris, Mgr de Quelen, and his colleague in Besançon, Rohan-Chabot, made no secret of their active support for ultraroyalism. Altar and throne had never been closer and it seemed increasingly that the throne took second place. The ultra concept of the interlinked institutions of church and monarchy bore little relationship to the *ancien régime* situation. They held a pre-absolutist theory. Louis XVIII had been a frequent disappointment to them. It is significant that in the department of the Gard, where the richest third of the population was Protestant and where the 1789 Revolution and subsequent years had been marked by frequent murderous interchanges between Protestant and Catholic communities, Catholic royalists favoured green, the colour of Charles X, not white, the more usual symbolic colour of the Bourbons.[6]

Criticism of this growing influence existed among royalists themselves, however, both in government and out, and even among clerics, echoing long-standing rifts, exacerbated by divisions within the church during the revolutionary period. Some clerics, particularly older ones who had seen service during the Empire, were disturbed by the strident political declamations of more recently appointed seniors and the intolerant ardour of junior colleagues. Others, heirs of Gallican tradition, feared that evangelism meant an upsurge in the power of Rome and a dilution of the autonomy of the French church. The *congrégation* was certainly inspired by the Jesuits and the evangelical movement benefited Rome more than the Bourbons. The papacy saw no reason to alter the Napoleonic *concordat*, for it contributed favourably to the extension of papal power over the French church. Thus there were divisions within the Restoration church and inherent contradictions between moderate royalists, who constituted the vast majority, and the evangelical movement, although the prevailing official ethos was one of the harmonious fusion of interests between church and state. When one considers the anti-clerical attitudes of the succeeding regime, it is important to realise that the image of total church–state harmony before 1830 was only a piece of ultra wishful thinking, perpetrated primarily by some of Villèle's policies and the aspirations of Charles X and Polignac.

Between 1817 and 1821 Restoration governments had battled with the papacy over the expansion of the number of bishoprics and the degree of papal control of the church. However devout, most of those who exercised civil power were determined to retain the upper hand, including Charles X himself, despite the contemporary cartoons of him in clerical garb. Conflict re-emerged during the Martignac administration in 1828. To placate the liberal parliamentary majority and elements within the church itself, non-certified religious orders were banned from teaching in secondary schools. This was a direct attack on the Jesuits who by 1828 were running eight secondary schools. These schools were put under the control of the University of Paris. In addition, restrictions were placed on the number of pupils to be admitted to the *petits séminaires*. Only three bishops obeyed these ordinances; seventy openly defied the government, led by the archbishop of Paris himself. Although Martignac secured the partial support of the pope to enforce the new regulations, his government fell before steps could be taken to implement them and the succeeding Polignac administration had a very different attitude towards the church. Thus, although Restoration governments had worked closely with the church, even during this period the delineation of church–state power had been a sensitive matter.

Anti-clericalism became a not insignificant aspect of liberalism, but was very different from the anti-clericalism of the 1790s. It contained no hint of anti-religion, which was associated with popular unrest and the violence and bloodshed of the Terror. Religion, circumscribed within established parameters, was perceived as a guarantor of the social order. Anti-clericalism crystallised during the Restoration, partly in response to Bourbon policies in two main areas: education and politics. There was lively opposition to the growing influence of the church in all aspects of education. The prominence of ultra clerics in the church and in politics and the unashamed electioneering on behalf of right-wing candidates was resented. Pamphlets and newspaper articles stressed that the church should confine itself to spiritual affairs. The Restoration liberals were circumspect in their anti-clericalism, however. Given their antecedents, including the degree to which supporters had bought church property in the 1790s, liberals were inextricably tied to an anti-clerical tradition. Nevertheless, they were even more committed, as the name *doctrinaire* implied, to the maintenance of the settlement of 1814. In areas like the Midi department of the Gard, where the large and wealthy Protestant minority lost the influence they had gained during the revolutionary and imperial years, liberalism was closely associated with the Protestant notables, although even here, from 1827 onwards, they were joined by moderate Catholic royalists, aware of the utility of the charter. Liberals were keen to make political capital out of criticising the revived influence of the church in politics and educational affairs. Since there was no threat to the revolutionary land settlement, however, and anti-clerical attitudes had mellowed somewhat (perhaps assisted by the European-wide, and not exclusively Catholic, contemporary religious revival), the anti-church views of the liberals were conducted through a fairly controlled war of words.

The revised constitutional charter of August 1830 accurately reflected the more muted and restrained anti-clericalism manifest in the nineteenth century. The new regime declared itself tolerant of all religions, as had been its predecessor, but the status of the Catholic Church was reduced from its Restoration position as the state church to its designation in the revised charter as the religion of the majority of French people. This carried no financial penalty, but was clearly a psychological blow. The Orleanists undertook to pay the salaries of the officials of other churches, including the Jews, and promised to develop a lay system of education. In the provisions made immediately after the July Days the emphasis was on tolerance of all religions. 1830 was often depicted by more extreme Catholics as a Prostestant revolution. Guizot became the first minister of the interior. In the Gard, the Protestant elite resumed its revolutionary and imperial ascendancy. The last Restoration prefect left Protestants in provisional control of the senior posts.[7] In the aftermath of the revolution anti-clerical feeling went much further than the more conservative Orleanist notables intended.

The violence of the July Days unleashed extreme manifestations of popular anti-clericalism which were re-enacted repeatedly during the second half of 1830 and the early months of 1831. In the department of the Gard this assumed the quality of a potential civil war between Catholic and Protestant communities; at the end of August seven people were killed and twelve wounded in clashes, and an all-out fight between Protestants and Catholic peasants from the rural areas around Nîmes, armed with pitchforks, was only narrowly averted.[8] Property associated with senior clerics who were well-known ultras and had gone into exile after the revolution figured prominently in successive riots, as did seminaries associated with missionary priests and the crosses erected during their visitations. The palace of the archbishop of Paris was sacked during the July Days and scandalised liberals described how they had seen vestments floating in the Seine and precious articles carried away by looters. Hartmann, deputy for Alsace, related in a letter to a friend how he had rescued some precious books abandoned by the crowd. He enclosed a scrap from an episcopal robe, which his correspondent, professionally interested in fabrics, attached to his diary entry.[9] The bishop of Nancy, Forbes-Jansen, was a well-known patron of the evangelists who had fled abroad at the revolution. His palace and the seminary, which had been a centre for evangelical priests, were attacked several times, both during the July Days and again in November 1830, when there were rumours that the seminary might reopen on the fête-day of St Charles, a tactless choice at best. The leaders of the crowd who marched on the seminary in July were acquitted when brought to trial and the seminary was closed by the prefect until all the evangelical priests had been sent away.

Official reports of anti-clerical riots sometimes mention that members of the National Guard took part, or were unwilling to quell disturbances; otherwise the rare details about participants mentioned artisans and humble people. After the looting of the seminary in Nancy at the end of July in 1830 seventeen men were arrested, including five cotton operatives, four shoemakers, a painter and a carter. The police commissioner was keen to note the state of inebriation of a minority of those detained.[10] The targets were political, however, and it seems very unlikely that these riots were spontaneous. 'Popular' sentiments were massaged by anti-clerical officials. After the students of the *petit séminaire* in Langres had let off fireworks to celebrate the fête of St Charles, the sub-prefect demanded the closure of the establishment.[11] His superior in Chaumont was no less hysterical, claiming that the *grand séminaire* was the heart of a conspiracy to smuggle priests to Switzerland.[12] Seminaries were a frequent target for demonstrations, because of their association with the missionaries. Sometimes the complaints against members of the teaching orders were petty. The *juge de paix* in Nogent complained in August 1830 of a 'scène facheuse' involving one of the teachers in the local *petit séminaire*, in which the teacher had confiscated tricoloured *cocardes* worn by the pupils in class.[13]

Even more provocative to agitated crowds were the new missionary crosses. There were countless examples of these being forcibly felled, usually by the National Guard, often encouraged by the new mayor. They were then moved to church land and replaced by the revolutionary symbol, the tree of liberty, and occasionally crowned with a *bonnet rouge*. Occasionally the missionary cross would also be set on fire.[14] Such unrest typified rivalries that often existed between mayor and priest. There was much resentment that the crosses had been erected on communal and not church property and that the missions had been overtly anti-revolutionary. On other occasions, such as the unrest in Nancy and Besançon, the problem seemed to lie specifically in the virulence of the anti-clerical attitudes of officials, often prefects. What tended to happen was that unrest flared up in towns where the leading official was an old Bonapartist, out of office since the Hundred Days and apparently keen to stir up resentment, perhaps to assuage his own frustration after spending fifteen years in an administrative wilderness. In Dijon the bishop was a very conciliatory and co-operative individual, but the new prefect was intensely anti-clerical. In the Haute-Marne the prefect, who had served in the same department during the Hundred Days, was extremely hostile to the bishop, an elderly and rather harmless man. The prefect in Nancy was equally intransigent and made a difficult situation worse. Some new sub-prefects adopted similar attitudes, as did mayors and National Guard commanders.[15]

On the other hand, the official policy of the Orleanist regime was one of formal tolerance, but no one doubted that the first three governments, of August and November 1830 and March 1831, were all, to varying degrees, anti-clerical in their basic assumptions. The separation of the two functions of *ministre des cultes* and *ministre de l'instruction publique* was an indication of future plans, promised in the revised charter, for legislation to encourage state education, which were certain to cause deep offence to the church. The Orleanists were determined to control the power of the church over society and above all over education. They were very conscious of the political commitment of the church to the Bourbons and were also convinced of the need to secure, in form at least, the church's acceptance of their regime. Bishops were asked – or ordered – to ensure that prayers for the welfare of the new king were said in church. Later the minister ordered that the fête of Louis-Philippe should be celebrated and that the anniversary of the July Days should be marked by church services. These orders, demanding a formal expression of obedience towards the new government from the clergy, were the cause of much resentment, most, but not all, emanating from the clergy. Some officials, notably outside the most 'active' Catholic areas such as western France, claimed that religious toleration ought to have introduced the total separation of temporal and spiritual matters, so that state officials should not be 'officially' party to religious ceremonies in one particular type of church.[16] Many *curés* refused to say prayers for Louis-Philippe and they and their superiors were masters of evasion. In the months after the revolution the central government frequently found itself in the position of moderator between mutually antagonistic bishops and prefects. Complaints against clergy multiplied up to March 1831. Unquestionably, the frequently expressed fears of the clerics – that the revolution constituted a danger to the church – were fed by the attitude of a vocal minority of new local officials who, unlike the central government, were willing to support and, indeed, sometimes provoke attacks on church property.

The attitude of the clergy, both younger evangelical priests and senior clerics, contributed to the intensity of the reaction, by confirming the apprehensions of their critics. A common initial response to the July Days was to claim that the church was in danger. A number of archbishops and bishops followed Charles X into exile, some to Fribourg, some to Rome. The bishop of Nancy, a prominent organiser of the *congrégation* was amongst them, as was the archbishop of Besançon. The archbishop of Paris went into hiding and then fled abroad. A few retired from their posts. It was in such dioceses that the number of complaints about the behaviour and attitudes of the clergy tended to grow into double figures.[17] Most bishops remained, however, and offered no active resistance to the replacement of Charles X. The lower clergy, who were largely a post-revolutionary generation, were often obstructionist and uncooperative. The *abbé* Tressé, a staunch supporter of the *congrégation* in the Haute-Marne, was infamous locally for his denunciation of the new regime and his condemnation of the election of the new sub-prefect's father, Toupot de Béveaux, senior, as deputy, as a 'punishment from heaven'.[18] The most vigorous opponents of the change of dynasty were found among young priests, the products of the *congrégation* and the evangelical movement. There were many anxious meetings of priests to discuss their changed situation. Ministerial, prefectoral and lesser bureaucratic files burgeoned with complaining missives, which were not reduced by the assumption of the faithful that the tenor of the new regime was bound to be anti-clerical. Even allowing for the release of repressed hostility to the church, there is no doubt that the church itself displayed an active dislike of the revolution. Evidence was assembled claiming that there were well over 600 justified complaints against clergymen in the early months of the regime.[19]

Most controversy concerned specific church–state relations, with the Orleanists demanding recognition of the regime while the church, alarmed and worried about its own security, was reluctant to accept the permanence of the new monarchy. Municipal councils asked priests to bless the *tricolore* and their National Guard emblems and the government asked them to say prayers for the new king. Unless one assumes that the requests were made merely to inflame clerical opinion and produce a confrontation, which seems unlikely, or that Orleanist officials, particularly mayors, were trying to assert their authority, which is quite likely, there was an assumption that a religious blessing would confer respectability on a regime born of revolution. It would appear that the sanction of the church was genuinely sought, perhaps out of superstition, perhaps out of real belief, which is not the approach one might expect from anti-clericals. Along with an attempt to bully the church into acceptance of the revolution, there also seems to have been either a naïve, or deeply cynical calculation that for the clergy to swap kings overnight would be a matter of no consequence, that in reality the claims of Charles X to be king by divine right had been taken lightly by the faithful. Many priests refused to offer prayers for the new king and continued to perform traditional acts of piety associated with the former regime. Understandably bishops paid little heed to complaints about their subordinates and were reluctant to order them to chant prayers for Louis-Philippe. In Besançon the prefect tried to prosecute the *abbé* Doney,[20] described by him as 'Le Lamennais de Besançon'. Doney was a supporter of the *congrégation* and wrote a pamphlet criticising the prefect, who reciprocated.[21] The court was so packed with legitimists, however, that the *abbé* was acquitted.[22]

The difficulties experienced by the Doubs prefect – the support from local officials for the felling of missionary crosses, attacks on church property and so on – began to be an embarrassment to those politicians in Paris who were anxious for stability above all and an end to repeated riots and popular unrest. Although liberal politicians were suspicious of senior members of the church hierarchy (and their fears were confirmed by Restoration government documents examined during the trial of the former ministers of Charles X, which revealed the extent of ultra electioneering done from the pulpit)[23] there was nothing to be gained by exciting continued violence towards church property. But no clear directive emerged from Paris during these months and local officials were left to pursue their own vendettas against individual clerics. Neither did senior churchmen provide their members with a positive lead, either for conciliation or hostility.

This period of uncertainty, in which some clergy continued to pretend that there had been no revolution and official attitudes to the church were ambiguous and often conflicting, came to a head on 14 February 1831 when the traditional memorial service for the Bourbon heir to the throne, the duc de Berri, murdered in 1820, was held in Paris. Because the duc de Berri's murder had been blamed on the liberals and a wave of anti-liberal legislation had followed, the celebration of a memorial service, however much the norm it had been in the Restoration,[24] was likely to be a political firework after the revolution, particularly in view of continued tension. At the very least such services would be an embarrassment to the new regime. In effect several provincial memorial services were held without public comment, even in towns like Lyons and Besançon where church–state relations had been strained. There was no secret made of the intention to hold the usual service in Paris and notable legitimists obtained the consent of the *curé* of St Roch, a church near to the Louvre, for the occasion. Apprised of the fact that provincial services had been held, however, the previously indecisive Laffitte government asked the archbishop of Paris to withdraw his permission, which he did.[25] The issue had thus become one of political significance. Either tactlessly or provocatively, the organisers persuaded the elderly *curé* of St Germain l'Auxerrois, who had attended Marie Antoinette shortly before her death, to conduct a service. It would appear that the officials of the archbishopric were not informed of the arrangements, but they were public enough for there to be a congregation of 150 leading legitimists the following morning. The congregation at the memorial service included de Berryer, de Couzy and de Boisbertrand, as well as a sprinkling of members of the National Guard and some police agents.[26] There was nothing exceptional about the memorial service, and the collecion of 3000 francs for the poor indicated the prosperity of the worshippers: clearly the elite of Parisian legitimists.[27] The service was no less than an open defiance of the regime. Towards the end it became positively treasonable. A young student from the Ecole St-Cyr placed a portrait of Henri, duc de Bordeaux, the duc de Berri's 'miracle' son, born posthumously and referred to by legitimists as Henri V, on the catafalque. To it he added a crown of leaves, which was subsequently broken up and distributed to the congregation, which then dispersed.[28] The service typified a rather sentimental and ineffectual aspect of legitimism.

Later that day the church was sacked, as were other Parisian churches, the archbishop's palace and his country house.[29] Some members of the National Guard deserted when ordered to control the crowds or guard buildings, which meant that there was no obvious body of men to restore order. Nor was the unrest minimal. Several Parisian churches were so devastated that they did not reopen. The palace of the archbishop of Paris was so badly damaged that, despite his protests, rebuilding was deemed impossible and he was offered alternative accommodation. A new wave of anti-clerical riots spread throughout France but nowhere experienced the degree of destruction found in capital. Some remaining missionary crosses were replaced with trees of liberty. In Dijon the tree was ornamented with both a red cap and a tricoloured one, inscribed 'Freedom or Death!' Excited crowds chanted 'Long live the republic!' and sang both 'Ça Ira' and 'La Carmognole', recalling memories of the 1790s. The crowd was left in control of the streets, the military commander considering that the presence of the gendarmerie would risk antagonising people. In the event the most serious consequence was that the performance in the local theatre was delayed for an hour and the audience was 'entertained' by a gang of youths waving flags and singing revolutionary songs. For one sub-prefect the worst consequence of the planting of yet another tree of liberty was the decision of whether to alter the inscription on the flag that adorned it from 'Liberty! Equality!' to 'Liberty! Public Order!' or not.[30]

In Nancy the seminary and the bishop's palace were again threatened, after excitement reached a high point with rumours that a memorial service was to be held in the church. Up to this point, although some liberal notables had been concerned about the extent of what appeared to be spontaneous popular anticlericalism, no official steps had been taken to prevent such disturbances. In Nancy the threatened buildings were occupied by a mixture of troops and members of the National Guard, who profited exultantly from the discovery of the wine cellar. The seminary was evacuated and the walls of the buildings were inscribed 'public property', ostensibly to preserve them and their occupants (the bishop was still in exile) from attack.[31] In Paris the rioters proceeded unmolested. The accelerated scale of rioting after February meant that continuing official indecision began to be seen as a threat to the regime, an ever-present nightmare for Orleanists given the origins of their own power. Steps had already been taken to gather information on public opinion from *procureurs*, prefects, gendarmerie commanders and so on and these were stepped up, with more precise instructions provided on the type of information sought. Local and national archives bristle with these reports, which were obviously referred to repeatedly, with summaries and digests being made to an unprecedented degree, presumably indicating genuine alarm within the administration. Fortnightly departmental reports were compressed to assemble a regional picture. No such detailed reports were made at any other time during the July Monarchy. Memories of the *grand peur* of 1789 and the civil war of the 1790s made members of the government anxious to prevent isolated riots merging into a general conflagration. Officials were clearly more fearful for the security of the regime than at any other period of the July

Monarchy although it soon became apparent that the religious question was only one component in the increased tension, the continuing economic crisis being more fundamental to the issue of popular unrest.[32]

The Laffitte government, already in disarray, following unrest in Paris after the trial of the former king's ministers, wavered between total indecision and tacit tolerance of the ensuing anti-clerical backlash. In these years episodes like the memorial service, in effect little more than an ill-judged, pointless pinprick to the new regime, were exaggerated by governments into major conspiracies. It was suggested that the modest sentences imposed on members of Charles X's government and the tolerant attitude of the Laffitte administration towards left-wing demonstrations had encouraged legitimists in the belief that they could return to power and that the memorial service was a high point in this optimism.[33] Twenty of the paricipants in the service (none of them important legitimists, one should note) were arrested and charged with conspiring against the regime. They were all acquitted.[34] The fact that other services were held was offered as confirmation of the conspiracy theory. The homes of known legitimists were searched for arms that might be assembled for a rising. From the scanty evidence this search revealed it would seem that there was no substance to these claims. In effect the searches were conducted very tardily; opponents had plenty of time to cover their tracks and investigation was called off completely after three weeks. A warrant was issued for the arrest of the archbishop of Paris. It was suggested that although he had refused the original request for the service, he had approved in private. Typical of official bungling over the whole episode, when the archbishop protested, from his hiding place where he had been concealed since the revolution, the warrant for his arrest was withdrawn and the new minister made a public statement of the archbishop's lack of complicity.[35] The *curé* of St Germain was also arrested but later released, no charges being made.

How can one explain these fluctuations in government policy? In the aftermath of the service, there was indecision and confusion. Thiers, who was undersecretary in the ministry of the interior, did not try to stop the anti-clerical riots, nor did Odilon Barrot, Parisian prefect of police. Barrot was dismissed, but otherwise the Laffitte government dithered. The government's indecision contributed much to the subsequent problem. The original service had been banned. Why was not the revised scheme also halted? It is reasonable to assume that the government knew of the change beforehand, or if not, it was certainly evident when rows of carriages bearing famous legitimist crests drew up opposite the side entrance to the Louvre. The service could have been halted, or precautions taken to guard against unrest. There were at least three spies in government pay in the church. Not only was no attempt made to stop the service, nothing was done to interrupt the riot that followed until the destruction was complete. Even the simple precaution of locking churches, which had been observed during the July Days, was neglected until several days too late. Nor did the government order the arrest of the rioters, or attempt to discipline the recalcitrant members of the National Guard. Odilon Barrot complained that he was left without orders by the government. On 15 February, however, the government was quick to despatch telegrams ordering an investigation into a supposed legitimist plot. Why did the government ignore the fact that the rioters seemed to be more subversive than the legitimists? It was claimed that action against the rioters might have provoked an escalation of violence. The explanations offered in the Chamber of Deputies in a subsequent enquiry were little more than a series of mutual accusations adding up to a picture of great confusion and contradiction.

The appointment of Casimir Périer marked a change in Orleanist policy towards the church, but it was more a matter of degree than fundamental alteration. Périer took a more conciliatory path in his relations with the church. Prefects were ordered to inform all mayors that 'If the clergy ought not to be involved in politics, likewise equally mayors should abstain from interfering in religious matters.'[36] Officials who had been overtly and actively anticlerical were dismissed. Conservative Orleanists sought a working compromise with a church which, apart from its preference for the Bourbons, was reassuringly conservative. In particular they were eager to establish positive relationships with bishops. The number of complaints about intransigent clergy dropped in the nine months after Périer's appointment to just over one-third of those of the earlier months of the regime and remained high[37] only where there was a particularly difficult bishop who either stayed in exile, as in Besançon, or was demonstrably unwilling to reconcile himself to the new regime. Périer continued to ask bishops for formal ceremonial support for the fête-day of the king and the anniversary of the revolution. Clerical resistance withered, but some officials persisted in their criticism. In particular, National Guard officers resented the imposition of a three-line whip on church attendance. By 1834 the requirement was withdrawn, attendance being left to the individual.[38] Numerous local wrangles persisited such as rivalry between *curés* and mayors, hostility to the absence of university control over the *petits séminaires* and criticism of individual ecclesiastical school-teachers, particularly Jesuits.

In areas where the link between the Bourbons and the Catholic Church had been cemented by the experiences of the 1790s, particularly in the west and parts of the Midi, Catholic legitimists responded to the 1830 revolution both by a policy of non-co-operation, failing to take the oath of allegiance to Louis-Philippe, introduced at the end of August, and by continuing to support the religious ceremonies of the Restoration, hence the affair of St Germain l'Auxerrois. Only 252 of the 430 deputies and 114 of the 365 peers had assembled to debate the new king and constitution in August 1830 with most Bourbon supporters, or legitimists as they came to be called, pursuing what became, for a time, an accepted policy of withdrawal from politics, or 'emigration à l'intérieur'. A third restoration of the Bourbons was another matter. Legitimist landowners and businessmen controlled a high proportion of the wealth of France, as recent studies have shown.[39] It is somewhat curious, then, that the high point of their support for the Bourbons after the July Days was merely a memorial service held in February 1831. There were, apparently, identity problems surrounding another restoration. Whom should they restore? Charles X abdicated in favour, not of his younger son, Angoulême, but his grandson by his elder son, the duc de Bordeaux. Some of the older generation of legitimists refused to accept Charles' abdication, some refused to acknowledge the renunciation of Angoulême. It is true the more influential recognised Henri, the 'miracle' child, but their support amounted to little more than pilgrimages to Prague where he was being educated.[40] Charles himself, who died in 1836, denounced any thought of an attempt at a further restoration. Another problem lay in an effective split, rarely acknowledged, between elite and popular legitimism. Legitimist landowners proved as socially conservative as their Orleanist contemporaries, despite the efforts of Genoude, editor of the Parisian *Gazette de France*, and his imitators in a number of provincial clones, to urge legitimists to favour universal suffrage as the most effective basis for a future restoration. Most legitimists would not countenance democracy. Popular violence was even more distasteful. It is notable that in a department like the Gard, where Catholic ultraroyalists had sustained a secret private army of former members of the National Guard in Artois' colours during the reign of Louis XVIII (leaving local drapers permanently out of stock of green serge), these peasants and weavers were not employed in large-scale battle against Orleanist supporters, even when the prefect Chaper used government engineers to fell the missionary crosses in Nîmes.[41] Nor were the Catholic weavers of Nîmes encouraged to rebel in imitation of Lyons weavers in November 1831. Orleanist fears of a rising in the west were replaced by far more credible complaints about the problems of local weavers trying to survive on low wages.[42] Local officials never considered the possibility that local legitimists might be as appalled as they were by a Lyons-type insurrection. Universally, the legitimist elite preferred to contain the potential unrest of the Catholic poor by charity distributions in times of hardship, laundered through ostensibly purely charitable foundations such as the St Vincent de Paul Society, founded in 1834. Violent popular demonstrations of legitimism were not considered desirable.

Aristocratic, neo-medieval conspiracy on the model of Walter Scott was another matter. Quatretaillons, one of the most murderous ultra bandits in the Gard, who was surrounded and shot by gendarmes in December 1830, was actually compared to one of Scott's characters in a biographical pamphlet. Many legitimists were imbued with a sense of being heirs to a tradition of aristocratic rebellion against central authority reminiscent of the seventeenth-century *Frondes*. In the months after the 1830 revolution, legitimists formed secret groups, modelled on a decidedly amateurish version of the *charbonnerie*, to plan a third restoration. Orleanist officials were at least as well informed of membership lists as their own supporters. An armed rebellion, planned for the spring of 1831, failed to materialise. There was no support from foreign powers, as there had been in 1815, and popular and official reaction to the memorial service of St Germain, which may have been a signal, caused intense pessimism. The duchesse de Berri, however, who had been formally adopted as regent in January 1831, was bored with her exile in Holyrood and persisted, despite advice, with the plan to land near Marseilles and attempt a Bonapartist-style march through the Midi. Unfortunately, the police were so well informed that, far from a triumphal entry, she was smuggled, with increasing embarrassment, from one safe house to another. Legitimist leaders, who had been arrested initially, were released without charge.

The departments of Loire-Inférieure, Vendée, Maine-et-Loire and Deux-Sèvres were put under a state of siege in June 1832. Large posters appeared justifying the step: 'Considérant que de nombreux rassemblements armés ont troublé la paix publique, tenté de renverser le gouvernement nationale et causé l'effusion du sang français.'[43] All hunting weapons and war arms were to be turned in, except for those held by the National Guard. Army conscripts frequently failed to report for service and were concealed by country folk, despite new penalties of six months imprisonment and fines of 20–200 francs for those who condoned desertion or who employed deserters.[44] More troops were demanded for the west and there were wild rumours of large bands of *chouans* (the term used locally to describe monarchist and clerical rebels in the civil war of the 1790s) financed by local notables. The area was kept in a state of siege until June 1833.[45] Although there were *chouan* bands, they were tiny, like the 20–50 men located by the police in the Loire-Inférieure, some ex-Restoration soldiers, with a mere eleven rifles between them (not the rumoured seventy-five), who passed a miserable existence sleeping rough.[46] Such groups might ambush local opponents, although one 'political' murder of a *débitant de tabac* was dismissed by the local gendarmerie commander as an accidental fall from a horse by a rather elderly and unsteady individual.[47] The cost of lodging and feeding the extra troops was resented but the conspiracy took on an air of farce when, after her arrest in Brittany, the duchesse de Berri gave birth to a daughter and was escorted to the frontier.[48] Even with the help of a whole library of romantic novels, conspiracy could never recover from such a débâcle.

The emphasis of most politically active legitimists subsequently turned to the protection and enhancement of provincial rights against the encroachment of centralising bureaucracy, which often meant the exploitation of the resources of that bureaucracy for their own advantage. They developed tools more promising than anachronistic conspiracy, including the recently enlarged electoral franchise. In the 1790s royalists had attempted to resurrect (and in some cases invent) the tradition of provincial liberties to combat the centralisation of the revolutionaries. During the Restoration a new weapon was added to their armoury, when they absorbed the potential of the electoral principle to sustain the claims of the localities against Paris, although the proposal for elected local councils aborted during Martignac's administration. The pope, with obliging rapidity, absolved them from any feelings of guilt in swearing the necessary oath to Louis-Philippe and legitimists immediately began to take full advantage of the extension of the electoral principle to municipal and other local councils from the spring of 1831. 'Emigration à l'intérieur' was a transitory phenomenon, with not a touch of frustration for the Orleanists in the consequences. There were pressing and advantageous economic considerations behind legitimist involvement in politics. The de Surville family, bankers and businessmen in the Gard as well as local landowners, turned from conspiracy to buy the Montpellier–Nîmes railway concession.[49] In areas of traditional legitimist dominance they quickly re-established a say in municipal councils, the influential post of mayor, *arrondissement* and departmental councils. Membership lists, which had been purged to allow control to loyal Orleanists in August 1830, reverted to a more legitimist complexion between 1831, when municipal councils were elected, and 1833, when other local councils were elected for the first time.[50] As Tudesq has shown in his magisterial study, by 1840 'emigration à l'intérieur' was little more than a folk memory, even within the field of parliamentary politics.[51] Orleanist officials began to speak of 'légitimistes ralliés', but were always more or less aware that their association with the new regime was merely one of convenience. However, it was an alliance actively sought by Orleanists like Chaper, successively prefect in the Gard, Côte-d'Or and the Loire-Inférieure, who was very conscious that some legitimists were prepared to bargain between a compact with either Orleanism or republicanism. In a number of departments it was vital for the Orleanists to woo potentially 'rallied' legitimists if they were to retain a credible political position. It is interesting to note that there was sometimes a social distinction between legitimists who actively exploited the Orleanist system and those who remained aloof. The *ralliés* tended to include recently ennobled families and those with entrepreneurial as well as landed interests.

Within the church hierarchy also, conflict abated as each new bishop was appointed. The age of the noble–cleric was over; the bourgeois–bureaucrat bishop had arrived. Louis-Philippe, predictably, chose far less socially elevated bishops and concentrated on individuals with a proven record as efficient administrators. Increasingly the episcopate took on the character of the religious arm of the bureaucracy. It became the norm to promote the incumbent senior vicar-general to a vacant bishopric. The decline in the number of noble bishops also reflected the reduced appeal of the church to that class after 1830. The lower clergy, including *curés*, or *desservants* as they were termed, and *vicaires*, were largely drawn from the peasantry, as before, and subsisted on very modest salaries. A *desservant* was paid 800 francs a year, a *vicaire* 350 francs. They had virtually no expectation of rising within the hierarchy. The church continued to speak for the notables, however, to respect established social hierarchies and to echo elitist and paternalist assumptions.

Although the clergy would have preferred a Bourbon monarchy, the political complexion of Orleanism was tolerably reassuring. Orleanist officials and senior clerics, like their Restoration predecessors, were equally keen to maintain the conservative character of the church and discourage speculative thought. Lamennais' reform movement, represented by his newspaper, *L'Avenir*, in which he urged Catholics to adopt radical, even revolutionary, attitudes to social change, earned him a papal condemnation and found hierarchy and civil authority in complete accord. Lamennais was hounded from the church, which limited itself to a reactionary role for most of the nineteenth century. A limited number of individual Catholics began to join the growing chorus of those who deplored the social effects of urbanisation and industrialisation. Villeneuve-Bargemont, a relative of the former Restoration prefect, in an influential and pioneering study, depicted industrial workers as the victims of an evil system.[52] Since the Orleanist regime could be seen as approving the growth of industry, Catholic legitimists could condemn both phenomena. But all Catholics and all legitimists did not share this concern. The leading legitimist paper, the *Gazette de France*, was oblivious to social questions.[53] As an organisation, the church made no attempt to convert or care for the new industrial working class, with the exception of a handful of individual bishops, such as Belmas, bishop of Cambrai, and Affre, archbishop of Paris in the 1840s. Officially the church continued merely to offer limited charitable help to the poor. In the past the regular clergy had supplied and organised this arm of the church's social role. In the nineteenth century the female lay members of the church, who formed an increasing proportion of each congregation, took on the provision of nurseries and poor relief.[54] Once the Orleanist regime was securely established the most pressing issue for the clergy was the decline in religious observance. Attempts to arrest the increasing absence from the churches, especially of men, often betrayed the ignorance, superstition and bullying tactics of some priests: women were urged to leave the marital bed if husbands would not attend confession and were informed that children were better dead than raised outside the church.[55] The clergy found it difficult to separate their fight against indifference from their fear of revolution.

Official departmental correspondence reveals that anti-clerical attitudes remained and that the approach of the clergy, especially in western France, continued to worry officials. Underlying mutual suspicion remained, to flare up in 1833 with the publication of Guizot's education law, which encouraged the growth of primary schools run by the communes and the setting up of higher primary schools and teachers' training colleges on a departmental basis. Guizot did not intend, and certainly did not attain, the elimination of diocesan schools and those run by religious orders, both of which continued to thrive. The church, however, was suspicious of the increasing role of the state in primary education and antagonism grew between representatives of lay and clerical authority in education. The Guizot law, despite its initiator's intention to encourage both church and state to develop education, undoubtedly contributed to making education the leading element in church–state antagonism or, more specifically, the mutual hostility of *curé* and mayor. In other respects anti-clericalism was of decreasing significance after 1830. The church never recovered its political and social eminence of the *ancien régime* or even its rather anachronistic pre-eminence of the Restoration. Only in the 1890s with Leo XIII's *Rerum Novarum* did it try to mount a sustained attempt to reconvert the population. For most of the century it was content to serve principally the female aristocratic and bourgeois section, typified by the emphasis on the cult of the Virgin Mary. Anti-clericalism had depended for its vitality on the existence of a threatening and powerful adversary. After 1830 the deterioration in the position of the church removed much of this danger, except in the area of education where church-run schools continued to prosper and attract growing numbers of pupils, especially from the wealthiest legitimist families.[56] It should not be forgotten that the nearest French equivalent to the English public school was not the *lycée*, but the Jesuit college.

7
The Bourgeois Revolution

The one 'fact' that everyone remembers about the 1830 revolution is that it was 'bourgeois', continuing the developments of 1789. What were the social dimensions of 1830? In order to answer this question, one must consider first the legacy of 1789. Questioned about the origins of the concept of a bourgeois revolution, the educated layman would probably refer to the theories of Karl Marx, but Marx diverged radically from earlier commentators, including the socialists. His own views were considerably embroidered by his disciples. A Marxist interpretation of both revolutions dominated French historiography until recent years. The revisionism of the last generation of historians of 1789, which has effectively disproved the wilder Marxist theories, has also almost deprived the first Revolution of social content. However, the implications of revisionist thinking has had only a limited impact on French attitudes to 1830. It is the aim of this chapter to evaluate these developments.

Nominally *ancien régime* France was a society of privilege, divided into estates or orders. By 1789 the feudal categorisation of society into 'estates' – the first being the clergy, the second nobles and the third theoretically made up from the rest, but in reality representing only the middle classes – had ceased to hold much meaning. Many nobles and parish priests were too poor to be considered advantaged, while the blanket term 'third estate' provided no description of the bulk of the population. It would be a gross oversimplification to claim that privilege was the prerogative of the first two estates before 1789. Wealthy bourgeois families owned venal offices, bought feudal rights and exercised various corporative privileges, according to their professions. Enlightened writers questioned the rationality and utility of inherited and purchased privilege. On the other hand, increasing commercial, industrial and demographic growth seemed to necessitate new ways of describing social divisions, and Adam Smith and others began to use the term 'class'.[1]

The discussion of privilege and the significance of social

groupings, old and new, was sharpened and simplified by the decision to try to solve the financial problems of the crown by calling a meeting of the Estates-General, which had not met since 1614. The *abbé* Sieyès contributed a formidably influential pamphlet, 'What is the Third Estate?', to the pre-election debate. The third estate, he said, constituted almost the entire nation, measured numerically, but counted for nothing. It had a right to be heard and consulted. Sieyès was in effect the spokesman for one section of the whole, those who could be loosely called the 'bourgeoisie' or 'middle class'. He found a ready audience among the educated, property owning non-nobles. Influenced by the American Revolution and aware of the writings of the *philosophes*, they anticipated that the financial embarrassment of the crown would be their opportunity. Typical of Sieyès' reasoning, and in tune with the ambitions of the traditional middle class of lawyers, doctors and other professionals who sat in the first revolutionary assembly, was the contradiction between its theoretical and practical statements. The Declaration of the Rights of Man of August 1789 asserted that all men were equal. The events of that one night of 4 August 1789 abolished far more than had been intended when the session of the assembly began. It saw the abolition of traditional social privileges, although the holders of feudal, corporative, venal and ecclesiastical privileges were to be compensated for their loss. Yet two years later, in the first constitution, the assembly distinguished between active and passive citizens; only prosperous property owners would actually take part in the political process. The creation of new forms of privilege by restricting voting rights was hallowed by all subsequent constitution makers, apart from the disastrous experiment with democracy in the Convention of 1792. The revolutionaries of the 1790s were determined to enhance the political and social power of an elite defined not by birth or inherited privilege, but the ownership of property.

This middle class, who wrote the various constitutions of the 1790s, were motivated by fear of mass violence, although they justified their restricted definition of the political nation with rational-sounding arguments. They found that revolution had its own momentum, which many detested and which was not easy to control. Repeated popular violence unleashed a force unforeseen by the educated and prosperous. The democratically elected Convention and its Committee of Public Safety were compelled by the imperative to survive in a time of civil and foreign war to honour the *sans-culottes*, the leaders of popular unrest in Paris. Robespierre genuinely tried to find a new platonic-style rationale for society and government in a rule of 'virtue', which respected no bounds of privilege or wealth.

The unpredictable and irrational suspicions, denunciations and violence of the era of the Jacobin clubs and the Terror finally emboldened more cautious politicians to act. After the overthrow of Robespierre and the Committee of Public Safety, the middle class revolution battened down the hatches on further experimentation, issued a frankly oligarchical constitution and asserted the privilege of wealth. The political framework of bourgeois rule and its moral justification were in tatters. Power was yielded to a successful general, who published succesive constitutions which were the negation of all political consultation. France remained politically neutered until after Napoleon's fall and the educated and wealthy presumably connived at this emasculation out of fear. Thus the political inheritance of the bourgeois revolution, was, as we have suggested, confused and negative. Thanks to the Revolution, however, it was possible to create a constitutional regime to accompany the Bourbon Restoration in 1814 in which the institutional changes of the years of revolution and empire were retained unchanged.

What of the social revolution? The 1789 Revolution was intensely anti-clerical and progressively, although not initially, anti-aristocratic. In a sense the increasing hostility to the aristocracy was inspired by the political orientation of some conspicuous nobles who defended the church and the rights of the crown. Yet some even more conspicuous nobles favoured reform. The events of the night of 4 August represented self-sacrifice, not theft. From the outset, however, it was clear that social grievances and social objectives were part of the Revolution for a wide range of people who now began to define themselves in groups in ways that they had not done before the constraints of traditional authority had been challenged. The momentum of the revolutionary atmosphere and process made the unthinkable possible. In the time of revolutionary upheaval it seemed possible to turn the old world upside down. Long-standing social tensions, which before seemed a natural part of existence, now appeared both unbearable and soluble. How could one attack some privileges without an escalation of the process? Nobles were deprived of their feudal rights, titles and citizenship and denied the vote. All *émigrés*, including the most numerous, the nobles, were subject to the sequestration of their land. The definition of what was an aristocrat, however, increasingly came to depend less on social position than on whether an individual was thought to be an enemy of the Revolution.[2] The Revolution became violently anti-*aristo* and almost anti-bourgeois, for a time. Babeuf argued that 'liberty' and 'equality', the political slogans of the revolutionaries, were irrelevant until a social revolution had occurred, which would involve a democratic redistribution of the land of France. Such sentiments found little favour among revolutionary leaders and Babeuf was killed for his beliefs. The distinction between 'privileged' and 'ordinary' private property was always ambiguous, especially as the ownership of feudal rights was by no means confined to the traditionally privileged orders. No consensus on a new social order ever emerged, despite a short desultory experiment in the use of the term 'citizen'. The reaction to fears of political and social levelling during the Terror caused a stampede not only toward military dictatorship but also toward the abandonment of radical social objectives. Napoleon was a willing ally of those anxious for social reconstruction. He worked hard to rebuild the parameters of a social hierarchy based on wealth and both traditional and new titles.

Did this elite constitute the essential bourgeois social revolution? A wide range of those involved in revolutionary and subsequent politics, from Guizot to the early socialists, believed that it did. In post-Napoleonic France, commentators of all political persuasions were convinced that the revolutionary and imperial years witnessed a bourgeois revolution. The evidence on the statute book was abundant. Traditional privilege had been eliminated. New administrative and legal institutions seemed to offer greater opportunities than had the old venal and inherited arrangements. Talent was proclaimed as the successor to privilege in the *lycées* and the new *grandes écoles*. New codes of law established a rational and egalitarian basis for society. The vastly expanded bureaucracy offered unprecedented opportunities, as did the new national conscript army. France was a more open society than ever before, a view popularised by novelists like Stendhal in *Le Rouge et le Noir*. There were obvious limitations to this optimistic interpretation. Julien Sorel himself thought only the army offered really democratic opportunities before 1815 and only the church afterwards. The social and economic power of the nobility remained unchecked and if anything, had been reinforced by the setbacks to the economy experienced during the war years. Except for the extreme right, to whom all of these developments were anathema, the bourgeois social revolution was seen as a positive achievement, an indication of the progress of mankind, although, for the early socialists, it was merely a half-way house, which, they hoped, would lead to the liberation of the whole nation.

Early nineteenth-century commentators did not connect a bourgeois revolution, political or social, with specific economic change. The typical 'bourgeois' was seen as an educated man of substance, who would almost certainly own land, might be a member of the bureaucracy, of the professions or be involved in business or industry. Early socialists, disgusted that an elite of wealth had replaced an elite of birth, did not differ from this definition. Marx, and far more systematically, his disciples, introduced a totally new element. He deplored the dominance of various sections of this bourgeois elite and emphasised revolution as a vehicle for continuing social change, ultimately unseating middle class pre-eminence. At root messianic rather than logical, socialists nonetheless asserted that their interpretation of history was based on rational, scientific analysis. They claimed that economic imperatives were more compelling than political ideas and ambitions, and that the development of capitalism would lead to a shrinking entrepreneurial element and a burgeoning working class which would, in time, dictate the timetable of revolution and the consequent take-over of the centralised state by the proletariat.

The socialists asserted that 1789, in its genesis, its course and its results, was part of an inevitable process of change from a feudal, aristocratic, landed society to a capitalist, entrepreneurial bourgeois one. For Marx 1789 was only the first stage in this process, while his successors developed increasingly structured theories of revolution, dependent on 'rising' and 'declining' classes, which made greater claims for the progress of 'their' revolution in 1789. Superficially, aspects of revolutionary attitudes, legislation and policy seemed to fit the theory that 1789 was primarily a stage in the decline of the feudal aristocracy and the development of the entrepreneurial capitalism. One could cite the anti-*aristo* stance of the revolutionaries in the 1790s, the *loi le Chapelier* of 1791 which forbade coalitions of workers and the attack on communal institutions which accompanied the abolition of feudal dues. Such legislation could be seen as embryonic capitalism. For Marxists, the new bourgeois elite that emerged fitted their belief in the development of an ascendant entrepreneurial bourgeoisie. Not only 1789, but all subsequent nineteenth-century revolutionary movements, seemed to dovetail into a persuasive analysis. During the Third Republic this interpretation became a revolutionary dogma, dominant in universities and schools and seldom questioned. The development of socialism as a major force in western European states by 1914, and even more, the Bolshevik Revolution in Russia, were seen as further stages in the seamless web of the triumph of Marxist theories. French republican historians welcomed the parallel and enlarged on such concepts arguing that political and social change was determined by the evolution of capitalism and the perpetuation and elaboration through bureaucratic intervention of the centralised state. Revolution was thus a progressive and optimistic phenomenon, the result of which would be the strengthening of the state. Ultimately, however, by some unexplained process, the state would wither away and class differences, which for so long had fired revolutionary upheaval, would disappear. Historians on the right, out of the mainstream of the academic historical community in the Third Republic, were also very conscious of the social tensions set up by modern capitalism and consistently described all revolutions as stages in social and political collapse in which a self-interested bourgeoisie undermined traditional French values. Thus in the early decades of the twentieth century the concept of a bourgeois revolution was supreme, detested by the right and revered by the left.

The actual development of communism in Russia, however, especially the purges of the 1930s and the Russo-German Pact, shook French confidence in the orthodox Marxist revolutionary catechism. But the challenge to the concept of 1789 as a Marxist bourgeois revolution was launched not in Paris, but in London, by Professor Cobban in his inaugural lecture as professor of French history at University College in 1955.[3] Cobban pointed out that the empirical research into actual members of the eighteenth-century elite by, among others, George V Taylor and Robert Forster, did not support the view that late eighteenth-century France was rent by ineluctable conflict between aristocratic landowners and an entrepreneurial bourgeoisie. The work of the last generation of historians has shown that the elite was an amalgam of noble and non-noble wealthy families, who intermarried and

The Bourgeois Revolution 127

shared most economic, social and cultural interests and norms. It had been suggested that privilege, feudal and otherwise, had become an issue in 1789 because of an aristocratic or feudal reaction in the second half of the eighteenth century which operated on two levels.[4] It has been argued that feudal dues were being collected in a more business-like manner and were detested by peasants who had to pay. There was an attempt to reassert the faded dominance of nobles in high office in state and church, while the value of purchased, venal office declined. Social conflict thus lay in recent developments and the criticisms they had aroused, rather than in a Marxist-style decline of feudalism. The middle class resented these tendencies but they were not a new entrepreneurial bourgeoisie. Forty-three per cent of the third estate deputies in May 1789 were members of the traditional professional and office-holding middle class.

Although traditional historians in France, like Soboul, were appalled by this challenge to Marxist orthodoxy, branding criticism as anti-national and a belittling of the 1789 Revolution itself,[5] the new generation of Marxists, in their own empirical research into detailed aspects of social change, were beginning to present a more nuanced picture. They also perceived the complexity of social groups and development in *ancien régime* society and the limitations of generalisation in social analysis.[6]

If Marxist theories on the outbreak of 1789 fail to stand the test of empirical analysis, this does not necessarily render the whole concept of the bourgeois revolution a nonsense. We have seen that much of the legislation of the 1790s was designed to undermine traditional privilege and undoubtedly served the interests of the bourgeoisie. Unquestionably, this was not a Marxist middle class, but that does not negate the considerable significance of revolutionary legislation in reinforcing and enlarging the role of the more traditional bourgeoisie of professionals, bureaucrats and landowners. Although Tocqueville asserted the continuity of *ancien régime* and post-revolutionary institutions,[7] the appearance of similarity, in the stress on centralisation for instance, belied the radical character of change, both in norms and in institutions.

Many contemporaries, and both right- and left-wing historians, believed that the Revolution and Empire together created a new bourgeois ruling elite. The Revolution witnessed an unprecedented increase in the size of the bureaucracy. The Directory was equipped with a quarter of a million civil servants, five times as many as before the Revolution. The central core grew by a staggering 850 per cent.[8] In this lay a very visible change. The personification of this phenomenon as a bourgeois revolution was by no means confined to Marxists. Such claims seemed to be borne out by the array of dynasties that dominated nineteenth-century administration and government.[9] Thanks to painstaking recent research, we now know that Napoleon's notables were not a new group, but that roughly one-third of his officials had held similar office before the revolution.[10] Nineteenth-century prefects and law court officials could, not infrequently, trace the role of their families in administration and the judiciary to the fifteenth century. Such claims (the ability to cite that one's family had served the *parlements*, for instance) figured high on the lists of qualities recommended in those applying for posts and promotion.[11] There were new families and dynasties, many of whom entered the lists via Napoleon's army, but continuity rather than change seems to be more in evidence.

The Napoleonic and nineteenth-century elite was an amalgam, not only of *ancien régime* and revolutionary families, but was also drawn from both noble and bourgeois stock. Revisionists like Tulard, Chaussinand-Nogaret and Bergeron in their work on the 1789 Revolution and Empire, and Tudesq writing on the first half of the nineteenth century, have stressed that, far from being in conflict, the noble and upper bourgeois groups were so similar in interests that they really formed a consolidated body, for which the contemporary term 'notable' seemed the best description.[12] Throughout the eighteenth century the acquisition of land and government stocks had been as absorbing for the bourgeoisie as for the nobility.[13] Revisionists have been keen to ridicule the Marxist categorisation of an entrepreneur, observing that before 1789 it was the aristocracy as much as, if not even more than, the bourgeoisie that was in the van of capitalist development.[14] The French Revolution of 1789, particularly in its later Napoleonic manifestations, actually served to increase the unity of the group. Historians have also shown that the noble, landowning fraternity lost far less during the Revolution than used to be believed, their holdings falling from about 25 per cent to 20 per cent of the land of France. In areas where they had been dominant, they remained so in the nineteenth century.[15] Some noble families actually increased their holdings by purchasing *biens nationaux*, but the largest group were the office holders, compensated for their loss of venal office by the revolutionaries. Many of them were bourgeois.[16] Their purchase of land was no radical departure: most were already substantial property owners. The bourgeois social revolution thus involved the extension of the role of the traditional middle class in land ownership and state service. Entrepreneurial capitalists, whether bourgeois or noble, tended, with some exceptions, to suffer serious set-backs as a result of civil and prolonged foreign war, in which as many men died as in the First World War (out of a much smaller population). The revolutionaries may have cleared the ground for capitalist development by some of their legislation, but the war ensured that it would remain barren for the foreseeable future. Far from transforming France from a feudal aristocratic society into a capitalist one, the Revolution retarded the process.[17]

Thus, for revisionist historians, the scope and dimensions of 1789 are very different from those portrayed by Marxists. The bicentenary celebrations of the Revolution have concentrated on the political aspects of the events.[18] This change is partly a consequence of the empirical testing of the Marxist dialectic, but it also reflects radical developments in the study of history. The concept of what was meant by social history has itself altered substantially. A rather generalised traditional approach to social history, in which it was sometimes merely an extension of the Marxist dialectic, began to alter, influenced by the methodology of other disciplines, including sociology. Adding machines and, later, computers facilitated detailed research of social groups, using documentary material previously unplumbed, such as notarial records.[19] An excellent pioneering example of such research was the work of Adeline Daumard on the Parisian bourgeoisie.[20] Such endeavours increasingly reveal the complexity of social groupings. The chronological scope of social history has also altered. French historians have stopped dividing history into small chronological doses, like some unpleasant medicine. 'Histoire de la longue durée' became fashionable in the 1960s. In the study of social change in particular, the student was urged to be aware of the gradualness of all change. A revolution, however significant and dramatic in its impact, could not have been the catalyst for the sudden demise of a landed noble group and the rise to power of a bourgeoisie, entrepreneurial or not. Given the experience of the twentieth century, class conflict began to seem less a determinant of historical change.

Revisionists may have disposed of the Marxist 'bourgeois' revolution of 1789, but investigations into the acquirers of *biens nationaux*, into the 'new' elite and a consideration of the institutional legacy of the revolutionary and imperial years, reveal the determination of the traditional bourgeois group to consolidate and develop their power. What of the 1830 revolution? Curiously, despite the eloquence of the revisionist industry, the standard Marxist concept of rising and falling classes is quoted without comment with regard to 1830 in a revisionist survey of elites.[21]

It will be beneficial to consider the label as applied to the 1830 revolution in three ways. First, was the liberal opposition to Charles X in any exclusive sense bourgeois? Second, can the July Days thus be categorised? Finally, what were the social consequences of 1830? Did the political conflict at the end of Charles X's reign have social dimensions? Did the liberals represent the bourgeoisie? In the late 1820s official reports on political attitudes were frequently couched in class terms. Prefects often commented that the industrial and commercial middle classes were wholly hostile to the regime. The law of the double vote had been passed in 1820 after the murder of the heir to the throne, the duc de Berri, giving the richest quarter of the voters a second vote on the assumption that this would guarantee a right-wing chamber. At first the new departmental electoral colleges performed as expected, notably in 1824. In 1827, however, and even more in 1830, extreme wealth was equated with a right-wing vote only in limited areas, such as the Catholic west.[22] One of the four ordinances that triggered the revolution planned to reduce the electorate by 75 per cent, deliberately eliminating, it was hoped, precisely such unreliable voters and enfranchising only the very rich landowners. The ultras were incorrect in believing that rich landowners were loyal monarchists and that opposition was limited to a less well-off bourgeoisie, as a survey of the membership of the Chamber of Deputies in 1827 indicated.[23] Only the very wealthy qualified as candidates, with the hurdle of a minimum annual tax bill of 1000 francs. Of the 432 deputies, 202 were centre-left or left wing in their political sympathies. Of the fifty-seven richest, who paid over 3000 francs in tax, thirty-eight were centre-left or left, while only nineteen were centre-right or ultra, of whom merely nine were actually ultraroyalists. Restoration governments were quite mistaken in cleaving to the richest voters.

Regional differences were more significant than class or wealth in determining electoral patterns. Paris and eastern France were predominantly liberal, the west more inclined to ultraroyalism. The generalised view that the bourgeoisie was hostile to the monarchy was an ultra myth, nurtured by the implacable hatred of the latter for the French Revolution and an *emigré* ignorance of political reality. The ultras were political romantics, who would have liked to destroy all memory of the Revolution. Ultras dreamed of a France ruled by king, church and aristocracy, even though not all ultras were aristocrats and the majority of royalists were not ultras. In the hierarchical view of the ultras the bourgeoisie were natural enemies of the traditional order. The ultras defined political conflict in simplified class terms, forgetting that a number of nobles had rallied to the Empire and many Restoration officials began their careers under Napoleon.

Why should official reports have reiterated such a naïve interpretation? The explanation lies partly in the inexperience of a section of the prefectoral corps in the late 1820s, when frequent reshuffles occurred to try to obtain more right-wing royalist election results. Charles was even more intent than his predecessor to appoint nobles to official posts. The attempt to construct a noble administrative, clerical and military elite antagonised bourgeois officials, whose promotion was blocked or who were kept out of office when they made the wrong choice during the Hundred Days. They were often the fulcrum of liberal opposition in their region. The worsening economic crisis added another dimension to liberalism. Many industrialists blamed the government's commercial strategy and the majority of industrialists were both bourgeois and liberal. A fair number of the richest were noble, however. More important, the industrial and commercial middle class may have been united in blaming the government for the crisis, but they were very divided over whether the best solution was to reduce or increase tariffs on imported goods. The liberals constituted far more of a political than a social opposition to Charles X. Some of them were titled, just as some ultras were bourgeois. Most were not the entrepreneurs of the ultra prefect's fancy, but landowners, professionals and bureaucrats. The aristocratic–bourgeois duel was not simply the product of the ultra publicity machine, however. Liberal leaders were equally convinced that 1789 had permitted the political maturation of the bourgeoisie: Guizot, Tocqueville and Rémusat refer to the close connection between the middle classes and the Revolution. Even liberals who were nobles enjoyed the 'bourgeois' label. Those who considered themselves the political heirs of 1789 took pleasure in believing that the Revolution inaugurated a period of social progress of which the middle class was the fulcrum.

The label 'bourgeois revolution' was initially pinned to the July Days not by a jubilant liberal notable, nor by Marx, but by contemporary republicans and socialists, expressing their disgust that what was in their view an artisan revolt was quickly filched from the fighters, leaving the old elite still in control. For them, 1830 was 'une révolution escamotée',[24] a revolution smuggled away from the real victors; 'bourgeois' because the bourgeoisie remained in charge, making none of the social reforms desired by the socialists. The socialists were correct in their claim that little was altered. In its electoral arrangements this was indeed a bourgeois regime, as was also that of the Restoration. In exploring the July Days themselves, we have seen that most of those who took part, in Paris at least, were certainly not middle class. Blanc and Cabet were correct in characterising the fighters mainly as artisans. Their complaint was not that the artisans were prevented from forming a government – this would have been as inconceivable to these two educated, bourgeois journalists as to Périer or Guizot – but that the new government failed to consider the problems and interests of those who took to the streets in protest against high food prices and scarcity of work. This was in some respects a fair accusation and one to which we shall return. On the other hand, the label 'artisan' revolution belies much of the character of the July Days. The real critics of the Restoration had been parliamentary notables and the July Days themselves, as we have seen, were restrained, controlled, almost contrived. Throughout France, the immediate response of the liberal notables to popular disorder had been to reconstruct the National Guard to prevent further disturbances. 'Order and Liberty' was the 1830 equivalent of the slogan 'Liberty, Equality and Fraternity' of 1789. There is no doubt that the liberal notables and the artisans and peasants who took part in popular disturbances in and after 1830 had little in common. But whom to characterise as the revolutionaries is another problem, and one whose solution awaits the investigation of the grievances of artisans and peasants.[25]

In opposition to earlier French socialists, Marx asserted that 1789, 1830 and 1848 were all stages in the bourgeois assumption of power. 1830 brought a wealthy business class to prominence:

'It was not French bourgeoisie that ruled under Louis-Philippe, but one faction of it: bankers, stock-exchange kings, railway kings, owners of coal and iron mines and forests, a part of the landed proprietors associated with them – the so-called finance aristocracy.'[26] The narrowness of the electorate, still based on a high tax qualification and the elevation of two bankers, Laffitte and Périer, to be successive heads of government in 1830 and 1831 seemed proof of this to Marx. The industrial bourgeoisie, on the other hand were in opposition to Guizot. Marx was thus quite specific in his delineation of the Orleanist ruling elite in which he included landowners. He postulated that the revolution of February 1848 merely enlarged the size of the middle class political community. June 1848 was seen as the first indication of the intervention of the working class in politics. The Paris Commune of 1871 was heralded by Marx, after some hesitation, as the first proletarian revolution. Marx's followers adopted the concept of the bourgeois revolution in an even more generalised form, eliminating landowners from the bourgeoisie and describing 1830 as the victory of an 'ascending' entrepreneurial bourgeoisie and the defeat of a 'declining' landed aristocracy.[27]

Was 1830 a social revolution in its consequences? First, was it anti-aristocratic? At one level, this question can be answered in the affirmative. Of the 365 members of the Chamber of Peers, 175 refused to take the oath of allegiance to Louis-Philippe and were excluded, along with peers nominated by Charles X. As promised in the immediate aftermath of the revolution, in December 1831 the hereditary right of membership of the Chamber of Peers was abolished. Members were to be appointed by the king from a list of specific categories. The upper house became bourgeois. Louis-Philippe used the right to nominate to the Chamber of Peers to reward well-behaved bourgeois bureaucrats, including 235 generals.[28] The attempt of the ultras to construct an aristocratic ruling elite was reversed in a dramatic 'émigration à l'intérieur'. Shrewd conservative Orleanists soon set out to woo legitimist notables, however, rather than risk the formation of a legitimist–republican opposition alliance. By 1840 the legitimist elite was firmly back in harness in local government, particularly in western France.[29]

Nobility itself had become a political issue, especially in Charles X's reign and many of those who secured official posts after the 1830 revolution were men whose career had been blocked at the second Restoration or subsequently. Thus there was mutual antipathy. On the other hand a substantial proportion of those involved in politics held noble titles throughout the period of constitutional monarchy and the 1830 revolution had no marked impact on numbers. In 1821 58 per cent of the Chamber of Deputies had titles; in 1827 this figure was 40 per cent and in 1840 just over 30 per cent. A title was seen as sufficiently desirable for many to be invented; in 1840 forty-five of the titles in the chamber were spurious. Contemporaries were very conscious of the distinction between different types of title and when they were awarded, however. Louis-Philippe's nobles were of Bonapartist stock. 1830 made a substantive difference to the role of the traditional nobility in halting Restoration attempts to make the ruling elite and the nobility synonymous. Just as Charles X fell because he refused to separate his fate from that of his government, so loyalty to the Bourbons and to the Catholic Church split the notables and excluded one section from national power politics. That does not mean, however, that 1830 was a stage in a general decline of the landed nobility. We have already noted that in economic terms this was far from the case. In the 1840s 235 of the 512 richest notables were landed aristocrats and in political terms the ultra hope of equating the ruling class with the nobility was never more than a dream, though it may have been a nightmare to the liberals. The nobility continued to make a substantial contribution to entrepreneurial activity of all kinds.

The events of 1830 split the elite in political rather than social terms. Does this mean that the elites of the Restoration and July monarchies were socially indistinguishable? Marx's assertion that 1830 saw the triumph of a finance aristocracy was one which met with considerable contemporary sympathy, not only from the left. It is certainly the impression conveyed by Balzac and other novelists, including Flaubert in his portrayal of the influential financier Dambreuse in *L'Education Sentimentale*. The image of the hard-nosed businessmen grinding the poor with the enthusiastic backing of the government is also echoed in the criticism of a wider range of grasping and unscrupulous bourgeois citizens in Daumier's cartoons. Art seems to support Marx. Research on electoral lists, however, shows that voters and deputies were primarily landowners, both before and after 1830. Marxist claims that 1830 gave power to big businessmen are not borne out by analysis. In 1829 14 per cent of the deputies were businessmen; in

1831 17 per cent; in 1840 13 per cent. France was primarily a prosperous agrarian country and much entrepreneurial activity was developed directly by large landowners from the produce of their estates. Men qualified as electors through their tax contributions. The most onerous direct tax was that on land, so it is not surprising that the bulk of voters were landowners both before and after 1830. In 1827 60 per cent of voters and 73 per cent of candidates were landowners. An 1837 survey in the Haute-Marne, then France's biggest iron producer, showed that only 114 out of 1064 electors qualified on their *patente* (the tax on industrial or commercial property – not profits) alone. Indeed the total *patente* bill for the department, just over 60 000 francs, was barely more than 25 per cent of the total tax collected, which was nearly a quarter of a million francs.[30] In 1829 31 per cent of deputies were landowners and 23 per cent in 1831. But the most often cited occupation, before and after the revolution, was civil servant: 40 per cent in 1829 and 38 per cent in 1831. Statistics show that few deputies were professional men: 5 per cent in 1827, nearly 9 per cent in 1840.[31] Such figures are misleading. Most candidates would list more than one occupation, yet only a sophisticated computer analysis can take adequate cognisance of the fact that a man would be quite likely to be a landowner, a forge owner and a mayor, for example.[32] There is no evidence to suggest that the elite of the July Monarchy differed markedly in occupation from that of the Restoration. Economic change was proceeding far too gradually for that to be the case. The most striking feature of the Chamber of Deputies in both periods is not the proportion of entrepreneurial or professional deputies, but the dominance of paid state servants.

It has been suggested that it was within the realm of paid state servants that the real revolution occurred in 1830, although the most recent American account viewed the administrative purge as more Bonapartist than bourgeois.[33] It is a curious irony, given the drama of the First Empire, the charismatic glamour of David's epic paintings and the romantic image of the lost liberal hero conveyed in the memoirs Napoleon wrote while imprisoned on St Helena, that the only whiff of Bonapartism apparent in 1830 was the return from moth-balls of a substantial number of the emperor's bureaucrats. There was a considerable army of disaffected former Bonapartist bureaucrats, particularly those unwise enough to return to Napoleon in the Hundred Days, who hoped, whatever the political form of the new regime after the July Days, that their own unwillingness to serve the Bourbons, which had disqualified them for work during the Restoration, would now be considered a glowing recommendation. The Orleanist regime's reputation for dynamic change lies, not in the form of government, the conduct of politics, or even the degree that it was a liberal regime, but in the administrative revolution that followed the July Days. We shall now consider the reorganisation that followed the 1830 revolution in order to evaluate the political and social characteristics of the new administrative elite in Paris and the provinces.[34] The Revolution was followed by a couple of years of prolonged political infighting and jostling for position accompanied by a worsening economic crisis and noisy, if ineffective, republican sniping. These conflicts were reflected in not one but repeated changes of officials, culminating in a profile that was more conservative than Bonapartist and in which the predominant concern would appear to have been to represent the interests of local notables rather than the views of one particular Parisian government.

No paid servant of the state was safe after July. All of the generals commanding the nineteen military districts were replaced. Only ten of the thirty-four Bourbon counsellors of state survived. The judiciary was thoroughly purged. It was recognised that *procureurs* were wholly vulnerable to the politics of the moment, and in reality judges were no more secure. This was in conformity with the practice of the Restoration. The Declaration of St-Ouen of May 1814 made by the returning Bourbons, specified that only judges nominated by the king were secure and this point was reiterated in the constitution a month later (article fifty-nine). After the Hundred Days, 294 magistrates had been replaced in nineteen appeal courts, despite the arguments of liberals like Royer-Collard that an appointment ought to be for life on a basic principle of natural law.[35] Many of those with judicial qualifications were members of the Chamber of Deputies and closely involved in the fortunes of different governments. They might survive ministerial reshuffles, but a new regime did not regard its predecessor's officials as sacrosanct. After the 1830 revolution 426 members of the judiciary were replaced, including 178 of the 361 *chefs de parquet de tribunaux*. In addition there were many resignations of men who refused the oath: 132 magistrates on *cours royaux* and 81 in *tribunaux* by December 1830. The largest number of resignations were in Rennes, Besançon, Bordeaux and Lyons. The motives behind the changes were varied.

In the July Days some courts went on strike when they heard of disturbances in Paris, ostensibly because they no longer knew in whose name to deliver verdicts. Once the new government had been installed, the obvious intransigence of many magistrates made a reconstruction of the corps essential, so that cases could be tried and law and order maintained. Some magistrates with lifetime appointments refused to take the oath of allegiance to Louis-Philippe and thus lost their jobs. In Besançon only three members of the *cour royale* actually resigned after the revolution, four others were promoted but the residue finally refused to take the new oath. This was exceptional. Most magistrates and court officials had elastic consciences. Many took the new oath and held onto their posts, irrespective of the person of the monarch. A member of the tribunal in Bar-sur-Aube remarked with some surprise in his diary of the existence amongst his colleagues of a political conscience. He had held office continuously since 1789 and could hardly believe that anyone still attached importance to an oath of allegiance.[36] The honorary president of the Besançon *cour royale*, who died in office in 1834, had begun his judicial career in the *parlement* before the 1789 Revolution.[37] Such continuity was common among those who held the most senior posts. The honorary president on Dijon had also been in almost continuous public service as a magistrate since before 1789, as had the vice-president of the tribunal in Chaumont. It is true that for both promotion had been blocked at the second Restoration, but they survived to take the oath to Louis-Philippe in 1830. The Dijon president had a particulaly impressive run. *Avocat* in the *parlement* in Dijon before 1789, he was then in almost continuous employment, apart from two years of the Restoration.[38] Most leading magistrates had long pedigrees, reaching back into the *ancien régime* judicial system. Typical was the president of the *cour royale* in Besançon, whose family had been notable in the town since the fourteenth century. A *parlementaire* himself, he had been an active ultra and, rather exceptionally, resigned in 1830.[39] Another leading ultra in Dijon, the *president de chambre* in the *cour royale*, died in office in 1834. *Conseillers auditeurs* rarely resigned, which caused some embarrassment to the *procureur-général* as the representative of a government with very different views. His solution was no different from that adopted during the Restoration, simply to block the promotion of opponents and manoeuvre around the inconvenience of their presence.

Those members of the judiciary whose tenure was not for life were replaced fairly quickly. *Procureurs*, the most important link between Paris and the local courts, were dealt with first, attention being turned to other officials during September and October. Twenty-three of the twenty-seven *procureurs* were changed. Their role, which involved deciding which cases should be prosecuted and reporting on the state of public opinion, was intensely political. Officials within the service, who had been penalised previously for their liberalism, now gained advancement. Local deputies were obviously influential in determining appointments, but sometimes favoured rival candidates, as in the appointment of a *procureur* for Montbéliard, Doubs. The disappointed aspirant, who only had the backing of one of the four deputies, had to settle for a post elsewhere. Local notables sometimes worked to prevent change. In August 1830 twenty-eight local worthies in Neufchateau, including the provisional sub-prefect, petitioned their deputies to press for the retention of the *procureur*. In making their recommendations for dismissals and new appointments, *procureurs-généraux* were sometimes inclined to make light of the known legitimism of their subordinates, even in a town like Dijon, where sympathy with the deposed monarch was considerable. Neither he, nor his colleague in Besançon believed that divergent political preference was sufficient grounds for dismissal. The Besançon *procureur* remarked on the foolishness of removing capable magistrates on political grounds. It was not always possible to find suitably qualified men for lesser posts and bringing in an outsider could create far more problems than it solved. It should also be remembered that a proportion of resignations were for other reasons. The president of the *tribunal* in Remiremont, a man who had supported the 1789 Revolution, took the oath to Louis-Philippe, resigned and was promptly succeeded by his son. The degree to which the *garde des sceaux* was besieged with recommendations, and the speed with which replacements were effected, inevitably led to mistakes. Some of the new *procureurs* remained liberal as the regime became more and more committed to *résistance*. The new *procureur-général* in Besançon appalled the *cour royale* in his first speech in which he referred to himself as a child of the Revolution and apparently announced that the reign of stupidity was now at an end.[40]

There was an almost complete reconstruction of administrative personnel after the July Days, to the extent that one historian has judged that this was the most innovative aspect of the revolution.[41] Of 764 members of the prefectoral corps, the first minister of the interior, Guizot, replaced 83 per cent. Only seven Restoration prefects remained in office and these, apart from the immovable and legendary Jessaint of the Marne, in office since the creation of the system, had been appointed during the more moderate Martignac ministry. New men were assigned to all of these departments, although two had actually served Polignac and were rescued from the low-ranking departments to which he had demoted them. An even larger number of sub-prefects were changed, 88 per cent, or 244 out of 277. In France as a whole all the sub-prefects in fifty-three departments were dismissed; only the Loir-et-Cher kept all the Restoration nominees. Only twelve departments retained the same general secretary, the senior member of prefectoral council who substituted for the prefect in his absence. Over two-thirds of prefectoral councillors were removed.[42] Local consultative councils, all of whose members were appointed from Paris but which supposedly represented local views, experienced substantial changes. The mayoral revolution was particularly sweeping. Departmental, *arrondissement* and municipal councils were overhauled in the months following the revolution. Even the administration of forests and the postal services were purged. Thus few stayed at their post. But what did the changes signify?

The administrative revolution in the provinces was largely the work of liberal deputies or, if they had hastened to Paris to influence national events, of their electoral committees, still triumphant after the summer elections. Thus, although theoretically ministers were omnipotent, and leading liberals were besieged with requests for jobs, as Benjamin Constant complained,[43] most changes were completed on the spot by local notables. Their standing, as patrons of *fonctionnaires* rose even higher, for a prospective official needed an influential backer even more than legal and professional training. Members of the Chamber of Deputies figured high on the list of desirable patrons and they had an intimate, if not impartial, knowledge of their region, for most represented their own locality. The familiar scramble for office that accompanied a new government, let alone changes of monarch, was complicated by the embarrassing number, and sometimes the radical nature, of vacancies filled locally before the new Parisian regime had been established. As we have seen, often the entire range of official appointments was filled by the old electoral committee, as in the Puy-de-Dôme, for instance. Only the most senior post of prefect was left to Paris, and even then there were instances when the local liberals overrode a long-established tradition in regional administration which stretched back into the *ancien régime*. The liberal notables of the Meurthe persuaded Guizot to appoint as prefect a man who had been out of office since his dismissal as prefectoral councillor following the Hundred Days. There was more than the usual possibility of discord between the outsider who became prefect and local notables. In Metz the new prefect complained that the liberals had terrorised the Restoration men into resigning in order to divide up the jobs among themselves before Paris could intervene. Hastily filled posts sometimes went to individuals who proved radical and encouraged popular unrest and anti-clerical outbursts. Others retained Bonapartist attitudes and harboured old grudges embarrassing to a regime bent on finding a *juste milieu*. Yet others simply turned out to be incompetent, a quality not of course reserved for those who had been promoted by the old electoral committees. Thus the dismissals, resignations and new appointments of August 1830 were not the end of the story.

What distinguished the new prefects and other officials from their predecessors? Although none of the Restoration prefects survived, most of the new ones had prefectoral experience and three were returning to departments they had served in the past. It has been calculated that in France as a whole fifty-three of the new prefects had worked for Napoleon and/or the Restoration before 1820, while thirty were new men.[44] The new men were not without administrative experience, however. Chaper, honoured with an appointment to one of the most difficult prefectures, the Gard, had been mayor of his home town for ten years.[45] In these departments, all had been either imperial prefects or had served the more moderate Restoration governments. The new prefects in the Haute-Marne and Jura had run these departments in the Hundred Days and two others had seen imperial service. The rest had been Restoration prefects; two were returned to their old departments by Guizot in August 1830.[46] Thus, not only were Guizot's prefects experienced civil servants, there was a conscious attempt to give them back their old departments. Nor were the

Orleanist prefects new in terms of their family background. Most came from families with a long tradition of public service. For example the father and grandfather of Siméon, who became prefect of the Vosges, had also been prefects and earlier generations had held public office.[47] Indeed, many officials of the constitutional monarchy, before and after 1830, came from families who had been in state service for several centuries. Most of the new Orleanist prefects were of mature years and their administrative experience reached back to the Empire. Some received no official post after Napoleon's fall, while a small number had only limited, brief employment after 1814 in the more moderate governments. A handful had been prefects during the Polignac administration, but were demoted by him. Thus Guizot's choices seem less dramatic when looked at in detail. His prefects had all manifested liberal political attitudes, but they also had extensive administrative experience. Where purely political considerations dominated, as in the Haute-Marne, Meurthe and Côte-d'Or, where men out of office since the Hundred Days were appointed, the results were disastrous, with political intransigence accompanying administrative incompetence.

It was a rare sub-prefect who outlasted the revolution.[48] Active opposition to the Bourbons seemed to be a prime qualification for office under Louis-Philippe and two-thirds of the new sub-prefects fitted this bill. But the right balance of family rivalries and links actually predominated. The new sub-prefect of Pontarlier, Doubs, belonged to the leading family in the *arrondissement*. He had been mayor under Napoleon, a member of the Legislative Assembly during the Hundred Days and a leading liberal in the 1820s.[49] Most new sub-prefects were younger and far less experienced, but were trained lawyers and were from families involved in either law or administration or both. In the choice of sub-prefects social standing, wealth, local connections and experience in some aspect of administration or law clearly mattered. The deciding voice in appointments was that of the deputy who represented the *arrondissement*, hence the preponderance of liberal electoral agents in 1830. Political orientation was crucial.

The changes in personnel extended to local councils, which continued to be appointed by the king until they were all made elected bodies between 1831 and 1833. Although the function of general departmental councils, composed of local notables, was purely to discuss aspects of local administration, the execution of which was securely in the hands of the prefect, there was a far more thoroughgoing change in their membership after the revolution than occurred in 1833 when they were turned into elected bodies. Superficially they might appear to have been almost superfluous ciphers, meeting as they did for only a few weeks a year, but because they represented, quintessentially, the local notables, it was important for the prefect to know, understand, cultivate and satisfy their views. During the Revolution provisional commissions tended to purge all local councils and it would have been a foolhardy new prefect who disregarded their wishes. As minister of the interior Guizot stressed to prefects the need to find new members whose social and personal standing and influence was considerable. Councils were also meant to provide a fair cross-section of the professions and occupations of the wealthy in the area.[50] All but one member of the general council of the Côte-d'Or had been replaced by November 1830[51] and this was a typical pattern. Sympathy with the change of regime was essential in a new member, but in addition the Orleanist councils were more representative of their areas and the local economy than had been their predecessors. The landed interest remained paramount; all councillors owed a substantial part of their fortune to their land. But industry and trade were better represented than before; in the Côte-d'Or seven of the new men were ironmasters, six were businessmen, one was a banker. They were no less wealthy than the Restoration councillors; the majority had fortunes of over 10 000 francs. Incidentally, nearly half of them became *mouvement* supporters and a thorn in the flesh of the government for some time.[52] The far less important *arrondissement* councils were also purged. In the Vosges twenty-seven of the fifty-five councillors were replaced, although only nine had volunteered their resignation.[53] Of those retained from the Restoration, some were known liberals, like the *receveur des finances* in Epinal who had been threatened with dismissal by the minister of finance just before the Revolution because of his support for liberal parliamentary candidates.[54]

Municipal councils were actively purged. The new prefect of the Doubs remarked in a letter to Guizot that the municipal council in Besançon had only managed to pass a congratulatory address to the new government because so many members stayed away.[55] Many mayors were excluded for their political beliefs, but legitimists with very considerable local influence could survive.[56]

On the whole the only mayors who held their place were in tiny communes where a replacement would have been difficult to find. In the Doubs one mayor appointed in 1789 was still in office in 1831. He was exceptional.[57] In the more important towns mayors either resigned during the revolution or were forced out by the municipal commission. In a number of cases the new incumbent was the old Napoleonic mayor. Typical was Hernoux, mayor of Dijon in the Hundred Days and chosen by the municipal commission during the 1830 revolution for the same post.[58] The oath of allegiance occasioned many resignations and prefects were flooded with petitions to remove or retain mayors. A mayor came under vigorous attack if he had criticised the reorganisation of the National Guard or had been reluctant to fly the *tricolore*.[59] One reluctant patriot had even ordered that the newly planted tree of liberty should be dug up. Sometimes a mayor deliberately concealed news of developments in Paris.[60] The National Guard was often the instrument for ousting such incumbents. In the smaller communes personal and family rivalries were evidently as crucial as political ones. Many of the revocations were justified on the grounds that the old mayor was the pawn of the *curé*. In September the sub-prefect of Pontarlier compiled a list of two dozen mayors regarded as unsuitable for this reason.[61] As early as 14 October, 147 mayors, 81 deputy-mayors and 146 municipal councillors had been axed in the Vosges alone.[62]

The principle of election was extended to municipal councils in 1831. Although the king reserved the right to choose the mayor from amongst those elected, habitually the man with the most votes got the job. *Arrondissement* and departmental councils were opened to election in 1833. Local elections were conducted on the same franchise as national ones, but frequently the tax qualification had to dip well below 200 francs in order to have a sufficiently large electorate. In the Vosges, not one of the poorest departments, the franchise for municipal elections dipped as low as 1 fr. 49 in 1845.[63] Lest it should be thought that the extension of the electoral principle was an unusually radical measure for the cautious Orleanist liberals it should be noted that the Martignac government had attempted to change local councils into elected bodies in 1828. Then the proposal had foundered, despite widespread support across the political spectrum, because the liberals could not countenance the idea of enfranchising only the quarter most rich electors who qualified for a second vote in national elections. The introduction of local elections was regarded rather nervously by the more conservative of the former Restoration liberals turned Orleanist juste-milieu also. There were apprehensions that the composition of the councils would change, possibly allowing them to be swamped by the relatively poor. Chaper, prefect in Dijon, complained 'les paysans n'ont voulu que des paysans.'[64] In fact, the notables continued to dominate local councils in most cases. Where individuals who considered themselves outside the elite were elected, it was sometimes impossible to persuade them to serve. In 1837 the prefect in Dijon, himself very much a notable, struggled in vain to persuade the municipal councillor whom he considered the best candidate to be mayor to accept the post. Dumay, his man, replied to his entreaties, 'Everyone thinks of the position of mayor in Dijon as an aristocratic one. To be mayor one needs a certain standing, either through birth, or wealth; I am the son of ordinary country people, I don't even pay enough tax to qualify as an elector, I'm just a member of the proletariat.'[65] There were also worries that the local elections might become intensely political and lose sight of the fact that local issues were paramount for such assemblies. There need have been no such fears.

The normal diet of these councils – roads, bridges, abandoned babies – were enlivened by more passionate, but equally self-interested, discussions on the provision of primary schools and the siting of railway lines. Annual meetings of departmental and *arrondissement* councils were very formal and ceremonial, more a token representation of local opinion, in public at least, than genuine consultation of the popular will.[66] Electors might throw caution to the wind and restore legitimist local councillors, particularly in the 1840s and especially in western France. But this was more a recognition of the local standing and influence of the family than a legitimist political revival. In eastern France electors were more likely to prefer left-wing candidates. After 1833 the departmental council of the Côte-d'Or had a left-wing majority. The same was true for a number of municipal councils in the area and some were also blessed with positively left-wing mayors. However, there was little or nothing in the results of local elections to explain the implacable refusal of Orleanists to consider franchise reform for national elections in the 1840s.

At what point was this administrative revolution complete? The attraction of an active commitment to liberalism soon turned sour.

The victors of July had only been united in their opposition to Polignac. The rapid split into *résistance* and *mouvement* meant that appointments which were considered politically harmonious in August 1830, seemed dangerously left wing to the Périer government of 13 March 1831. A new 'prefectoral waltz' ensued. Périer dismissed one-fifth of the prefects in the twenty eastern departments: they were men who proved too anti-clerical and too sympathetic to extreme liberal views, especially those of Lafayette and the National Guard. But prefects did not only come to grief because they were too liberal for Paris. Others were too conservative for their departments. Local notables in the Moselle resented the nomination as prefect of the former Polignac nominee from Puy-de-Dôme. As in several other departments, personal and local rivalries became intertwined with the political issue. In the Moselle the notables had their way over every appointment below the rank of prefect and this had gone to their heads. In this case the prefect remained in office and when Casimir Périer became chief minister, several local notables lost their official posts instead. In at least two other departments the thwarted ambitions of local mayors who had aspired to the prefecture caused widespread resentment and non-cooperation, frustrating the efforts of the prefect who had been appointed.

In the months following the revolution a substantial proportion of new officials declared themselves in favour of the *mouvement*, as did a number of the deputies who had promoted their appointments. Criticism of the lack of reforming zeal came to a head at the end of 1830, but the *résistance* triumphed with the appointment of the Périer government. The administrative revolution was not really complete until after Périer's appointment and by then it had a very conservative aspect, with Paris asserting its control over the provinces. From the outset Périer insisted that officials back him whole-heartedly or resign: 'La première devoir du gouvernement est ... en laissant la liberté entière, de rétablir, l'ordre, et pour y parvenir, de rendre à l'autorité toute sa force et toute sa dignité.'[67] Divided loyalties in the first general election in the summer of 1831 led to the dismissal of several sub-prefects. Even the changes in departmental and municipal councils were modified to give more predominance to those with *résistance* views and where alteration to local councils was incomplete Périer urged the maintenance of the status quo, remarking that legitimist views as such did not disqualify a local councillor.[68]

There was an initial wholesale transmutation of individuals, but the changes were not really startling, novel or radical. It was more a case of retarding or accelerating promotion than one of replacing one set of individuals with another. Administrative appointments were highly political but, as we have seen,[69] recent research on the 1789 Revolution and Empire demonstrates the high level of continuity of personnel.[70] In 1830 the scale of administrative change appears colossal at first sight, but looked at in detail, one is aware of considerable underlying continuity, obscured by the necessary removal of some of Charles X's ultra nominations. Guizot played the same game of 'ins' and 'outs' with the same group of men as did the Restoration ministers of the interior. The years since 1789 had witnessed so many political changes that there simply could not be enough 'sets' of matching administrators for them all. Officials had learned to shift their political ground with alacrity and so survive. Potential charges of disloyalty were rendered inappropriate by an increasing reverence for professional skills and respect for the hierarchical system of administrative training set up during the First Empire. As we have seen, local councils were eagerly reshaped by liberal electoral committees, but after March 1831 Périer was keen to take cognizance of the influence of local property owners, placing liberal political affiliations lower in his list of priorities.

Thus the administrative revolution was somewhat less than revolutionary when seen at a local level. Its Bonapartist character was weakened by the intransigence or incompetence of some of those unemployed since 1815. In a recent study of the politics of the July Monarchy, it has been suggested that France was intrinsically Bonapartist, a spirit which the regime tried in vain to capture. The July Monarchy emphasised professional qualifications for officials, important in the First Empire and obscured during the Restoration, particularly in Charles X's reign. The array of personnel dossiers stored in the *Archives Nationales* reveals the continuity of families, dynasties as critics claimed, through the Empire with, perhaps, a break during the Restoration, but more typically, lack of promotion. Charles X's appointments stand outside the mainstream. In this sense, one could argue, as some eminent historians have done, the Restoration itself was almost Bonapartist, an 'Empire without Napoleon'. Even more concretely, the July Monarchy adopted Bonapartism as an emotional credo. Instead of the secretive and officially condemned hero-worship of the Restoration, there were open displays of Bonapartist memorabilia, not only medals, busts and the like, but also the very public honouring of Napoleon with the return of his ashes to *Les Invalides* in 1840. Louis-Philippe himself initiated and adorned this crescendo of sentimental Bonapartism.

What of the notion that the administrative changes represented a bourgeois take-over? The emphasis on continuity noted in the bureaucracy makes such a label a redundant fudge. One would not expect administrative changes to reflect a Marxist-style bourgeois revolution: Marx was inclined to disregard the significance of the bureaucracy and professional bureaucrats were unlikely to be drawn on a large scale from the Marxist entrepreneurial bourgeoisie at any stage, let alone at a time when the entrepreneurial element was still small compared with the landowning group (and often inseperable from it). On the other hand, the new administrative appointments of the July Days unquestionably advanced the careers of bourgeois bureaucrats belonging to the traditional, long-established bourgeoisie of trained professionals, landowners and state servants whose families had held public office often for centuries. In this sense 1830 was bourgeois, but as we have noted earlier, so was the Restoration to a large extent, with the notable exception of the Villèle ministry and the reign of Charles X. The ultras in particular had pressed for the appointment and promotion of nobles, from the most senior lineage possible, in the army, church and administration. The social complexion of these institutions had thus changed radically during the Restoration, with the unprecedented elevation of often totally inexperienced scions of noble houses. By 1830 45 per cent of all prefects were noble, while 70 per cent of all prefects appointed during the Restoration were noble, many of them from émigré families.[71] Out of the 100 prefects who had served Napoleon during the Hundred Days, only ten secured an official post of any kind again before 1830. Thus any investigation into the social origins of officials is bound to show a sharp swing from a majority of titled men before the July Days, to a majority of bourgeois after the revolution. It should be recognised, however, that this apparent social revolution was really a restoration of established norms.

It has been suggested that the real difference between the Restoration and the July Monarchy lay in the attitudes of the two regimes to economic and social questions: that the July Monarchy was more supportive of the industrial and commercial middle class and that its ethos was more profoundly bourgeois than the Restoration monarchy. Both regimes followed highly protectionist commercial policies at the behest of producers and both favoured the employer in his relations with the employee. Both had great respect for accumulated wealth. The economic crisis of 1827–32 aroused criticism of Bourbon commercial policies among producers but, as we have seen, there was no bourgeois consensus of condemnation of the economic policies of the Restoration, capitalist or otherwise. The priorities of different entrepreneurs were diverse, and continued to be so in the July Monarchy, when protectionist policies were pursued and strategies developed, as in the previous regime, in response to pressure from the most powerful economic interest groups. Just as the early 1820s had been a time of economic prosperity, so were the 1840s. It has been suggested that the Soult–Guizot administration was more constructive in its attitude to capitalism, but this may correspond with evolutionary economic change rather than contrasting government preoccupations.[72]

The only real difference between the elites of the Restoration and the July Monarchy lay in their attitude to the church and the house of Bourbon, particularly in the amount of respect they were accorded. The label 'bourgeois' was a trendy contemporary red herring. It led to a series of misunderstandings on the relationship between capitalism and revolution which lay undetected until actual revolutions failed to match Marxist expectations in the twentieth century. The development of society had allowed wealthy non-nobles to exercise some political influence long before even the 1789 Revolution. On the other hand, despite the abolition of the hereditary peerage in France in 1831, the social and economic power of the nobility remained very considerable and titles and many aspects of privilege remained embedded in social norms. These were untouched by revolution. Liberal sentiments cut across class lines and the political issues of the period were not exclusively class interests. The diverse elements of the middle classes – landed, bureaucratic, professional, commercial and industrial – were far from united in their goals, or even conscious of any commonality of purpose.

Finally as a postscript to the more nonsensical claims that the July revolution heralded a new bourgeois era, the king himself was often referred to as a citizen or bourgeois king. His father had, of course, temporarily abandoned his title, but not his wealth, when he called himself 'Philippe-Egalité' in the 1790s. Louis-Philippe gained his appellation not because he was a regicide like his father, but because of his lifestyle, his famous umbrella, the shops, whores and accessibility of the Palais Royal, because his sons went to school with the rest of the elite and because of the cosy domesticity of his private life. But one has to recall that he was the king's cousin, and that he and his sister were the chief beneficiaries of the indemnification of the *émigrés* to the tune of twelve million francs.

The July Monarchy was only slightly more bourgeois than the Restoration in the composition of the political nation and the ruling elite. During the Restoration the ultras, beleaguered dinosaurs in the modern world, tried to construct a golden age, to recreate what was not there even in 1789, an aristocratic ruling class. The illusion was sustained by *émigré* ignorance of modern France and by the romantic novels of Scott and others exploiting the need for anachronistic security in a medieval past. It is no accident that four of Scott's novels figured among the thirty best-sellers in France during Charles X's reign.[73] But mythology became confused with reality as the cascade of ultra-inspired legislation of the 1820s revealed. Temporarily the aristocratic image of the Restoration seemed more than an aura, transcending the fact that the regime was a continuation of the political and social compromise of the Empire. But the liberal notables were sufficiently secure in their land, official appointments, careers and businesses and knew it. 1830 was a political, not a social revolution. The Orleanist liberal elite enjoyed thinking of itself as bourgeois, which they equated with being modern, educated and industrious. They claimed to represent opportunity for all, an end to traditional privilege and the liberty of the individual. Perhaps they lived in as much of a dream world as did the ultras; within five years press censorship was more rigorous than before, even the word 'republican' was banned; all political associations, however small, were forbidden and the response of governments to the problems of the silk weavers of Lyons in the early 1830s was just as repressive as Bourbon attitudes towards artisan grievances.

8
Une Révolution Escamotée

The July Days were more the product of artisan unrest and the misjudgements of the Polignac government than the machinations of either republicans or liberals. The Orleanist monarchy was universally tolerated but agreement ended at that point. Radical and, more specifically, republican attitudes rapidly emerged among those who were not able to hoist themselves to power alongside the new king of the French. From the outset there was pronounced left-wing criticism of the revolutionary settlement, accompanied by a sharp increase in the incidence of popular unrest, which did not die down until the summer of 1834. This chapter aims to analyse both and to consider the relationship between the discontents of the elite and the grievances of the less well off.

During the Restoration political clubs were either secret, or subdivided into sections of less than twenty to side-step article 291 of the Penal Code,[1] or existed as loose pressure groups like *Aide-toi*. The events of the 1790s had set a tradition of prolonged heightened political awareness following a change of regime. The July Days saw the revival of clubs in the style of the 1790s, the names and language of that time serving as a direct example. In July the main opposition political organisation was *Aide-toi*. It had taken a leading role in the detection of official electoral malpractice and had established committees in thirty-five departments between 1827 and 1830. *Aide-toi* was no agent of revolution. After the July Days, some of its adherents, particularly those who had scrambled into office, considered the organisation redundant and resigned; some new officials retained their membership. The bulk of members were, however, those who had failed to gain advancement. Their continued membership may indicate more than a personal grudge; those whose political indications were radical were unlikely to prosper under Louis-Philippe. *Aide-toi* quickly came to represent the *mouvement* tendency in politics. It broadened its goals to include a larger electorate, economic and fiscal reform and universal education. It also retained its earlier function as a watchdog of elections. In 1831 the society backed a wide range of candidates, from the left-wing Hernoux to Cabet, soon to declare for a republic. Local committees vetted parliamentary candidates and were vigorous agents in national and National Guard elections. They continued their pamphlet campaign, now directed against their former allies, loosely grouped in the conservative Orleanist *résistance*: 30 000 such pamphlets were printed in 1832. *Aide-toi* remained an efficient electoral pressure group in the 1831 national elections, but it was never subversive and it never attempted to become a mass organisation. At the beginning of 1832, when Garnier-Pagès launched a membership drive in the provinces, the initial subscription was five francs, with an annual fee of twelve francs.[2] While not totally prohibitive for those who did not qualify as electors, it was unlikely to attract the less well off when one considers that 1 fr. 50 was a reasonable day's pay for a working man. This typified the restrained, elitist character of *Aide-toi*, which never sought to democratise politics.

Radical dissatisfaction with the extent of the 'liberal' revolution, appropriately grouped under the vague label *mouvement*, was also expressed in the period after the July Days by the emergence of transitory organisations devoted to specific issues. There was a coinsiderable overlapping of membership within all of these. Discontent with the limited political changes of 1830, a desire to underline their impatience with the conservatism of internal politics by trying to force the government to support revolution abroad, and to some extent nervousness that foreign powers might be tempted to restore Charles, generated 'patriotic' or 'constitutional' societies. They attracted men who had been leaders of *Aide-toi* committees, a substantial number of whom had received official appointments after the Revolution. The reasons why they continued their criticism were varied. There were those who had received a more minor post than they thought justified, like Micaud, a member of the provisional administration in the Doubs, who was thwarted in his ambition to be made prefect.[3] The patriotic society in Metz was set up to fight the appointment as prefect of one of Polignac's prefects. Its organisers were the three most influential members of *Aide-toi* before the revolution. They were the mayor of Metz, the general secretary of the prefecture and the first president of the *cour royale* and they gave their patriotic society considerable influence.[4] There were bound to be numerous personal grudges following a revolution when the provinces had been left to their own devices to make most of the new appointments, but there were broader objectives behind which disappointed ambition could also be concealed. These included the freedom of the press, religious liberty, the future of the National Guard and above all, the desirability of an extended parliamentary franchise.[5] In February 1831 a group of deputies, led by Salverte, organised a pressure group to fight for a substantial reduction of the 300 franc property qualification and they were very disappointed by the franchise of 200 francs agreed by parliament in April.

Initially, however, opposition concentrated on foreign policy. Revolutionary movements were underway in Belgium, Poland and the Italian states.[6] The first two Orleanist governments both wisely refused to offer help, but more left-wing politicians were sympathetic, especially to the Poles. Lafayette headed a committee in Paris,[7] with provincial affiliations, to collect money for them. The Polish committee in Metz, set up in February, was almost controlled by the patriotic society and headed by the first president of the *cour royale*. Sympathy for the Poles was not confined to government opponents, however, for the Metz group also included the *procureur-général*, who had founded a pro-government society to oppose the patriotic club.[8] Support for the Belgians came more exclusively from the left. General Lamarque, a Bonapartist veteran, Restoration opponent and supreme commander of the army in the west since August 1830, collaborated with Mauguin, deputy for Dijon, to organise a battalion of volunteers to fight in Belgium.[9] Shortly after the outbreak of the Italian revolts, the *Aide-toi* opened a subscription to provide help, supported by the *National* and others.[10] Most of those who expressed public sympathy for foreign revolutions were critics of their own government. They drew attention to the war of 'liberation' which, they believed, revolutionary governments of the 1790s had fought throughout Europe. They denounced the peace treaty of 1815. They argued that as the July revolution itself was a defiance of that treaty, the new government should be consistent and help revolutions abroad.[11] It was beyond dispute that, by the terms of the Treaty of Vienna, the allies were pledged to maintain the Bourbons on the throne. It was only twelve years since the last occupying forces had left France. Although the possibility of a third restoration of the Bourbons by the allies was purely theoretical, if the new regime had sent military assistance to the Poles, it might well have found itself, like the Poles, at war with Russia. Likewise active support for the Belgians risked the intervention of both Britain and Prussia. A domestic interpretation of revolution was therefore a necessity in France. Non-intervention to prevent invasion and war was the keynote of the foreign policy of successive foreign ministers.[12]

The Chamber of Deputies, which often sat with a bare quorum and no spectators, was packed for debates on foreign affairs. The theme of threatened foreign invasion was played on by government and opponents alike as a device for enlisting support. However, there seems to have been genuine panic, especially in frontier departments during the winter. Prefectoral circulars, designed to calm fears, often had the opposite effect. The Doubs prefect was surprised at the alarm engendered when he urged his fellow citizens to discount rumours that Austrian, Prussian and Russian troops were all mobilising.[13] Military reports from the east were full of comments about Prussian troop movements. The military commander in Metz remarked on the bellicosity of the Prussian press, reported that Prussian fortifications on the Rhine were being repaired and, finally, that a camp of 30 000 men was being established 'for the coming war'. At the beginning of April he seemed to fall prey to total panic, in one day writing letter after letter filled with often quite unsubstantiated rumours.[14] Local people also believed that invasion was imminent. *Procureurs-généraux*, with orders from February 1831 to send regular fortnightly reports to Paris because of the degree of unrest and effervescence throughout the country, stressed the fear of war all along France's eastern borders.[15] Fears were exacerbated by the lack of readiness of the frontier garrisons.[16] Voluntary recruitment to the army increased[17] but the National Guard was inadequate. Only the larger communes sported a battalion and this was frequently unarmed and more disposed to fight against the regime than for it.[18]

Fear of foreign intervention, and the political capital made of it by critics on the left, was not the only destabilising factor. The lack of direction of the Laffitte government of November 1830, which contained a mixture of *résistance* and *mouvement* supporters, created a sense of widespread uncertainty. The trial of Charles X's former ministers on a charge of causing the revolution contributed to raise the political temperature in the capital and led to frequent popular demonstrations, in which members of the National Guard were prominent. A national defence association was launched by loyal government supporters in Metz in February 1831, the *Union des départements de l'est pour la défense de la patrie*. They urged the patriotic, if painful, early payment of taxes. In Metz nearly a hundred notables promised to do so, while some officials offered to renounce part of their salary, merchants their profits and farmers their horses. They also covenanted money, jewels and arms in case of war. The Metz *Union* consisted of the government-supporting element in the former *Aide-toi* committee, with the *procureur-général*, the *procureur du roi* and senior members of the *cour royale* as its leaders. The *Union* also sent friendly encouragement to the Italian revolutionaries and two of its organisers were on the Polish committee.[19] Even so, they counted themselves government supporters.[20]

Left-wing critics like Lafayette attacked the conservatism of the new regime and claimed that the pusillanimity of the government made Orleanism vulnerable to a legitimist onslaught. As we have seen, one result was increasing anti-clerical violence, often condoned and even openly encouraged by officials.[21] Following the most lawless displays after the memorial service at St Germain l'Auxerrois, the pressure for national defence organisations took a new turn. On 6 March 1831 a rival National Association was set up in Metz for the defence of France from foreign and domestic enemies. Posters advertising the new society appeared during the night. The committee began to recruit vigorously and a membership list was carried from door to door.[22] The committee urged other towns to follow their example to band together to ensure that the Bourbons were kept in permanent exile.[23] The idea spread quickly through eastern France to Paris. By 11 March a group in Beaune, Côte-d'Or, had chosen its committee.[24] On 14 March, the day after the strongly *résistance* government of Casimir Périer was announced, Parisian left-wing papers, including the *National* and the *Journal de Commerce*, welcomed the formation of an *Association Nationale pour la défense du territoire* in Paris, and the election of a committee, the *Patriotes du département de la Seine*. They recognised the Metz group as their inspiration.

The Périer government immediately condemned the new formations; the *Union* in Metz was quick to comply, transforming itself from a society into a mere subscription. Within less than a month, however, over sixty departments had set up patriotic defence organisations. Prefects tried to convince themselves and their superiors that only the insignificant joined,[25] but this was not so. By 30 March forty deputies had either joined the Parisian society or formed groups in their own departments.[26] They were all critics of the Périer government. Bouchotte, the *mouvement* deputy for Metz was a leading figure, as was Hernoux, mayor and deputy for Dijon. Six of the deputies for the Seine were on the local committee. *Mouvement* deputies were almost invariably the inspiration. The associations attracted, and were often founded by, local officials, especially mayors and members of the judiciary. In Metz the mayor, Emile Bouchotte, nephew of the deputy, headed the committee, which also included five of his municipal councillors; in Dijon there were seven municipal councillors, including the mayor.[27] The local mayor was prominent in every committee whose membership lists have been traced. Affiliations were proclaimed very publicly in newspapers. In Beaune all of the officials appointed since the July Days were on the committee. The *procureur du roi*'s deputy was president. In Nancy, de Merville, the prefect dismissed by Périer, headed the committee which also included a member of the prefect's council, the mayor and the local left-wing deputy.[28] In the Doubs three members of the general council of the department helped to found the society.[29] The participation of such notables gave prestige to the organisation, but was a source of discomfort to the regime and was perceived as a threat to the existing government, which it was almost certainly meant to be.[30] Equally disturbing was the prominence of officers, both of the National Guard and from local regiments.[31] If the motivation had been unadulterated patriotism, their participation would have been welcome to Périer. However, the National Guard had frequently shown its dissatisfaction with the new regime. Lafayette, its popular commander and hero of the July Days, was obliged to resign after National Guard demonstrations when Charles X's ministers had escaped the death sentence. He joined the National Association of the Seine. Often the local commander of the National Guard shared the leadership of the society with the mayor, as in Nancy, Dijon and many other communes. In Dijon, the National Guard headquarters was one of the society's recruiting centres. In the Puy-de-Dôme most of the officers were sympathetic to the association.[32] Sometimes the whole committee were Guardsmen.[33] Many of those who joined the Seine society as ordinary members were in the Guard, while in Lyons whole companies joined as a body. Local army commanders were alarmed by the attraction of the society for their junior officers. High-ranking officers also joined, including Lamarque and de Pire, commander of the second military division.

The National Associations were taken up by the opposition press. Newspaper backing was their only means of publicity, as the government soon pointed out that advertising a political concern by means of posters was illegal. Newspaper editors figured prominently on the committees. Six national papers were represented on the committee for the Seine. Carrel, editor-in-chief of the *National*, and Paulin, the owner of the paper, were members. Cauchois-Lemaire and Dumoulin spoke for the *Constitutionnel*, Chatelain for the *Courrier Français*, Fabre for the *Tribune*, Guillemot for the *Journal de Commerce* and Fazy for the *Révolution*. Provincial societies were also dependent on the support of the press. The pivot of the group in Epinal was the *Sentinelle des Vosges* and its editors, Gerbaut, Mathieu, Deblaye and Turck, were former *carbonari* and future republicans.[34] In St-Dié, Vosges, a printer who joined the committee generously produced all their leaflets free of charge. Carion, an influential local printer in Dijon, who edited the *Journal de Carion*, was on the committee. In the Doubs the society was supported by the *Impartial* and in the Moselle by two local papers.[35] Newspapers were excellent for publicity, especially as in some cases none of the local papers backed Périer. Membership lists were kept in the newspaper offices for enrolment purposes. The paper that provided most coverage was the *National*. Carrel printed detailed membership lists for the Seine, as well as news of local groups. When the government publicly condemned the organisation, he issued a special supplement in its defence. Other Parisian papers whose editors were on the committee were less consistently enthusiastic. The *Constitutionnel* abandoned the society after a half-hearted article on 23 March.

In Paris large numbers of students from the *École Polytechnique* joined, as did a considerable number of those who had fought in July. The social composition of the society is interesting and far from consistent with that portrayed by Périer's officials. Most of those who joined, and certainly most committee members, were notables. Anyone could join, but membership was not free. Wild rumours circulated at the end of March that the vast funds at the disposal of the association were a threat to the stability of the government. Salverte's estimate of a total of 300 000 francs, while substantial, only represented a subvention of three francs from each member. His calculation was pure supposition, however, for there is no evidence that such funds existed. Members were asked to contribute twenty-five to fifty centîmes a month, although some groups asked for contributions according to the member's means. The money was apparently destined to be used to equip poor members of the National Guard, but as the society was shortlived, its funds were presumably incorporated into those of the various organisations of which it was an offshoot. The associations do not seem to have tried to attract the poor who were suffering most acutely in the worsening economic climate, although there were a large number of artisans in the Seine society. The associations were the first attempt to organise opinion nationally since the July Days and to attract mass participation. Even unsympathetic officials had to admit that they were fairly successful in this aim. The Metz prefect estimated that 800 joined the local group initially and that 1200 had enrolled by 20 March when the first general meeting was held. In Paris the society had to be subdivided to cope with the large numbers. From 19 March Paris had its own organisation. The *National* printed lists containing 1600 names and held an additional secret list for those who wanted to conceal their patriotic intentions. In the Saône-et-Loire 200 enrolled in two days. Even in the east, some areas were less enthusiastic and everywhere membership was an urban phenomenon. The prefect in the Vosges wrote disparagingly of 'notre petit club d'Epinal',[36] and in Besançon there were merely thirty adherents, while the list circulated in the department attracted only fifty signatures.

The *National* claimed that, at its height, there was a National Association in sixty-six departments. The editor was either a little optimistic, or the evidence has disappeared. Speaking in the Chamber of Deputies at the end of March, Salverte calculated that there might be 100 000 members. The societies were too shortlived as National Associations for a more precise estimate to be made, but it is significant that no one contradicted Salverte's figures. The eastern departments bordering Prussian territory were most affected, but the society also attracted support in the capital and surrounding departments and in the west.[37]

The National Associations of 1831 were formed at a time of real and imagined internal crisis, in response to a transient situation, the war scare, the fear of legitimist revival and the setting up of a fiercely *résistance* government. Their aims were correspondingly limited. They represented, however, long-standing discontents and traditional attitudes. Many members looked back, nostalgically, to the revolutionary wars. A number believed that Napoleon's final defeat and the invasion of France might have been prevented by the formation of popular defence societies like their association. The societies were particularly large in departments which had been occupied after the wars. During the lengthy parliamentary debate even opponents recognised that a real fear of war prompted their genesis. There were also specific factors. The first association in Metz was clearly generated by the setting up of the *Union* a few days earlier by rival members of the former *Aide-toi* committee. It was a continuation of a vendetta launched by a section of the notables against the prefect. The issues raised were much broader, however, for the response in many areas was immense. The Metz society stressed both foreign dangers and the domestic threat from both the legitimists and republicans. They claimed that their main purpose was to protect France by informing the government of local attitudes. The existing government, the association alleged, was hesitant, unreliable and incompetent. The people had to compensate for these deficiencies by uniting in mutual defence and by working to establish those reforms which should have followed the July Days. Some groups concentrated their attack on the government's domestic policy and, like the societies in the Rhône and the Côte-d'Or, urged the development of republican institutions within the popular monarchy.[38] Many branches expressed support for the Polish and Belgian revolutions.[39] Carrel condemned the Périer government as a ministry of peace at any price. The National Association represented patriotism; the government pusillanimity. Clearly the ministers could not ignore such allegations, especially as they were made in part by their own officials, some of whom tried to argue that their membership did not imply political opposition.

The government took the National Associations and contemporary popular unrest seriously. On 18 March Périer introduced a bill to try to prevent the formation of mobs, *attroupements*, such as the one which had wrecked the church of St Germain a month earlier. The debate, which began on 28 March, swiftly turned to an analysis of the disturbed state of the country, and of the legality of the associations, which were different in structure from any previous societies, as they neither tried to be secret, nor to subdivide into small sections to circumvent the Code. Périer did not question their legality.[40] For the government they raised three main issues, one concerned with foreign affairs, the other two with domestic policy. These were the questions of war or peace, of what the revolution meant and of the degree to which individual governments should expect the total loyalty of their subordinate officials. The associations dominated debates in the Chamber of Deputies for nearly a week. None of the issues raised were new. Conservatives wavered between the view that the societies constituted an unofficial government[41] and the fear that they were a vast, probably republican, military conspiracy. Périer accepted that their motivation was patriotic. He drew a distinction between the members and their leaders, whom he accused of war-mongering. He noted the paradox of urging the government to support foreign revolutions while preaching that France was in danger of invasion: the first would undoubtedly lead to the second. The societies divided France. In war they would be dangerous, in peace superfluous. He was determined to keep the peace.

The second issue raised, the significance of the revolution, exacerbated divisions within the liberals of the July Days. Périer saw the revolution as an unpleasantly violent change of government, necessitated solely by the ordinances, not a revolution inspired by fundamental grievances involving consequent radical political change, as the organisers of the associations claimed. Their leaders sought a wide variety of reforms in order to achieve the monarchy with republican institutions which Lafayette and others had spoken of since July. In 1831 most still accepted the monarchy, but they resented the way in which political control was slipping from their hands. When they spoke of their fear of counter-revolution, they were thinking not only of the memorial service at St Germain l'Auxerrois, but also of the new conservative government.[42] They were right to be apprehensive, for Périer did not tolerate opponents holding official posts. Périer was also right to be nervous, but for himself, not the king.

The most disquieting aspect of the National Associations for Périer was the support they received from officials. He pointed out to his subordinates that it was their duty to fight against any faction which threatened to divide the country and disturb the peace. When this observation had little impact, he condemned all societies, whatever their politics, and ordered everyone to choose between club and job. Other ministers followed suit. Many officials resigned from the association, some from their posts. A few tried to have it both ways, like de Pire, commander of the second military division, who announced in the *National* that, although he had been forced to resign from the association, he was still with them in spirit. Périer had no choice but to dismiss the rest. In the Seine alone there were sixty dismissals at the beginning of April, including the prefect, Odilon Barrot. In Metz the mayor and the first *avocat-général* in the *cour royale* lost their jobs and events followed a similar pattern elsewhere. Some army officers were dismissed, including Lamarque, hero of the left. The commander in Metz was also removed. The associations were either dissolved, or, more often, took on another name. In Metz the committee remained intact. On 5 April all but two members signed a published defence against Périer's charge that they were hostile to the monarchy. The *Indicateur*, a sympathetic source, claimed that there had only been fifteen resignations from the association. There were demonstrations in Metz on the news that members had been stripped of their official appointments, but they were occasions for speech-making, not rioting. At the end of April the military commander was still harassed because a number of junior officers refused to give up membership. Subsequently there was no mention of any such association in the *National*, but during the summer the Lyons society was composed of 150 National Guardsmen with elected leaders.[43] A society with the same name still existed in Dôle and Arbois at the time of the troubles in the Vendée, although by this time both were republican clubs.[44]

The government congratulated itself that, with the dissolution of most National Associations at the end of April 1831, systematic opposition had disappeared. Many members had never intended their adherence to be a fundamental rejection of the regime. The more radical, mostly deputies and journalists, had moved on to a more topical project, the elections. A general election was imminent once the new electoral law had been passed in April. National defence associations were a transient stage in the crystallisation of opposition and the definition of formal divisions within liberal groupings never renowned for solidarity. A substantial number of the liberal deputies who signed the address of the 221 deputies condemning the Polignac government, also joined the association, which expressed a similar lack of confidence in Périer. There is a striking resemblance between the list of journalists who signed the protest against Charles X's ordinances and those who joined the Seine committee in March 1831.[45] The Parisian committee of the association was drawn from the *Aide-toi*; eight of the latter's Italian committee were members, including Garnier-Pagès, Carrel, Cauchois-Lemaire and Chatelain. Indeed the *Aide-toi* and the association issued joint recruiting pamphlets and circulated their electoral propaganda together. However, the association was not an offshoot of *Aide-toi*; it was more a case of adoption. Indeed the original association in Metz seems to have had links with the more left-wing *Amis du Peuple*. A prolonged debate on which particular existing society, if any, first thought of the idea of a network of patriotic clubs is rather academic. Organisations were fluid, created to suit circumstances, but they appealed to a fairly consistent clientele of government critics.

The National Associations were a stage in the evolution of opinion. They have been called 'associations pre-républicaines'.[46] Some leaders became active republicans within a year. Many of the newspapers that supported them also became republican. One of the founder members in Metz, Dornès, who for a short time after the July Days had been general secretary of the prefecture, later became an editor of the *National*. Together with another member of the association, he took part in the defence of those accused after the so-called republican conspiracy of 1834. Some associations were transformed into societies linked to the *Amis du Peuple*.

The *Amis du Peuple* was a very different kind of political organisation from either *Aide-toi* or the National Associations although, as we shall see, there was a very considerable overlap in membership. Its name deliberately recalled the club of the 1790s, which was associated with a radical, divisive and bloody phase of the Revolution. It began on 30 July 1830 as a public society, with no limit on numbers and with headquarters in *rue* Montmartre. The *Amis* held large, noisy meetings in a riding stable. It condemned the new regime for its failure to call a constituent assembly after the revolution. Placards challenging the legality of the Chamber of Deputies led to the arrest of Hubert, the first president, Thierry, their treasurer, and David, their printer. Prison sentences followed. The society, which had only 150 actual members, was forced to retreat into secrecy, both by the government and by the hostility of local tradesmen, who judged them bad for business because of the disruption caused by their meetings. They moved to a building owned by the freemasons. They were implicated in the riots which followed the judicial decision to merely imprison the ex-ministers of Charles X after they had been found guilty of causing the revolution. Nineteen members were arrested, including Godefrey Cavaignac, Guinard and the doctor, Trélat, but they were acquitted. Members joined in the Belgian revolt of 1831 and were involved in a number of public protests in France. The *Amis* were regarded, and thought of themselves, as 'jacobins', revering the Convention and even resurrecting the language of 1793. The Paris doctor, Raspail, who became president, stressed social and educational issues, urging each member to undertake to support the education of half a dozen poor families in the capital. The *Amis* encouraged the formation of provincial groups. Because it was a secret and fairly fluid organisation the number of provincial clubs has sometimes been underestimated but they were numerous in eastern France.

The *Société des Droits de l'Homme* was also founded shortly after the July Days as a radical offshoot of the *Amis*. After the June insurrection of 1832, when the *Amis* were pursued by the government, the *Droits de l'Homme* took over as the main republican club. The groups of the *Amis* then became sections within the other organisation. The *Droits de l'Homme* appears to have tried to be a very structured and rather bureaucratic society. There was a central committee of eleven directors, with twelve commissioners for each *arrondissement* of Paris and forty-eight for each *quartier*, who had the responsibility for the organisation of the sections. Each section had a separate name and could claim to be an independent club in order to evade the law. In April 1833 the leaders of one section were arrested and the whole society declared illegal by the courts, but the decision seems to have had little immediate impact. The *Droits de l'Homme* made a positive effort to establish provincial clubs. A special committee was formed to promote local affiliations and correspond with them. A number of the provincial clubs modelled themselves on Parisian sections, but were independent. In 1833, when he urged parliament to take more decisive action against such clubs, which he believed were making nonsense of the authority of the regime, Guizot estimated that the *Droits de l'Homme* had about 3000 members.

In addition to these two main clubs, there were other, sometimes short-lived organisations set up to publicise such issues as press freedom and universal education. An association to provide free

Une Révolution Escamotée 163

education for the poor was headed by Dupont de l'Eure, Arago, Cormenin, Barrot, Lafayette, Carrel, Garnier-Pagès, Cabet and Mauguin. In 1833 2500 people were enrolled in its fifty-four classes. With such a leadership, it was predictably republican in spirit, but because of its direct involvement with the Parisian poor, issues of social, rather than political reform were emphasised.[47] In Paris these different societies were separate, with overlapping membership lists and with close links between them. In provincial towns there was often only one club, usually with several sections. Typical was the Republican Circle in Dijon, which corresponded with both the *Amis* and the *Droits de l'Homme* in Paris.[48] It was a focus for other local groups, corresponding with and sending representatives to societies in Beaune, Semur, Nuits and St-Jean. The prefect commented ironically, 'In the country districts, people like to spread the rumour that there is a huge secret organisation in all parts of France which will control our destiny.'[49] Republican societies grew mainly in eastern France with large clubs in Metz, Strasbourg, Epinal, Colmar and Nancy. Further south there were active groups in Franche-Comté and Burgundy, with energetic and substantial clubs in Besançon, Arbois, Dijon, Chalons, Beaune, Seurre, Grenoble and Lyons. In contrast there was little republican enthusiasm in northern France and predictably, after the events of the 1790s, in the west, with the exceptions of Rennes, Nantes and Poitiers. Clubs and newspapers were more plentiful in the Midi; not in Bordeaux, but in Toulouse, Montauban, Auch, Bayonne, Perpignan, Montpellier, Hérault, Marseilles, Aix and Var. There were a few republican formations in the centre; Trélat edited the *Patriote* in the Puy-de-Dôme and there were clubs in Clermont-Ferrand and Moulin.[50]

What sort of people became members? They attracted some notables, professional men, landowners and industrialists, who had been in the liberal opposition to Charles X, and moved on to the *Association Nationale* and were unhappy with the conservative direction the regime had taken. But most were young, particularly in the *Amis* and *Droits de l'Homme*. The founding members of the *Amis* included Cavaignac, Blanqui, Buchez, Trélat and Raspail. Others were law and medical students, young clerks, shop assistants, members of the National Guard and some artillery officers. Most groups had a central core containing a high proportion of lawyers. In Dijon the president was a *notaire* and Demontry, another committee member and departmental organiser of the

Amis and *Droits de l'Homme*, was also a lawyer.[51] The *procureur du roi* and his deputy in the town were so sympathetic that prosecution of the club was impossible.[52] Doctors were prominent members, including Raspail, Trélat and Turck. Local left-wing journalists often set up the clubs. In Besançon the president was the editor of the *Patriote*. Gerbaut, the editor of the *Sentinelle*, was a leading figure in republican circles in the Vosges.[53] National Guard officers and men figured prominently in some clubs; in Dijon all the committee members were officers, and here, as in smaller communes like Arbois, the participation of the Guard made it impossible to use them as an auxiliary police force against demonstrators.[54] Republican clubs also attracted soldiers, especially junior non-commissioned officers. One battalion, stationed in Dijon, had to be moved because of the activities of republicans amongst them, Demay, in particular, who was decorated for his contribution to the July Days, but later dismissed from the army for his republicanism.[55] In Strasbourg thirty of the one hundred members of the republican society were officers in the forty-ninth regiment and many students from *École Militaire* enrolled.[56]

In these respects, apart from the presence of a younger generation, the republican clubs were socially not unlike the more moderate organisations, and indeed were sometimes National Associations or *Aide-toi* groups under another name, perhaps losing some of their older and more conservative members along the way. However there were distinct social differences between moderate and republican organisations in some areas. Some clubs, and not exclusively those in Paris and Lyons, positively encouraged the less well off to join. The *Société Patriotique et Populaire* in Metz, led by local notables like Bouchotte, the mayor, had a high proportion of working men among its members, including young cabinet-makers and stone-cutters, trades well represented among the revolutionary fighters during the July Days in Paris. Although the society was split into the usual sections, meetings regularly attracted an audience of around 200 people.[57] In Strasbourg the 500–600 workers in the tobacco industry supported the club. In 1839 144 of the 204 men included in the prefect's list of republicans were artisans or involved in wholesale or retail business, but it is not possible to gauge how prosperous or otherwise were the brewers who occupy so prominent a place on the list.[58]

One might be tempted to see the presence of artisans as typical of more industrialised areas, but interest was not confined to urban workers. A great proportion of contemporary industry was rurally based with many workers combining industrial and agricultural activities. The most energetic of all the republican clubs, that of the small rural commune of Arbois, was composed of winemakers, but also included weavers, plasterers, carpenters and other tradesmen.[59] The Dijon club encouraged the growth of forty rural offshoots. The prefect commented, 'On gagne dans les villages une certaine importance, lorsqu'on peut se dire membre d'une société, quelque soit.' Membership flaunted defiance of the mayor or local big landowner.[60] The republicans of Lyons, bourgeois and irredeemably split into quarrelling factions – called 'girondins' and 'jacobins' by the prefect and others – did not turn the silk weavers into revolu-tionaries, but they did try to enlist worker support. The *Glaneuse* orchestrated the republican campaign, misdirected, at first, by re-publicans who were anxious to endorse concepts of modernisation, until they realised that the *canuts* (silk weavers) were fighting against change and embryonic capitalism in their industry. The *Droits de l'Homme* set up a democratic central committee in Lyons directly elected by all members. Club affiliation cost a mere fifty centîmes a month. Members had to swear allegiance to Robespierre's version of the Declaration of the Rights of Man. Later branches were added in Vienne, Villefranche and St-Etienne.[61] The republican club in Metz offered even cheaper membership in March 1834, reducing its annual subscription from ten francs to two francs. But the societies did not try to enrol the indigent.[62] Indeed the Dijon society was very offended when the prefect issued the needy poor of the town with hats similar to those worn by the republicans, black with red bands, which could be unfolded to reveal the motto 'Vive la République'.

Republican clubs all adopted a semi-secret structure, reminiscent of the freemasons and that used by the *charbonnerie* a decade before. The Dijon club was split into *centuries* and *décaries*, each with about eighteen members. In 1834 there were about sixty-seven such sections, thirty-nine of whose members were known to the government.[63] Thus, in the Côte-d'Or there may have been about 1000 members. Occasionally large meetings were held, particularly in the crisis surrounding new repressive legislation in 1834. The Metz club held sessions with 200 present in March 1834. In Chalons the *Droits de l'Homme* had 1500 members and regularly held meetings of 400–500.[64] The parent group in Paris claimed a total membership of 4000 in 1833.

Newspaper publicity was crucial to the emergence of republican clubs, both in the capital and in about fifty regional centres. The *Tribune des Départements* welcomed the designation 'republican' on 31 July 1830. The *National* gave measured support to republicanism. Cabet's *Populaire*, with an annual subscription of ten francs, less than a third the cost of most papers, set a new trend and consciously appealed to workers in its weekly editions. There were also some bourgeois republican periodicals like *Paris Révolutionnaire*. In the provinces left-wing newspapers flourished for a time after the revolution, but there were only a limited number with pronounced radical views and most of these were published in the eastern and south-eastern departments. They were often called *Patriote* or *Sentinelle*. The papers launched membership drives for the clubs. In its first edition the *Patriote* in Besançon praised *Aide-toi* and kept the membership lists of the society in its offices. The *Patriote* in Dijon conducted successful publicity for the *Amis*. In the Vosges the society found a sympathetic agent in the *Sentinelle* and its editors, Gerbaut and Mathieu. In 1832 Gerbaut was acquitted for the third time on a charge of having insulted government and king. Only three jurors voted for a conviction, the rest were apparently nervous of being ridiculed and having their names and addresses printed in the paper if they condemned him.[65] In January 1834, when the *Patriote* in Besançon was acquitted after it had published an article claiming 'the younger branch of the Bourbons has bestowed honours only on thieves and criminals', the editors printed an account of the trial both in the paper and as a separate pamphlet and included names, addresses and occupations of jurors, who could rarely see any substance in press offences compared with murder, assault or even theft.[66] The *Association pour la liberté de la presse*, whose membership was very similar to that of the clubs, tried to encourage readership by setting up *cabinets de lecture* which could then subscribe and a single paper reach many readers.[67] Pamphlets were a popular and relatively cheap form of publicity. The *Amis* specialised in short, simple pamphlets to appeal to less well-educated artisans.[68] In Epinal the local club was so poor that handwritten material had to suffice.[69] Pamphlets were sold in the countryside by hawkers, *crieurs publics*, who would sell anything that was easy to carry and likely to find a market. They were a useful way to reach country people, who were accustomed to buying a wide range of items from them, from ribbons to the outpourings of the *bibliothèque bleue*.[70]

Disappointed personal ambition, disillusion with the degree of liberalism demonstrated by the new regime, singly or in combination, might tip the balance to turn a Restoration liberal into a supporter of the *mouvement*. Others were sufficiently disenchanted with Orleanism to prefer a republic. Cabet, a former member of the *charbonnerie*, accepted an official post in the early months of Louis-Philippe's reign, but the Périer government turned him to republican and socialist ideas. For junior officers in the army low pay, relative inactivity, lack of promotion prospects and the boredom of provincial life made a republican club, like the *charbonnerie* in the 1820s, an interesting alternative to sitting around in cafes in total idleness.[71] For others, in particular the less well off who joined, their own economic problems were paramount. The club offered the opportunity to attack the fiscal and commercial policies of the government. Governments, whether Bourbon or Orleanist, were blamed for the cyclical depression, criticised for maintaining high tariffs and maligned for retaining high indirect taxes, especially on wine. The centralised state was attacked by the poor for undermining communal traditions in the countryside: the forest laws of 1827, for example, took the supervision and management of communally owned forests out of the hands of the commune and brought them under the control of central government. Joining a republican club hit out at the centralised state.

How politicised and distinct was republicanism? How much was the term, when used by educated contemporaries, themselves members or aspiring members of the political elite, more than a theoretical and abstract recollection of the confused and contradictory republican experiences of the 1790s? In what sense were they spokesmen of democracy? What were the main policies of republicans? In terms of political ideas they all identified philosophically with the political concepts of the early 1790s, but they could not agree on their precise model. Some looked back to the Convention, others to Robespierre in particular, and their failure to agree caused many arguments in the early 1830s. Following their disappointment with the 1830 revolution, their main political goal was universal male suffrage, or as the Dijon Republican Club put it, the sovereignty of the people. The Arbois club petitioned the Chamber of Deputies to enfranchise all tax-payers. Even the *mouvement* society *Aide-toi* pressed for a larger electorate and in 1833–4 *Aide-toi* and *Droits de l'Homme* together launched a franchise reform campaign. Also, in common with the *mouvement* deputies and later banquet campaigners, republicans demanded that office holders should be excluded from the Chamber of Deputies. In 1830 the liberals had insisted that deputies who accepted a public appointment, should seek a renewed mandate from their constituents, but this became a mere formality and in no way guaranteed a deputy's independence. In 1846 40 per cent of the members of the chamber were office holders. Republicans also sought payment for deputies and the abolition of the 500 franc tax qualification for parliamentary candidates.[72] In addition to petitions, pamphlets and press campaigns, republicans, like the electoral reformers a decade later, held banquets. One held in Dijon in December 1833 was attended by 600 diners, including mayors from nearby communes.[73] After the meal there would be speeches in favour of reform from politicians such as Garnier-Pagès or Cormenin. Electoral reform, even a democratic ticket, was not specifically, or intrinsically republican, especially if one recalled the political history of the First Republic. The concept of a republic was publicised by vague and generalised panegyrics; a peroration on the theme of the ideal republic was standard form for the final speech for the defence in all republican trials at this time. Listeners were usually told that the perfect republic would not be a product of bloodshed and revolution, but of peaceful and gradual change through the education and enlightenment of people.

For some republicans evolutionary change was too slow and they believed that revolutionary action was the only means to attack the regime and further their cause. Sections of the *Amis* and *Droits de l'Homme* were supposed to be armed, and some were. Members in Dijon, Beaune and elsewhere were instructed to provide themselves with a gun and ammunition, and this must have been fairly easy for members who were in the National Guard or who were soldiers. Clubs were ordered to drill and hold target practice; the Arbois club even claimed that such exercises were not subversive. It was not all practice, however, and there were a number of violent demonstrations in the early 1830s in Paris and elsewhere, which did nothing to promote the image of republicans as peace loving. There was pressure from rank and file members in the summer of 1832, after the death of Périer, for an armed uprising, though the leaders resisted. The funeral of general Lamarque, another cholera victim, on 5 June gave the opportunity for which some members had hoped. They expected help from the *mouvement* opposition, but none came. The demonstration that accompanied the funeral was suppressed with great brutality. Paris was put in a state of siege, the arrested were charged and the leaders ultimately deported.

Did republican writers and activists want to create a mass movement, a view certainly conveyed by Weill and other turn-of-the-century historians? Or were the republicans rather aloof and condescending in their awareness of the need to educate the poor and concern themselves with their welfare? Was the tone of the republicans towards the poor very different from the paternalism of conservative Orleanists? Did they believe that the poor, to whom they referred in very general terms, had an equal right to be part of the political community and merit equal consideration of their economic and social grievances? To what extent did they try to understand the grievances of peasants and artisans? Did they appreciate the impact of economic change and urbanisation on poor people? Were they aware that these changes made the circumstances of the 1830s qualitatively different from those of the 1790s?

Economic and social reforms were discussed. At this stage there were links between republicans and early socialists, although many socialists were later to be disenchanted with republicans and republicans to dismiss socialists as utopian dreamers. Trélat and Raspail were moved by the miserable state of the poor and, like a number of other republican medical men, did not confine their views to words. They provided a free medical service to communities totally bereft of all help. Raspail's dedication to republicanism denied him the prizes and honours which would otherwise have been his during the July Monarchy.[74] Poverty was seen as an evil inflicted by the wealthy and in particular by the evolution of a capitalist system of exploitation and 'free competition'. The poor had no defence against the demands of employers that they work for lower and lower wages in order to maximise profits. In the early 1830s the republicans offered no structural solution, but were willing to be the champions of the poor. The first manifesto of the *Amis* committed the society to the defence of the interests of the lower classes and improvements in their moral and physical condition. The *Patriote* in the Saône-et-Loire commented in 1834, 'The republic offers upward social mobility, even to the poorest worker.'

The grievances of the poor in the industrial and agricultural depression, 1827–32, led to widespread popular unrest, manifest in traditional forms such as bread riots, obstructing the free movement of grain and burning the files and, if possible, the offices of tax officials. On occasions popular grievances and republican agitation found a common cause. The republicans of the early 1830s were aware, as were more conservative politicians, that recurring economic crises and gradual changes in the structure of industry unleashed misery for many families entirely or partially dependent on their earnings as industrial workers. They had some understanding of how economic crises affected the poor, and claimed that their impact, even their occurrence, could be alleviated by less selfish employers and a change in government policy. Their initial grasp of the impact of industrial change was less accurate. They praised the benefits of genuine competition and the blessings of technical changes, such as mechanised printing. The consequent suspicion of republicanism shown by working people brought a gradual change in these 'progressive' views. Parisian printers, already appalled by the introduction of mechanical presses, saw the July Days as an opportunity for Luddism. Bourgeois radicals, it was argued, were wrong to claim that mechanisation would benefit the poor by making books cheaper and boosting literacy. On the contrary, the mechanised presses were used to produce the books read by the elite, which were impossibly expensive. The more modest works read by the poor were no cheaper and skilled men were left without jobs. The cause of literacy and of the poor, therefore, would best be served by opposing mechanisation.[75] The early forays of republicans into the problems of the Lyons silk industry also led them to praise free competition, until they realised that the master weavers who were at the centre of strikes and protests were falling victim to the merchants. The latter were changing from 'middle men' to embryonic capitalists, lending money to weavers to buy the new and expensive Jacquard loom. Increasingly, merchants were able to dictate the price they would pay for cloth woven by the weavers and thus undermine their independent status. It was not until the late 1830s that early socialists began to propose artisan-led structural changes in industry to protect them from capitalist exploitation. In these years organisations like the *Droits de l'Homme* offered primarily political solutions. They suggested that workers should first combine in societies to press for democratic government.[76] Apparently they believed that democracy would, in some vague and undefined way, resolve the social and economic grievances of the poor. In other respects, the general approach of bourgeois republicans to artisan grievances was fundamentally paternalistic rather than participatory. They would do 'good' to working people, with free medicine, evening classes and copies of their pamphlets for the unemployed,[77] but they wanted to control demonstrations, shape them to their political ends, and they did not yet expect working people themselves to take an active role in their own liberation.

Republicans were even more uncomprehending of the long-term grievances of peasants. The problems of country people related both to short-term crises and the impact of structural change. Republicans were not alone in blaming the high food prices that accompanied harvest shortfall on the unwillingness of governments to permit the free import of foreign grain. Likewise the hardship suffered by wine-makers was attributed not just to climatic disaster but also to the protectionist commercial policies by which France's iron and textile industries were shielded from competition, thus exposing her wine industry to victimisation by foreign nations. Even more immediately damaging were the indirect taxes imposed on wine. Radical politicians, *mouvement* and republican, joined wine producers in repeated protests against the *droits réunis* in the second half of 1830, and expressed sympathy, but perhaps more muted, for those suffering from high bread prices. Republicans, like other educated men, could understand these problems. In Dijon in 1833 the republicans organised a society to oppose the detested indirect taxes on salt and wine, a movement initiated in Paris, the details of which were brought to Dijon by their republican deputy, Etienne Cabet.[78] The *Patriote Franc-Comtois* orchestrated the campaign in Besançon and the editor was charged with undermining the regime. He was acquitted and said in his defence address,

> We were keen to show that a republican isn't a troublemaker, does not want to steal and plunder, does not want bloodshed, but a man of his times, who wants to make things better for the poor, without threatening the position of the rich, whose aim is universal happiness and who firmly believes that the way to achieve this is to involve everyone in government.[79]

On the other hand, peasants were left alone to argue their case against rural modernisation. The revolutionaries of the 1790s had intensified the demolition of the 'feudal' system in France, which intimately involved an attack on communal rights. Subsequent regimes pursued similar strategies in the name of modernisation and of property owners. The Forest Code of 1827 created a new government bureaucracy to administer state, crown and communal forests. There was to be no pasturing of goats or sheep. Restrictions were placed on the annual 'cut' allowed for fuel and repairs, which could be bought by an individual, rather than, as had been the custom, shared by all members of the commune. Peasants protested by persisting in their traditional right to pasture animals and gather wood from communal forests. Wood prices were soaring and communal rights eroded by those with the capital to invest in an increasingly valuable asset. Peasant wood gatherers were treated as thieves and were resisted with force by the authorities. The issue was regarded as strictly 'non-political'[80] by the new Orleanist officials. In areas where the resources of common lands, especially the forests, were an indispensable item in the economy of the poor, peasants hoped that the victors of July would take their side. In Ariège, Pyrenees, in particular, the 'demoiselles', men dressed as women, struggled to defend communal rights. But the revolutionary regime was unyielding.[81] There was never any question that the Orleanists might abolish the law of 1827, rather the reverse. The cause of the poorer peasant was never espoused by the republicans; rather, they showed deference for the rights of private property. Later in the decade early socialist writers like Fourier and Proudhon suggested that there was virtue in communal ownership, but they were not totally convinced about the virtues of innovative modern communalism. Phalange members were to be allowed private property. The socialists did not seem to notice that a traditional communal system existed, which was vital to the survival of poor families and whose erosion was provoking profound peasant unrest. No one took up the cause of the poor peasant. Peasant protestors, whether concerned to try to defend traditional practice against the relatively new concept of a national free trade in grain, or rioting to try to enforce traditional ideas of a 'just' price, or in sporadic and often pathetic attempts to defend the beleaguered communal system, attracted neither the sympathy nor the support of republicans.

While it is possible to reconstruct what contemporary literate republicans, many of whom were professional writers, thought was their inspiration and motivation, and with equal facility explore the Orleanist (over)reaction to the movement, one is left with an obviously incomplete story. The world of secret societies is always somewhat make-believe, especially when the inevitably ubiquitous government spies are paid by results.[82] But the most difficult problem is to discover what the artisans and peasants themselves believed, their problems being only partially understood by radical politicians. We can judge their attitude to the economic and social problems discussed above by the frequency of popular protest in these years, but the paucity of written records, apart from the still-rare artisan newspaper, makes the link between the protest of the poor and the political sophistication of the radical educated groups a matter of surmise. Did artisans and peasants who joined republican clubs and whose strikes and demonstrations seemed to coincide with republican protest share the political aspirations and assumptions of bourgeois republicans? To what extent were the less well off, whose grievances in the late 1820s and early 1830s provided the disturbed background for the movement, and who, from time to time, make an appearance in it, motivated by any appreciation of the theoretical benefits of republican democracy, mass education and social reform?

A number of studies of peasant communities have been undertaken in recent years. Agulhon was a pioneer in his accounts of the Var,[83] where he detected a strong municipal political tradition. He explained the radicalism of the less well off as a response to the process of modernisation of the rural economy, which reduced the role of rural industry and undermined communal traditions and with them the domestic economy of the poor. Thus the inspiration for their radicalism in the years, both before and after 1848, was seen to be their attempt to preserve what would be regarded by the educated as archaic traditions in the face of capitalist development. Corbin pursued this theme in his history of the Limousin,[84] and Aminzade has looked at the radicalism of artisans in Toulouse,[85] where there was no immediate or obvious threat from a developing factory industry. Historians no longer assume either that the poor were embryonic Marxists or that they were motivated solely by immediate economic concerns. When simplistic deterministic Marxist notions are reassessed, the historian is still on unsure ground in identifying artisan motivation. Underlying the work of this recent group of French historians is the assumption that the less well off emerged in 1848, after scuffles with the authorities over issues like forest rights, into fully-fledged, self-conscious, modern and forward-looking democrats, wholly aware of the relevance of socialist ideas to their own situation. Jones, in his well-rounded analysis of the society of the southern Massif Central, questions this interpretation, which involves a Pauline crystallisation of peasant and artisan opinion in 1848. He stresses that in the Massif Central local economic difficulties and the ideas of 1789 had more impact than the concepts of the early socialists and republicans.[86] These regional studies clearly begin to put flesh on the previously vague and one-dimensional cardboard image of popular motivation. So far historians have mainly concentrated on the poorer areas, where radical views only seemed to coalesce in 1848. What of regions where factory industry was developing and where an embryonic political movement was manifest in the early 1830s?

In the absence of artisan and peasant explanations of their motives, one must rely on the evidence of popular protest itself. There were three distinct changes after the July revolution. The incidence of popular unrest increased and became more varied, reaching three peaks, in the weeks after the sacking of the church of St Germain, in the spring of 1832 and in late 1833 through to the summer of 1834. The July Days were a mere incident in a long chain of unrest,[87] the nature of which – market riots, protests against shipment of grain, strikes against wage reductions and so on – have been described during the earlier discussion of the outbreak of revolution. The motives of the rioters were more precise and more wide ranging than before the July Days. The physical dimensions of the riots were also greater; cities and departmental capitals were held by protestors, often joined by members of the National Guard, for up to a week.[88] The case of the bread riots in Lorient, Morbihan, on 16–18 October 1830 may be taken as typical of the very many episodes that could be cited. A crowd of about 1200 workers from the port, including carpenters, shoe and leather workers, led by a longboatman and a blacksmith and including many women and children, invaded the *hôtel de ville*, shouting 'long live the king!' and 'lower bread prices!' When the mayor refused to try to bring down the price of bread, a woman led them off to the nearest bakery, threatening pillage and murder of all bakers. Three other women, including an onion seller, supported her in dividing up the bread as the baker himself fled. The National Guard and troops were brought in. The crowd went on to invade other bakeries. Arrests were made, houses were searched for weapons and National Guard and gendarmerie patrols were instituted.[89] These riots differed from many others in that the National Guard remained loyal and the crowd actually expressed itself favourable to some form of monarchy.

Unquestionably economic problems were important. The harvest of 1830, following an arctic winter in 1829–30, was disastrous, 1831 was little better and the spring of 1832 augured ill for the coming harvest.[90] The uncertainty created by the revolution further weakened confidence in financial and commercial circles and industrial production slumped even more, with building and the luxury industries suffering disproportionately. The increase in popular protest was thus comprehensible, but there were political dimensions. There was optimism that the revolutionary government could miraculously solve France's economic ills, a naïve expectation given the record of the early 1790s, but an understandable one. In particular, the less well off hoped that dues on imported wheat would be cut and that *droits réunis* on wine would be abolished. Some temporary grain imports were authorised, in line with the established regulations.[91] A number of officials themselves argued that the indirect taxes on wine should be abolished; the *droits réunis* were resented by rich as well as the many poorer wine producers.[92] Some prefects were so confident of reform that they suspended collection of the tax. Modest reductions were introduced after much delay but too late to prevent the prolonged rioting of the late summer and autumn of 1830.

The government assembled detailed local evidence of the scope of the industrial depression in 1831–2. However, ministers were convinced that the problems were the result of a temporary loss of confidence caused by the revolution. Their duty was to stand firm, not to intervene.[93] Temporary relief was provided for the unemployed. The Restoration had relied on municipal and private charity. As the situation grew worse after July, the central government was forced to accept responsibility. In the capital Luddism, strikes and demonstrations urging the restoration of former wage rates became more intense.[94] Two million francs were assigned to public works projects in Paris and 6000 people were found work in workshops set up in the capital, but the number of unemployed far exceeded resources. There were complaints that many of the beneficiaries were not Parisians. By the end of December work had been found for over 10 000 with 6500 on a project to develop the Champ-de-Mars alone. The city of Paris was handing out 15 000 francs daily, four times the original estimate. At the end of December an additional fund of 100 000 francs was voted when funds ran out completely. There was fear of additional popular violence (the government had just weathered the riots after the trial of the ex-ministers) if wages could not be paid. The final cost of the workshops to the city was 1 290 000 francs. Six years later it was still trying to repay the central government.[95]

Grants were given to stricken departments to set up workhouses or to start road-building programmes. The money did not arrive until December, too late to relieve the misery of the winter.[96] It was often used to run temporary workshops, as in Paris. The Doubs received 23 000 francs,[97] the Haute-Marne[98] and the Vosges 10 000 francs, which was pathetically inadequate to resolve the problems of the latter, a rather poor department.[99] The sums requested were higher in 1831. In November an additional eighteen million francs was set aside for workshops in needy areas.[100] In February 1832 in St-Dizier, normally a prosperous small commercial town busily shipping goods to Paris, 75 per cent of the workforce were entirely dependent on the workshops.[101] These projects were never seen as more than very temporary expedients, often supplying more of a charity handout than real work. They were closed down as soon as possible. The government was also forced to intervene over the problem of grain and bread prices. By 1832, despite the implementation of the sliding scale for importing grain, it became clear that many poor people could not afford the price of bread. In the Côte-d'Or bakers were subsidised by the prefect so that they could sell to the poor at lower prices, but the scheme was not popular with the bakers themselves.[102] Some communes bought grain and sold it to the poor at a loss; some distributed both grain and bread. Sometimes the free distribution of bread was forced on towns fearful of unrest.[103] These were panic measures.

The regime was bitterly attacked for its failure to attempt to help the poor in more structured ways, such as a defence of worker associations. On the contrary, troops were employed to 'maintain' order against strikes and worker demonstrations. The poor did not need Cabet to tell them that 1830 was 'une révolution escamotée', smuggled and stolen away from those who had fought on the barricades. It was no accident that the numerous trees of liberty, echoing the hopes of the 1790s, which were erected in the place of missionary crosses, were crowned with 'bonnets rouges'. The Orleanist governments were surprised by the force of anti-clerical feeling in the popular protests of this period. On the other hand, there is scant evidence of popular sympathy for the deposed king. In November 1830 the sub-prefect of Sables d'Olonne, Morbihan, fretted a little about rumours of the revival of *chouannerie* and the possibility that some army recruits might refuse to serve.[104] But, as we have seen, even this most royalist area of western France failed to support an attempted legitimist rising in 1832. Where the political sentiments of the poor were visible, they were either critical of government policy, or looked back to the republic of the 1790s in simple, symbolic terms. A final difference between the period after the July Days and the previous years was the involvement of some workers in political clubs set up by the better off. The link was tenuous and temporary, broken within a few years by the direction of the new socialist movement, which was to alter the radical tradition of the 1790s beyond recognition.

There is no doubt that the economic crisis helped to sustain popular unrest, republican agitation and government apprehension. The Laffitte administration of November 1830 was sometimes ambivalent and hesitated to crush popular demonstrations that engaged the sympathy of some newly appointed local officials. Casimir Périer, in office from March 1831, took a firm line, combining the dismissal of those public servants compromised, especially in the recent anti-clerical riots, with thorough investigation and repression.

Governments were afraid that political criticism and economic grievance might merge. In November 1831 the silk weavers of Lyons rioted and took over the city for several days, driving out the indecisive prefect and the troops of the local garrison. The prefect, Dumolard, had, in fact, intervened in the long running conflict between the merchants who, increasingly able to dictate rates of pay, were thus reducing both the status and the economic position of the previously independent weavers. The prefect had given the weavers the impression that he would intercede in their dispute with the merchants to help them negotiate more stable and beneficial rates. When tartly informed by Paris that the government's policy was to remain neutral, he backed down and lost Lyons and ultimately his job in consequence.[105] The government was at pains to emphasise in 1831 that the silk weavers were not politically motivated.[106] The Lyons rising was a particularly dramatic illustration of the type of worker protest of the period but it was not isolated. In December 1831, following tension between pin and needle workers and their employers over wage reductions and the introduction of new machinery, there was a demonstration of 300 workers, some armed with staves, in Rugles, Eure. Only 24 of the 231 National Guardsmen reported for duty to repress the riot and it was left to the gendarmerie to cope. Extra troops had to be called in. The prefect, very conscious of the situation in Lyons, was inclined to brand the affair a conspiracy, but the captain of the gendarmerie claimed that there was wrong on both sides. The manufacturers were exploiting the misery of their employees. Like Dumolard, he argued that the government ought to intercede between worker and employer.[107] There was no sympathy for this view in Paris, where 'freedom' was always seen through the eyes of the employer.

The hypocrisy of government policy and violent repression of worker unrest, combined with active support for those who were seen as the representatives of employers, saw links forged between republicans and workers. Périer envisaged republican groups as 'artisans de trouble'. The weapons of the government were observation, propaganda, the National Guard, the gendarmerie and other military reinforcements. A new membership drive by republican clubs in March 1832 brought the immediate response from the government: 'The first responsibility of the administration is to maintain public order, by offering those political groups which threaten it an invincible resistance.' Périer ordered his prefects, 'Ne cédez rien à la force, ni à la menace.'[108] National Guard and soldier participation in republican groups and the unreliability of the former in popular unrest meant that in reality prefects had to be circumspect in the use of force.[109] Detailed regular political reports were called for and prefects complied at length. The repeated investigations demanded of prefects after March 1831, aided by the informers they employed, presented a picture of

France, particularly of Paris and the east, riddled with large, armed, conspiring and dangerous clubs, although some prefects, like Chaper in Dijon, were rather more sceptical of the highly coloured conspiracies their secret agents reported. Clubs and newspapers were repeatedly prosecuted for contraventions of the existing law and almost just as often acquitted by juries, occasionally sympathetic but more often taking the view that there was no threat to the state in the expression of political opposition. To enlarge the scope of existing legislation might well be counter-productive and harmful to the image of a 'liberal' regime. However, even acquittals in such large numbers were a threat to the republicans, because of the cost of conducting their defence and the time devoted to it. The leaders of the *Amis* were constantly pursued in the courts, winning three major cases in 1832, but the high cost led to the collapse of the organisation. Litigation forced many local newspapers to close down.

The ending of the industrial recession during 1832, aided by a normal harvest, seemed to restore the government's confidence for a time. In 1833 worries over republicanism seemed to be over. Guizot concluded in February, 'les émeutes sont mortes, les clubs sont mortes, la propagande révolutionnaire est morte.'[110] Some military commanders and prefects continued to send anxious reports of subversive organisations and activities. In April 1833 a banquet planned to honour Garnier-Pagès in Lyons had attracted 6000 subscribers when the prefect nervously banned it.[111] The government, apparently convinced that it was still under threat, planned a three-pronged attack to stop the circulation of republican pamphlets, to close the clubs and to force their newspapers out of business. In February 1834 *crieurs publics* were forced to apply to the prefect for a permit to ply their wares, which could be revoked at any time. A law on associations, introduced by Barthe, minister of justice and a former member of the *charbonnerie*, was passed on 10 April 1834, securing a majority of 246 to 154 in the Chamber of Deputies. All societies, whatever their size or nature, were obliged to seek prefectoral sanction. The penalty for belonging to an illegal organisation was increased from a fine alone to one year's imprisonment and a 1000 franc fine. Whoever owned the property where an illegal meeting was held was equally liable.

What was the impact of the new legislation? Discussions about the proposed legislation and how to oppose it contributed much to stirring up a fading movement. Police informers seem to have done the rest, partly by fabricating conspiracies and partly by creating them by joining, or even starting, a republican club. It was in this atmosphere that officials found credible the idea that there was a major republican conspiracy in eastern and southeastern France.[112] The normal journeyings of Mathieu and other delegates to visit different clubs were logged, often with growing hysteria and naïve incredulity, perhaps in the hope that the worse the republican threat appeared, the more acceptable would be penal legislation and severe repression. It was in the material interest of police spies and informers in the clubs to reinforce the conspiracy theory that grew in 1833–4. One such spy, Mascarène, a member of a local regiment, egged Mathieu on to set up a club,[113] then repeatedly claimed that Mathieu was at the centre of a dangerous military plot. In effect Mascarène himself generated most of the activity that took place, to the extent that his commander, General Hulot, asked to have him transferred to Africa in 1833 because he was such a disturber of the peace. In February 1834 Mathieu travelled to Nancy and Chalons to assess the availability of men and arms for a concerted rising, publicly proclaiming his hope that a vast conspiracy would put government in the hands of the republicans. This was no more than wishful thinking, however. He took Mascarène with him, apparently unaware that his most active supporter was a double agent. Mascarène's commanding officer gave him permission to go, it would seem, because he hoped that Mascarène would be able to stir up trouble in the regiment stationed in Lyons. The government would then be able to justify dealing a crushing blow to the republican organisations.[114]

Lyons was seen as a pivot because of the pre-existing disaffection among the workers, particularly the weavers. At the beginning of 1834 the weavers were locked in yet another battle with the increasingly dominant merchants. Overproduction and the consequent low price of silk left the weavers vulnerable. In addition, the weavers, grouped in trade associations like that of the *mutuellistes*, feared that new legislation on associations would eliminate their only remaining defence against the merchants by compelling their traditional artisan formations to disband. On 14 February all 25 000 looms in Lyons came to a halt with the call of 'vivre en travaillant' but by 19 February the silk workers were forced to return to work through lack of funds.[115]

The government, by now quite paranoid about political opposition, convinced itself that the strike was the signal for the start of the much-discussed rising in eastern France. The *Droits de l'Homme* had made inroads among the weavers, but only on issues that affected them directly. There was no overt political aspect to the strike. However the imminence of the new legislation made a strict separation of economic and political motivation impossible. The workers were convinced that the new laws would even ban the *compagnonnages*, despite the government's repeated denials. The strike leaders were arrested and their trial fixed for the first week in April, when the law on associations was before the Chamber of Peers. Postponed, the trial opened on 9 April. Troops on duty around the *palais de justice* opened fire when stones were thrown. Barricades went up and the fighting continued until 15 April, leading to 300 deaths. There was never a chance of a takeover by the workers, as in November 1831. The weaving districts were bombarded by the artillery and fortifications built since the last rising effectively separated the outlying Croix Rousse weaving district from the inner-city areas. The weavers had virtually no reinforcements and initial heavy casualties among the troops were mostly due to their own inexperience in such fighting. Somewhere between 3000–6000 took part and 37 per cent of those arrested were weavers, mainly journeymen. The rest were mostly from other trades. Only 15 per cent were in either a political or workers' association. Of the one hundred arrested, only thirty-nine were republicans, and only eight were eventually tried.[116] Despite these figures the governments persisted in its claim that the unrest in Lyons was part of a massive republican plot.[117]

Mascarène had tried to oblige, stirring up the bored, underemployed soldiery wherever he could. Clement Thomas, a twenty-five-year-old junior officer stationed in Luneville, who had links with the *Droits de l'Homme* and leading figures like de Ludre, conceived a plan of leading the three Luneville regiments to Nancy and there linking up with the Nancy garrison to march on Paris. Following recent restructuring there were many discontented junior officers in these regiments. After a few meetings in local cafés with two other bored colleagues, Bernard and Tricotel, they decided to try their plan while Lyons was in revolt. Tricotel was despatched to Nancy to prepare the ground. On 16 April, after yet another meeting in a local café, the conspirators returned to barracks to prepare to march, but found that the plot was discovered. The leaders were arrested. Mascarène portrayed the affair as part of a concerted effort.[118] There were a few other isolated incidents and the Arbois club, true to form, declared a republic.[119]

There had been much talk of a rising in the capital, but the Parisian *Droits de l'Homme* hesitated. The government did not. Five hundred militants were arrested and the *Tribune* was banned. On 13 April barricades went up in central Paris, despite the opposition of the republican leaders. Within a day the attempt had been repressed with unnecessary bloodshed.[120] The massacre, depicted by Daumier with gruesome realism, turned the episode into a permanent altar of martyrdom for the left. The reputation of Orleanism for hard-faced brutality, the protection of the wealthy and degradation of the poor, was further reinforced. The pathetic attempts of local people to resist troops in the *rue* Transnonain emphasised that there was no organised conspiracy against the regime, although there was opposition to the new legislation against associations.

The government needed to invent a grand plot to justify otherwise irrelevant illiberal legislation. 2000 so-called leaders were arrested. After much delay 164 were finally brought to trial on 5 May 1835. Before the trial there was widespread sympathy for the incarcerated accused, as there did not seem to be much of a case to answer and as the court tried to dictate who could represent them. Some of the accused discredited themselves by bickering, however, and some refused to attend the hearings. The attempt on Louis-Philippe's life by Fieschi, a republican, robbed the accused of all public support, although he had no links with them at all. The trial ended uneventfully in January 1836. Trélat got three years and a fine of 10 000 francs for little more than a speech in which he declared, 'You are my political enemies, not my judges. You may condemn me, but not judge me, because you are quite unable to understand my ideas or my actions.'[121] Miran, the editor of the *Patriote* in Besançon, denied having any role in the supposed conspiracy, with the comment that he could not be condemned for his thoughts.[122] In fact the *Patriote* had published an article on the new legislation which concluded that a time would come to proclaim 'l'insurrection est un devoir'.[123] Several of those arrested, especially the young soldiers stationed in Epinal denied membership of the republican club, one said he only went to a meeting because he was rather drunk. Another young man replied that he never joined the society because his mother told him not to. Mascarène, not surprisingly, was acquitted.[124] It is clear from the evidence presented that despite Mascarène's inventions, there was no real case to answer. Some leading republicans escaped trial, including Cavaignac and Cabet who fled to England. In 1837 those who had been jailed were given amnesty and in 1840 those who had fled were allowed to return to France, which may indicate some official embarrassment at the exaggeration of the panic of 1834.

What of the clubs? In July 1834 the Dijon sections met to select candidates for the National Guard elections, which they habitually dominated, but the prefect commented, 'Il ne reste que les ouvriers et un petit nombre d'ambitieux déçus ou de fanatiques ruinés.'[125] The club had accumulated debts of 14 000 francs but by the end of the year it had regrouped as a *société d'harmonie* and gained official recognition.[126] Whatever their real aim, the name added a touch of humour, which the prefect would appreciate: he had long bemoaned the lack of such a society. The Dijon club was the only one to survive in the area and it was one of very few in the country. In the summer of 1835 the leader, Demay, was running a literary salon and bookshop in the town and was accused of selling seditious books. The local judiciary were too sympathetic to bring him before the tribunal, however.[127] The republican society also survived in Strasbourg as the *Cercle dit patriotique du café Faudel*. It was acquitted on charges of sedition in June 1835. In June 1836 they held a fund-raising banquet to help those jailed for political offences in the capital and raised 350 francs.[128] In 1839 the society had two hundred members, including twenty-three municipal councillors. The Chalons club re-emerged as a *société de bienfaisance* in 1835, and a branch of *Jeune Europe* was also set up with a subscription of fifty centîmes a month.[129] However, most clubs lacked the means, organisation or will to restructure themselves as legally constituted groups. Perhaps it would have taken the fun out of their distinctive hats and the dressing-up and posturing in the manner of Robespierre.

In September 1835 new press laws were brought in that increased the initial caution money to be paid by an editor, added to the range of possible crimes and certain punishments for refractory editors and removed press cases from the scrutiny of juries. Louis-Philippe could no longer be criticised for the policies of his governments and those who tried to do so risked a fine of 50 000 francs and a year in jail. No accounts of trials could be published and even the term 'republican' was banned.[130] Few opposition papers survived to experience the severity of the new laws. In Paris the *Tribune* had been pursued constantly since 1830 with 111 prosecutions, 20 condemnations, a total of 49 years jail for the editor and fines of 150 000 francs. The paper was forced to cease publication in May 1835. The *Réformateur*, similarly harried, closed a few months later. This left only the *National* and the monthly *Journal du Peuple*[131] to concentrate nervously on remaining circumspect, but sufficiently lively to hold their readers, and thus stay solvent. The new legislation was equally superfluous in the provinces. The *Sentinelle des Vosges* disappeared in 1833; the editor of the Besançon *Patriote*, accused of conspiring in April 1834, was sentenced to twenty years hard labour, only to be exposed as an embezzler who had lived in Besançon under a false name. His newspaper never reopened. The Dijon *Patriote*, acquitted on a charge of sedition in April 1834, survived until the new law, but with increasing difficulty; its sales fell from 470 to 354, 30 of which were actually given away. In the Puy-de-Dôme the *Patriote* survived the new laws; in Lyons the *Glaneuse* was almost bankrupt in January 1834 and closed down in March when its editor was jailed. Only the *Echo de la Fabrique* was still publishing out of a handful of earlier opposition newspapers.

The repressive legislation was unnecessary. Republicanism had never been a mass revolutionary movement and the popular unrest with which it coincided in 1830–32 faded as harvests improved and the economy recovered. Disputes over doctrine, the curse of the left, were self-indulgent, given the size of the movement. Supporters could not agree on whether the Convention or Robespierre should be their model, on the significance of social questions, on whether they should attempt to be a vanguard party and try to take power by force, or wait, as a pedagogical and philanthropic movement, for the rest of France to understand that a republic could unite as well as divide and could bring harmony and enlightenment. The republicans of the early 1830s were too dominated by republican history to understand and exploit the grievances of artisans and peasants.

Orleanist governments were momentarily nervous that such an alliance might develop, but they were more immediately concerned with the degree of opposition their policies encountered among their own officials, including prefects, mayors and members of the judiciary. Périer was ruthless in purging *mouvement* prefects. Interestingly, they were often the purest Bonapartists, unemployed since the Hundred Days, perhaps more rusty than radical.[132] The *résistance* government of March 1831 was more effective than any since the fall of Napoleon in selecting a reliable, efficient and reasonably intelligent prefectoral corps. Périer chose professionally trained administrators like Achille Chaper in Dijon, a friend of Rémusat, who sought to conciliate left- and right-wing opposition while maintaining his own authority intact. Having secured a loyal and stable prefectoral corps, Périer and his successors gradually eliminated the more radical men nominated after the revolution. By 1834 such purges were as complete as they could be, leaving radicals in only a few municipal councils, including some mayors, particularly where they were the only men who displayed an intelligent and willing aptitude for municipal affairs (in the view of the prefect). The officer corps of the National Guard, elected since 1831 by universal suffrage, also continued to be dominated by men who had run the republican clubs, partly because so few people showed any interest in the National Guard. In a few towns, such as Strasbourg, the Guard was so hostile that it had to be disarmed and dissolved.[133] More serious was the attitude of some members of the judiciary, because of their pivotal role and the permanence of their position. In both Dijon and Besançon the prefects hesitated to press charges of sedition against either republicans or legitimists, knowing that leading magistrates would oppose such cases and acquittal was certain. In Dijon several leading magistrates resigned over the law on associations, including the *procureur du roi*, a member of the *charbonnerie* before 1830, who refused to prosecute former friends. His deputy also resigned for the same reason, as did the *procureur* and his deputy in Semur, providing the opportunity to consolidate a conservative magistrature.

Probably most decisive in the fading of radicalism was growing confidence in the permanence of the existing regime. Few had believed that a republic was a practical possibility in 1830, but radical sentiments had been awakened quite widely among notables in the late 1820s by the anachronistic and counter-revolutionary inclinations of Charles X. His overthrow created a temporary ferment and led to the reawakening of revolutionary memories and traditions, among them a propensity to form political clubs, which inspired apprehension more because of the memory of the past than through the expectation of radical change in the present.[134] After some months of upheaval, the new regime developed a better technique of management than that of the Bourbons. Charles had tried to impose real central control and direction over the apparently highly centralised system he inherited. From 1831 the new regime effectively decentralised by accommodating itself to the views of the local notables and blocking the more radical attitudes of some sections of urban opinion, notably in Paris. This approach gave considerable freedom to local notables and the outspoken sympathy of some of them for radical views waned. However, although the comfortably-off liberal middle class supporters attracted by groups like *Aide-toi* were temporarily halted in their reforming zeal by the persistence of Orleanist repressive policies in 1834–5, some re-emerged as the backbone of the banquet campaign for electoral reform in the late 1830s and 1840s. The republicans were left as a small fringe, some middle-class lawyers and journalists, some modest businessmen and some artisans. A number of the more innovative thinkers, like Cabet turned from political action to utopian socialism. Republicanism did not escape its dictatorial, anarchic and bloody image, as the failures of 1848 and the Commune of 1871 were to show.

9
Conclusion

Far from being a bourgeois, Parisian and brief affair, the 1830 revolution emerges as one element in a multitude of popular disturbances which were conceptually diverse and geographically and chronologically broad in compass, and whose bourgeois dimensions were incompatible with Marxist theory, emphatically opportunist and anti-revolutionary. Let us lay to rest for ever that spectral and unconvincing species of an entrepreneurial middle-class revolutionary, but let us also question the existence of a dangerous and subversive species among artisans and peasants. Above all, we must dismiss the vision of insurrectionary artisans in alliance with the bourgeoisie to advance the cause of individual liberty and constitutional representative government.

There was no fundamental or structural reason why there should have been a revolution in 1830. The election results of 1827 and 1830 certainly catalogued the existence and success of the liberals but it was a very disparate and diffuse opposition. The liberals expressed the grievances of a tiny, wealthy elite. They were united in their criticism of the clerical policies of Restoration governments, they were hostile to restrictions on press freedom, they were suspicious of the indemnification of the *emigrés*. But Restoration royalists themselves were far from unanimous in their support for the unlimited revival of clerical influence; some ultras, like Chateaubriand, were also leading advocates of the liberty of the press and no one really believed that there was any threat to the revolutionary land settlement. To some degree the liberals were simply exploiting whatever political advantage offered itself. The resurgence of clerical influence was annoying and obstructive, but in so far as it was obviously part of the baggage of the ultras, it posed no real danger to the established social order while the ultras were a minority. The law of sacrilege was a piece of harmless anachronistic theatre. The accession of Charles X gave the church a higher profile, however. The ultras failed to increase their numbers in parliament to match the king's hopes, but there was no mechanism to prevent him shaping a government to his own taste, which he did in August 1829. Was there a real threat of counter-revolution, as liberals claimed? It seems unlikely: Charles was cautious and irresolute, but unpredictable. The ultras, even the group in office, were not in accord. In terms of official appointments, the answer must have seemed to be yes, as ultra aristocrats almost exclusively were appointed to vacant senior posts.

What united the liberals most of all were the almost ostentatiously public monkey tricks played by the government and its agents in falsifying electoral lists and elections themselves. Hence the formation of the cautiously legal *Aide-toi*. In the last resort, however, liberalism was far from solid. In many ways liberal criticism of the Polignac government was a facade: no one believed that the *ancien régime* could be revived and the liberals were almost as afraid as the ultras of the resurrection of the revolutionary ambiance of the 1790s. Only a tiny minority were prepared to make their war of words real and only when a ready-made riot presented itself under their noses.

If the liberals were not revolutionary, what of their opponents, the ultras? Restoration ultras were essentially innovative, being deeply hostile to the memory and institutions of the Revolution and Empire, but all but the most intransigent were aware that the 1814 settlement checked their worst terrors. The ultras were never more than a minority and were themselves divided and merged imperceptibly into the royalist majority. Was the extreme right genuinely afraid that the liberals were Jekyll and Hyde revolutionaries at heart? Or was this fear merely a pretence to win voters? Was the appearance of a right-wing attack on the constitution merely the result of ultra ignorance of the nuances of how the revolutionary years had affected political life? Or were the ultras very aware, despite their aura of reactionary romanticism, that the liberals were terrified of revolution and would therefore continue to allow themselves to be pushed around? Despite their small numbers in parliament, the ultras had secured a mass of favourable legislation since 1820 like the law of the double vote and the seven year law, not to mention blatant cheating in elections and the dissolution of the National Guard. Their greatest triumph was the appointment of a set of ultra ministers in August 1829, when the liberals were in possession of a comfortable parliamentary majority and, in terms of past practice, might reasonably expect to head a government themselves. The liberals appeared to be merely sound and fury and palpably the sound was a cacophony of discordant voices. Unquestionably Charles and his ministers hoped that the growth in opposition was merely the transient consequence of a short-term economic crisis. Some right-wingers seemed to expect to inherit the mantle of patriotism through the military success in Algeria, which they hoped would win support for Polignac. Were the four ordinances any more audacious than earlier press legislation and the law of the double vote? There was a chance that liberals would weigh the odds and that once more their own fear of insurrection would render them politically ineffective.

That the ordinances proved a catalyst for revolt was due not to the response of the parliamentary liberals, despite their large majority at the recent election, but to the fusion of two other factors, artisan unrest and the resistance of a section of the liberal press. What was the basis of artisan protest? In the traditional Marxist revolutionary catechism economic circumstances were the determinants of revolution. Any self-respecting revolution worthy of its name had to be accompanied by an economic crisis,[1] and fortunately the nineteenth century was well littered with examples of cyclical economic depression, with and without attendant revolutions. Contemporary ultraroyalists also believed that the opposition encountered by Charles X in parliament was a product of economic disasters from 1827 onwards. There is no doubt that the depression gave fuel to government critics. The Martignac government itself crystallised the debate in parliament by its official enquiries into the problems of major sections of the economy. The wealthy unquestionably and predictably blamed the administration of the day for their own difficulties. This did not, however, create a revolutionary situation. Firstly, because the entrepreneurial bourgeoisie were divided in their interpretation of both the causes of the depression and viable remedies. Secondly because they were anxious to prevent popular protests against short-time working, reduced wages and other measures because such riots harmed them most. Finally because the results of the elections show incontrovertibly that the Restoration prefects were wrong in claiming that the entrepreneurial middle class alone was liberal. By 1830 only 143 government supporters were elected in the whole of France. The Restoration had served producers of both agrarian and industrial goods faithfully, paying constant attention to their needs and demands. The years from 1818 until

1827 were ones of considerable prosperity and growth.[2] Martignac was visibly the least sympathetic minister in the period: the tone of his enquiry into the iron industry clearly implied that producers were at least partly to blame because they were unwilling to innovate and use coal for smelting. The point was not pressed. The liberal opposition was brought together not over economic matters, but political problems, specifically Polignac. It is in the response of the poor that the fuse of revolution can be detected. In Paris, in smaller towns and in the countryside there was widespread unrest during 1828–30. The 'shapers' who converted spasmodic, disconnected riot into revolution were the Parisian journalists, themselves enraged by the first of the four ordinances, which threatened long-term unemployment for them if enforced. They were the first to protest against the ordinances and their intervention was decisive. The deputies, on the other hand, were divided and proved timid and reluctant revolutionary leaders.

The revolution must be seen in a broader chronological, geographical and conceptual context than the political crisis alone. Popular unrest, not the quarrels of the elite, lost Paris for the king. What is more, this was not confined to the capital in the 'Three Glorious Days' but extended from the reign of Louis XVI until the 1850s and beyond. In the past the ubiquity and consistency of popular protest has been relatively uncharted, except when it coincided with the more concerted and coherent complaints of the better-off in periods of short-term depression occasioned by harvest failure and loss of confidence in financial circles. The poor were principally and consistently concerned about protecting traditional institutions and values. They opposed the modernisation of the economy and accompanying structural change. In doing so they were, in reality, always at odds with the better-off, educated men who became leaders of successful risings. If the poor were volatile and prepared to fight it was not for 'progressive', rational and enlightened 'reform', but the reverse. They fought the erosion of communal rights, which suffered most in the hands of the revolutionaries of the 1790s. They tried to defend the independence of the artisans and the integrity of guild formations, in whose destruction the 1789 Revolution was also an active agent. By the 1820s some became Luddites as new machines presented tangible targets, but by the 1830s there was open social conflict, for instance between weavers and merchants in Lyons. Early bourgeois socialists attacked the evils of 'competition' and sought ways to revive an artisan economy along communal lines. Such long-term grievances were instrumental in destabilising central government in conjunction with short-term economic depression produced by harvest failure, financial and commercial crises or war. This was evident in the 1790s, 1830, 1848 and 1871, but those who actually took part in physical protests were never the beneficiaries. The objectives of the poor were always at variance with ambitious politicians who used their grievances for political advantage. The politically astute were always modernisers themselves. In the past historians influenced by a Marxist dogma assumed that there existed some sort of alliance between the two. In reality central government, whatever its genesis, indeed the revolutionary variety in particular, was the enemy of those who did not want to move forward, but back to a perhaps romanticised, idealised, stable and just society in which the poor were protected by communal traditions. The Lyons *canut* was a reactionary, compelled to use violent, 'revolutionary' means to protect his livelihood. The volatility of nineteenth-century France compared with today can be related, in large part, to this social distress and protest.

The instability of nineteenth-century regimes was linked to more than the repeated volcanic onslaught of the poor. Why were governments able to retain control in some situations – 1817–18, 1830–34, 1839 and 1851 – while in others they failed to do so? Policing and psychology seem to provide an answer. Why were there too few troops in Paris in July 1830 and why were they poorly equipped and provisioned? One might envisage the answer in terms of the failure of management techniques or the accident of individual personalities. There is also the possibility that at times there was a crisis of confidence, a lack of conviction that a particular situation could be managed. From the 1790s there was widespread apprehension among property owners that anarchic revolution was an inbuilt element of any situation. Few believed in permanent stability. Most assumed that revolution brought real change. The extreme right was convinced that France was set on a downward path of decline into hell-fire as a result of the 1789 Revolution. Marxists argued that revolution was a permanent feature of social and political change, an upward slope towards an ideal and classless future. Liberals feared revolution, but assumed that progressive gradual change would preserve an elitist society. There was, of course, some element of credibility in such generalisations, but they were all too systematic and too rational. In a volatile situation, chance and individual panic could have a not inconsiderable impact, to be tidied, explained and organised by those who gained control after the event and aided and abetted by later historians. The shadow of the guillotine must have made a contribution to the rapid self-imposed exile of deposed nineteenth-century rulers. In 1830 there was the additional problem that the army still retained Bonapartist sympathisers, while lack of action and/or promotion accompanied by low pay created a predisposition to disloyalty in a tough situation.

The July Days displayed the fragility of the centralised state. France temporarily, but enthusiastically, dissolved into a multitude of municipal liberal republics run by their *Aide-toi* committees. Their decisions on new appointments were generally respected by the new government. France was a formally centralised state, 1830 was a revolution effected in the capital, but as Tudesq and others have demonstrated, it was the writ of the individual local notable that counted for most. A successful Parisian government wooed such notables rather than bullying them as Charles X had tried to do.

What was changed by the revolution? At the outset there was no consensus, apart from the need to avoid civil war, a repetition of the 1790s and foreign intervention on behalf of the Bourbons. This collection of pious negatives left the way open to the more conservative liberals, soon dubbed the *résistance*, to grab the best jobs and change as little as possible. The constitution of 1830 must hold the record for speed of completion. It is not entirely fair to see the victors as self-seeking cynics: their quarrel had been with Charles X and his ultra associates, not with the 1814 constitution. The anti-clericalism of the Orleanist monarchy was similarly consistent. Conservative Orleanists were appalled by the waves of anti-clerical protest following the July Days, bringing attacks on property, threats to individual ultra senior clerics, most of whom had the wisdom to leave France, and the hacking down of missionary crosses and their replacement by trees of liberty, often surmounted by the red republican cap. Such behaviour smacked of social chaos and anarchy, especially when encouraged by less conservative former liberals ensconsed in office. *Résistance* ministers like Casimir Périer were determined to crush violent demonstrations against the church. Churchmen and Orleanists shared some objectives, in particular the preservation of social conservatism. The church was, however, expected to be a passive organ of social control. Its officials thought otherwise and in the name of freedom of education fought the Guizot law that permitted the setting up of primary schools run by communes. Church–state antagonism was further stimulated by the success of the church in running a wider and more popular range of schools than did the lay authorities.

The Bourbons receded into the background. Legitimists were divided in their allegiance. Charles disdained any attempt at a third Restoration, Henri was too young to be an independent candidate and the exploits of his mother relegated the subject to the level of embarrassing farce. Legitimists were not passive hostile spectators, as has been suggested. Tudesq has ably documented the high level of their participation in local politics, as mayors, members of local councils and as deputies. Their hostility to the regime, sometimes sustained by co-operation with republicans in election campaigns, was kept alive by Orleanist educational policies.

Was 1830 a social, bourgeois or artisan revolution? The concept of a bourgeois revolution was acclaimed by the unusual unanimity of legitimists, Orleanists and left-wing critics. Only the legitimists believed that 1830 actually brought the bourgeoisie to power; the others claimed that the revolution merely confirmed their ascendancy. The bourgeoisie they described included many different elements, from landowners, civil servants and professionals to a small, but growing body of entrepreneurs. The legitimists put particular emphasis on the last element. Marx further emphasised the role of the businessmen, pointing to the elevation of two bankers as chief ministers within nine months of the revolution. Marxists subsequently slotted 1830 into a systematic theory of revolution dictated by economic imperatives. 1830 was supposed to be a stage in the ascendancy of the entrepreneurial middle class and the decline of the feudal landed aristocracy. All nineteenth-century revolutions, and finally 1917 in Russia, were knit together by the Marxists, optimistic that they had a total explanation of history. The right identified the same phenomenon, but interpreted it as an overwhelming disaster. They remained convinced that society was crumbling as a result of the rise of a capitalist and often Jewish bourgeoisie.

There was no real challenge to the 'bourgeois' revolution until after the Second World War. Revisionist reworking of 1789 necessitated a reinterpretation of later revolutions. Sherman Kent showed that the elite of the July Monarchy remained principally one of landowners. Tudesq exhaustively demonstrated this, defining the wealthy as notables, who shared many interests, whether noble or bourgeois in ancestry. The persistence of the nobility as the dominant wealthy group in nineteenth-century France seems to support the case of the revisionists, although the debate is by no means complete. In their determination to disprove the wilder Marxist claims, which most Marxists have long abandoned, the revisionists have overstated their case and fudged genuine social differences and divisions. While there can be little doubt that 1830 did not bring a capitalist bourgeoisie to power – their numbers were too small and most entrepreneurs were not over-eager for an active political role – 1830 was self-consciously and assertively a bourgeois revolution. Louis-Philippe was hailed as a bourgeois king, however silly that may sound; the hereditary peerage was abolished; the new rulers gloried in the idea of bourgeois power. To grasp the reality behind the myth, we must remember that Cabet, in this respect, was correct and that bourgeois rule meant stability, not innovation. The rule of the bourgeoisie meant the dominance of a traditional landed and professional middle class.

What of the 'révolution escamotée'? Was 1830 a social revolution in this sense? The answer must be both yes and no. The Parisian artisans were never more than a catalyst of political change and in 1830 had no expectations of direct political power. There was no distinct 'revolution of the people', subsequently smuggled away by the elite. On the other hand, without street fighting the Restoration regime would have remained. The dimensions of social grievance were very wide and chronologically extensive. In this sense there was a continuing revolt of the poor, out of tune with any central government, a volcanic factor in the genesis and nemesis of nearly all nineteenth-century regimes. It was a legacy which terrified its beneficiaries within the elite. Perhaps the most destabilising factor was the ever-present fear of those who governed as a consequence of revolution that their own authority was transitory.

Notes*

1 HISTORIANS AND THE REVOLUTION

1. J. L. Bory, *La Révolution de Juillet* (1972). In a brief article Agulhon pressed for a revival of interest in 1830 and urged that a less cynical view be taken of the sincerity of the liberal bourgeoisie's motives. M. Algulhon, '1830 dans l'histoire du XIXe siècle', *Romanticisme, Revue du XIXe siècle*, 28–9 (1980) 15–27. Reprinted in *Histoire vagabonde II. Idéologie et politique dans la France du XIXe siècle* (1988) pp. 31–48.
2. D. H. Pinkney, *The French Revolution of 1830* (1972).
3. C. H. Church, *Europe in 1830* (1983).
4. A. J-A. M. Prince de Polignac, *Etudes Historiques, politiques et morales* (1845) p. 319.
5. Ibid., pp. 255–6.
6. C. Lemercher de Longpre, baron d'Haussez, *Mémoires*, vol. II (1896–7) pp. 231–6.
7. P. D. comte de Peyronnet, *Discours de M. le comte de Peyronnet prononcé devant la cour des pairs, 19 décembre 1830*, p. 12.
8. J. B. S. G. vicomte de Martignac, *Défense de M. le Prince Jules de Polignac* (1831) p. 8.
9. Quoted in G. de Bertier de Sauvigny, *La Révolution de 1830 en France* (1970).
10. C. Drumont, *La France Juive* (1888) p. 16.
11. E. Beau de Lomenie, *Les responsibilités des dynasties bourgeoises* (1964).
12. F. P. G. Guizot, *Mémoires pour servir à l'histoire de mon temps*, vol. I (1858) p. 27.
13. A. Thiers, *La monarchie de 1830* (1831) p. 17.
14. P. L. Duvergier de Hauranne, *Histoire du gouvernement parlementaire*, vol. X (1857–72) p. 485. He was a left-wing opponent of Guizot and one of the organisers of the campaign for parliamentary reform in the 1840s.
15. Guizot, *Mémoires*, vol. I, p. 3.
16. F. Guizot, *Mémoires, pour servir à l'histoire de mon temps*, vol. II (1859) pp. 16–17.
17. Duc de Broglie, *Souvenirs*, vol. III (1886) p. 393.
18. C. F. M. de Rémusat (ed. C. H. Pouthas), *Mémoires de ma vie*, vol. II (1959) p. 367.

---

* For full details of the works cited in these notes see the extensive Bibliography, pp. 216–33.

19. Thiers, *La Monarchie de 1830*, p. 55.
20. A. de Tocqueville, *Recollections* (trans. G. Lawrence, 1971) p. 5.
21. P. Thureau-Dangin, *Histoire de la Monarchie de Juillet* (1884–92).
22. P. Thureau-Dangin, *Royalistes et Républicains* (1874) p. 327.
23. L. de Carné, *Des intérêts nouveaux en Europe depuis la Révolution de 1830*, vol. I (1838) pp. 30, 217.
24. L. Blanc, *Revolution Française. Histoire de Dix Ans* (1841) pp. 175–7.
25. Cabet, *La Révolution de 1830 et la situation présente* (1831) p. 119. He enlarged these views in a fuller study, *Histoire populaire de la Révolution française 1789–1830*, vol. IV (1840) p. 630.
26. J. P. A. Villeneuve-Bargemont, *Economie politique chrétienne* (1834).
27. L. R. Villermé, *Tableau de l'état physique et moral des ouvriers employés dans les manufactures* (1840).
28. L. Blanc, 'Organisation du Travail', in J. A. R. Marriot, *The French Revolution of 1848 in its economic aspect*, I, (1913).
29. E. Cabet, *Ma ligne droite, ou le vrai chemin du peuple* (1841).
30. P. Leroux, *De la ploutocratie, ou gouvernement des riches* (1848) p. 123.
31. K. Marx, *The Eighteenth Brumaire of Louis Bonaparte* (1852, 1926).
32. S. Charléty, *La Restauration* (1921) pp. 346, 370.
33. S. Kent, *Electoral procedure under Louis-Philippe* (1937).
34. A. Cobban, 'The myth of the French Revolution', inaugural lecture, University College, London, 1955; reprinted in *Aspects of the French Revolution* (1968). This began the re-examination.
35. A. J. Tudesq, *Les Grands Notables en France 1840–49. Etude historique d'une psychologie sociale* (1964).
36. T. D. Beck, *French Legislators 1800–34. A study in quantative history* (1974) pp. 133–45.
37. 'La reorganisation du ministère de l'intérieur et la reconstitution de l'administration préfectorale par Guizot en 1830', *Revue d'histoire moderne et contemporaine*, IX (1962) 241–63.
38. Pinkney, *The French Revolution of 1830*, p. 293.
39. H. A. C. Collingham, *The July Monarchy. A Political History of France 1830–48* (1988) p. 256.
40. Bory, *La Révolution de Juillet*, p. 701.
41. G. de Bertier de Sauvigny, *La Restauration* (1955) pp. 457–8. de Sauvigny compiled a useful survey of recent historiography: 'Quarante ans d'historiographie: 1940–1980', *Romanticisme: Revue du XIXe siècle*, 28–9 (1980) 69–84.
42. J. Merriman (ed.) *1830 in France* (1975).

2 THE POLITICAL CRISES OF THE BOURBON RESTORATION

1. *Compte annuel*, 1818. AN F1cIII Moselle 9. P. Leuilliot, *L'Alsace au début du XIXe siècle. Essai d'histoire politique, économique et religieuse, 1815–30*, vol. I (1959) p. 81.
2. P. Guillon, *Les complots militaires sous la Restauration* (1905) pp. 6–38.

3. P. Chalmin, *L'officier français de 1815 à 1870* (1957) pp. 69–73.
4. R. Holyrood, 'The Bourbon army 1815–30', *Historical Journal*, XIV (1971) 3, 540.
5. G. Weill, *Histoire du parti républicain en France de 1814 à 1870* (1900) p. 1.
6. F. Guizot, *Des moyens de gouvernement et des moyens d'opposition dans l'état actuel de la France* (1821).
7. P. Buonarroti, *Conspiration des égaux, dite de Babeuf* (1828).
8. D. W. Johnson, *Guizot. Aspects of French History 1787–1874* (1963) pp. 119–21.
9. Reports on *Conspiration de l'Est* can be found in prefectoral accounts of local happenings. For example in *AN*, F7.9682: *Situation des départements de 1814 à 1830*. This series is organised on a departmental basis. Judicial reports also occur in *AN* BB30 where they are grouped according to *cours royaux. AN* BB30.237 and 240 provide useful accounts.
10. A. Calmette, 'Les carbonaris en France sous la Restauration', *La Révolution de 1848*, X (1913–14) 135. J. A. Faucher and A. Ricker, *Histoire de la franc-maçonnerie en France* (1967) p. 274. U. Trélat, 'La Charbonnerie', *Paris Révolutionnaire*, II (1838) 275–341.
11. Report of *procureur-général* to *garde des sceaux*, 1 Jan. 1822, *AN* BB30.240. A. Brandt, 'Quelques aspects de la vie politique à Mulhouse sous la Restauration', *Bulletin de la société industrielle de Mulhouse*, 101 (1935) 351. L. Delabrousse, 'Les députés de l'Alsace sous la Restauration', *Revue Alsacienne* (1883–4) 62.
12. Faucher and Ricker, *Histoire de la franc-maçonnerie*, p. 271.
13. St-Die, *Les Amis Incorruptibles des Vosges*, 25 Dec. 1829. *Bibliothèque Nationale, Fonds Franc-maçonnerie*.
14. P. Barral, 'La franc-maçonnerie en Lorraine XIX–XX siècles', *Annales de l'Est* (1970) 15.
15. Report to minister of interior, 3 Jan. 1822. *AN* BB30.240.
16. To *garde des sceaux*, 5 Feb. 1822. *AN* BB30.241.
17. Prefect, Haut-Rhin, 3 May 1830, *AN* CC574. Evidence given at the trial of the ex-ministers of Charles X.
18. B. Fitzpatrick, *Catholic royalism in the department of the Gard, 1814–52* (1983).
19. P. Leuilliot, *L'Alsace au début du XIXe siècle. Essai d'histoire politique, économique et religieuse, 1815–30*, vol. I (1959) p. 7.
20. M. Hartmann, 'The sacrilige law of 1825 in France: a study in anti-clericalism and myth-making', *Journal of Modern History* (1972), 35.
21. *AN* F1cIII Nord 5.
22. *AN* F7.4352A.
23. Cf., ch. 3.
24. S. Kent, *The Election of 1827 in France* (1975) pp. 25–30.
25. Chamber of Deputies, 19 March 1829, M. J. Mavidal and H. E. Laurent, *Archives Parlementaires*, LXII, p. 637.
26. Leuilliot, *L'Alsace au début du XIXe siècle*, p. 516.
27. C. Charton, 'Souvenirs de 1814 à 1848', *Annales de la Société*

d'*Emulation des Vosges*, XIV (1872) 4, 229. Charton was *chef de bureau* at the prefecture.
28. 19 Jan. 1824, *AN* F1cIII Ardennes 4.
29. Nov. 1827, *AN* F1cIII Meuse 6.
30. *L'Impartial*, 11 July 1830, *AD* Doubs. The *Impartial* was the local liberal newspaper and rallied opinion against the wine taxes.
31. Cf., ch. 3.
32. Kent, *The Election of 1827 in France*, p. 65.
33. *Aide-toi, Manuel de l'electeur en fonctions*. *BN* Lb49.1330. There is a fairly representative collection of the *Aide-toi* pamphlets for 1827–30 in the *Bibliothèque Nationale*.
34. Prefect to minister of interior, 22 July 1830, *AN* F1cIII Nord 5.
35. *Dossier personnel* Nau de Champlouis, 25 Aug. 1829, *AN* F1bI.168i.
36. Cf., ch. 3.
37. *Aide-toi*, 25 Aug. 1829, *BN* Lb49.1096.
38. Prefectoral reports, Jan. 1829, *AD* Calvados M 16212.
39. D. L. Rader, *The Journalists and the July Revolution in France* (1973) p. 19.
40. I. Collins, *The government and newspaper press in France 1814–81* (1959).
41. *Journal de Carion*, 28 Oct. 1829.
42. *Association pour le refus de l'impôt*. A substantial correspondence exists in *AN* F7.6742 and F7.6754.
43. *L'Annonciateur Boulonnais*, 3 Dec. 1829, *AN* F7.6742.
44. His speech was circulated to all prefects: *AD* Puy de Dôme M62, for example.
45. Rader, *The Journalists*, pp. 208–9.
46. For example, *Aide-toi*, 15 April 1830, *AN* F7.6718.
47. 18 April 1830, *AN* F7.6718.

3 THE ECONOMIC CRISIS AND THE REVOLUTION

1. Cf., ch. 6 and P. M. Pilbeam, *The Middle Class in Europe 1789–1914; France, Germany, Italy and Russia* (1990), especially ch. 1.
2. E. Labrousse, 'Comment naissent les révolutions', *Actes du congrès historique du centénaire de la Révolution de 1848* (1948). Reprinted in F. Crouzet, W. H. Chaloner and W. M. Stern, *Essays in European Economic History 1789–1914* (1969), 4.
3. J. P. Gonnet, 'Esquisse de la crise économique en France de 1827–32', *Revue d'histoire économique et sociale*, XXXIII (1955) pp. 290–91.
4. de Sauvigny, *La Révolution*.
5. Pinkney, *The French Revolution*.
6. J. Merriman (ed.), *1830 in France* (1975).
7. J. B. M. Braun, *Nouvelle biographie des députés ou Statistique de la Chambre de 1814 à 1829* (1830) pp. 53–4.
8. P. M. Pilbeam, 'The growth of liberalism and the crisis of the

Notes 199

Bourbon Restoration', *Historical Journal,* XXV (1982) 2, 351.
9. C. Dupin, *Forces productives et forces commerciales de la France* (1827) p. xxx.
10. J. M. Dutens, *Essai comparatif sur la formation et la distribution du revenu de la France en 1815 et 1835,* vol. I (1842) p. 15. Dutens gives a total of 10 billion kilos for 1815 and 15 billion for 1835, but his supposed 1815 statistic was from J. A. C. Chaptal, *De l'industrie française* (1819), none of whose figures refer to beyond 1812.
11. Villermé, *Tableau de l'état.*
12. L. Mounier, *De l'agriculture en France d'après les documents officiels,* vol. 1 (1846) p. 291.
13. Grain imports 1821–33, *AN* F20.560.
14. Labrousse, 'Comment naissent les révolutions'.
15. *Grains et subsistances,* Gendarmerie reports, *AN* F7.6690, 6691.
16. *Journal de Nicholas Lebert.* This local *juge de paix* kept a diary which is largely filled with very detailed descriptions of the weather, apparently an absorbing passion for many contemporaries. Lebert has far more to say about the bad winter of 1829–30 and the hot July of 1830 than about the revolutionary events. *AD* Haute-Marne *Série J.*
17. *Ministère de l'Agriculture et du Commerce. Direction de l'Agriculture. Bureau des Subsistance. Récoltes des céreales et de pommes de terres de 1815 à 1876* (1878), 470.
18. To minister of interior, 20 April 1830, *AD* Eure 1M227.
19. E. Labrousse, R. Romano and F. G. Dreyfus, *Le prix de froment en France au temps de monnaie stable 1726–1913* (1970), p. xxxv.
20. Sub-prefect, Cambrai, to prefect, Nord, 24 April 1829, *AD* Nord M433/42.
21. L. Tilly, 'La récolte frumentaire, forme de conflit politique en France,' *Annales: Économies, Sociétés, Civilisations,* 27 (1972) i, 757.
22. *Procureur-général,* Dijon, to *garde des sceaux,* April 1829. *AN* BB18.1170.
23. Prefect of Nord to lieutenant of gendarmerie, Lille, 22 April 1829. *AD* Nord M433/42.
24. Prefect of Nord to minister of interior, 15 July 1829, *AN* F7.9685.
25. *AD* Ille-et-Vilaine. 1M98.
26. Gendarmerie report, Moselle, 27 May 1829, *AN* F7.6691.
27. *AN* F7.9685.
28. Romeuf, head of eighteenth military division to prefect of Haute-Marne, 17 May 1829, and reply, 23 May, *AD* Haute-Marne 146M1.
29. 8 Jan. 1830, *AD* Calvados M16212.
30. *AD* Seine-Maritime 1M162. Sympathetic comments from several mayors in the spring of 1829, including Elbeuf.
31. L. de Chateauvieux, *Voyages agronomiques en France,* vol. I (1843) p. 453.
32. 'Tableau par département de l'étendue et la culture de la vigne', *AN* F20.560.
33. Leuilliot, *L'Alsace au début du XIXe siècle,* vol. II, p. 130.
34. M. J. Mavidal and M. E. Laurent, *Archives parlementaires de 1787 à 1860* (2nd series), vol. LVIII (1888) p. 413.
35. Leuilliot, *L'Alsace au début du XIXe siècle,* vol. II, pp. 44, 121–8.

36. Mavidal and Laurent, *Archives Parlementaires*.
37. *AN* F20.744.
38. Mavidal and Laurent, *Archives Parlementaires*.
39. *Chambre de Commerce*, Clermont-Ferrand, 20 Jan. 1829, *AN* F12.2498.
40. *AN* C.2097.
41. Annual gendarmerie report, Côte-d'Or, 1829, *AN* F7.3970.
42. *AN* F20.560.
43. *L'Impartial*, 13 Sept. 1829, *AD* Doubs.
44. Gendarmerie report, 10 July 1830, *AN* F7.6778.
45. *AN* F7.4079. *AD* Haute-Marne 146M1.
46. *Procureur-général*, political report, 13 Oct. 1829, *AD* Doubs 13U8.
47. P. M. Pilbeam, 'Popular violence in provincial France after the 1830 Revolution', *English Historical Review*, XCI (1976) 278–97.
48. 1 Aug. 1828, *AN* F7.6772. See also A. Daumard, 'L'evolution des structures sociales en France à l'époque de l'industrialisation', *Revue Historique* (1972) 247, 329.
49. L. Ame, *Etude sur les droits de douanes et les traités de commerce*, vol. I (1867) p. 62, and G. Ellis, *Napoleon's continental blockade: the case of Alsace* (1981) p. 85.
50. E. Levasseur, *Histoire des classes ouvrières et de l'industrie en France de 1789 à 1870* vol. I (1903) p. 566.
51. Leuilliot, op. cit., vol. II, p. 375.
52. Levasseur, op. cit., p. 582.
53. A. M. Heron de Villefosse, 'Des métaux en France', *Annales des Mines* (1827) 42.
54. J. B. F. Faiseau Lavanne, *Recherches statistiques sur les forêts de la France* (1829) p. 91 and J. J. Baude, *De l'enquête sur les fers* (1829) p. 51.
55. Muel-Doublat, forge owner, Meuse, evidence to commission on iron industry, 29 Nov. 1828, *AN* F12.2530.
56. Becquey, *directeur-général Ponts et Chaussés et Mines* to comte de St Cricq, *président de bureau, Commerce et Colonies*, 2 Nov. 1825, *AN* F12.2531.
57. *Directeur-général Ponts et Chaussés et Mines*, 'Etat des hauts fourneaux allant à la houille 1825', *AN* F12.2531.
58. Becquey to comte de St Cricq, *AN* F12.2531.
59. Baude, op. cit., p. 47.
60. A. M. Heron de Villefosse, 'Mémoire sur l'état actuel des usines de fer de la France 1826', in J. G. V. de Moléon (ed.), *Recueil Industriel*, vol. III (1827) pp. 187–90.
61. 'Etat des hauts fourneaux', *AN* F12.2531.
62. An application to establish a new blast furnace at Anglus, Haute-Marne, in 1827, was fiercely contested by a group of local iron-masters on the grounds that the owner could supply only one-sixth of the wood he needed for smelting. *Journal politique, littéraire et d'annonces du département de la Haute-Marne*, 30 Dec. 1826, *AD* Haute-Marne *Bibliothèque Barotte*.
63. F. Danelle to Berthelin brothers, iron-masters, 7 Dec. 1831, *AD* Haute-Marne *Archives de la famille Berthelin* 6J150 and 'Charles Seraphim Joseph Gauguier au Mm. les maîtres de forges des

départements de la Haute-Marne, Meuse et Vosges, 22 Nov. 1829', *Archives de la famille Berthelin* 6J150.
64. AN F12.3532.
65. M. Levy-Leboyer, 'Innovation and business strategies in nineteenth- and twentieth-century France', in E. Carter (ed.), *Enterprise and Entrepreneurs in Nineteenth and Twentieth Century France* (1976) pp. 102–3.
66. M. Mieg, *Relation historique des progrès de l'industrie commerciale Mülhausen et ses environs* (1823) p. 19.
67. E. Dollfus, 'Rapport sur les métiers à tisser à la mécanique, 30 Oct. 1829,' *Bulletin de la Société Industrielle de Mulhouse*, iii (1830) 338–9.
68. M. M. Kahan-Rabecq, *L'Alsace économique et sociale sous le règne de Louis-Philippe* (1939) 14.
69. Dupin, *Forces productives*, vol. I, pp. 255–63.
70. AN F7.4137.
71. *Statistique Générale, Commerce Extérieure de 1787 à 1837* (1838) p. 433.
72. Gendarmerie report, Haut-Rhin, Feb. 1828, AN F7.4137.
73. Ibid., March and May 1827.
74. Ibid., March 1828.
75. Gendarmerie report, 16 Jan. 1830, AN F7.9685.
76. Dupin, *Forces productives*, vol. i, p. 263.
77. AN F7.6767.
78. Villermé, *Tableau de l'état*, p. 40.
79. A. Penot, *Recherches statistiques sur Mulhouse* (1843) pp. 152–3, 157.
80. N. Koechlin, *Enqûete Commerciale. Interrogation du Président du Chambre de Commerce de Mulhouse* (1835) p. 17.
81. R. J. Bezucha, *The Lyon Uprising of 1834* (1974) offers a sound and accessible account of the industry.
82. A. Blanqui, 'Extrait de la relation d'un voyage au midi de la France pendant août et septembre 1828', *Archives historiques, statistiques et littéraires du département du Rhône*, vol. IX (1828–9) p. 394.
83. J. A. F. O., 'Mémoire sur l'état actuel des soieries en France', in J. V. G. de Moléon, *Annales de l'industrie manufacturière, l'agriculture et commerce*, vol. I (1827) p. 80.
84. D. Truchon, 'La vie économique à Lyon 1814–30', *Revue d'histoire de Lyon* XI (1912) 205.
85. *Statistique Générale*, pp. 470–71.
86. AN F7.4144.
87. F. Dutacq and A. Latreille, *Histoire de Lyon de 1814 à 1940* in A. Kleinclausz (ed.), *Histoire de Lyon*, vol. III (1952) p. 60.
88. Report made by C. Dupin to *Académie de Lyon*, 17 Feb. 1829, *Archives historiques, statistiques et littéraires du département du Rhône*, vol. X (1829) pp. 99–101. See also Dutacq and Latreille, *Histoire de Lyon*, op. cit., pp. 555–60.
89. AN F7.6771.
90. J. Bron, *Histoire du mouvement ouvrier français*, vol. I (1970) p. 51.
91. AN F7.6771.
92. G. and H. Bourgin, *Le régime de l'industrie en France, 1815–30*, vol. III (1912–41) p. 268.
93. Ibid., p. 246.

94. AN F7.6771.
95. A. Chaptal, *De l'industrie française*, vol. I, pp. 178–9.
96. Levasseur, op. cit., p. 584.
97. 'Tableau statistique de l'industrie manufacturière 1825', *AD* Pas-de-Calais M1212.
98. 14 July 1828, *AN* F7.9685.
99. Prefect's reports, Aube, 26 Jan. and 26 Nov. 1829, *AN* F7.6767.
100. C. Charton, 'Souvenirs de 1814 à 1848', p. 234.
101. Ardennes, 26 Feb. 1830, *AN* F7.6768.
102. M. Agulhon, *La république au village* (1970), A. Corbin, *Archaisme et Modernité en Limousin 1845–80* (1975) and P. M. Jones, *Politics and rural society. The Southern Massif Central c. 1750–1880* (1985).
103. Villeneuve-Bargemont, *Economie politique chrétienne*, vol. I (1834) p. 17.
104. Cf., ch. 6.
105. Dupin, *Forces productives*, op. cit., p. 249.
106. L. Chevalier, *Classes laborieuses et classes dangereuses à Paris pendant la première moitié eu XIXe siècle* (1958, also in trans).

4 THE 'THREE GLORIOUS DAYS'

1. *Moniteur Universel*, 26 July 1830.
2. D. L. Rader, *The Journalists*, p. 230.
3. *AN* CC547.
4. de Sauvigy, *La Restauration*, p. 449. Pinkney, *The French Revolution*, p. 121, cites the official figures of 496 insurgents and 150 soldiers killed.
5. Pinkney, *The French Revolution*, pp. 252–73.
6. O. Barrot, *Mémoires posthumes*, vol. I, p. 106.
7. Beck, *French Legislators 1800–34*, p. 133. Beck identifies a generational divide within the new Orleanist elite.
8. A. Esler, '"Youth in revolt": the French generation of 1830', in R. Bezucha (ed.), *Modern European Social History* (1972) p. 326.
9. N. Newman, 'What the crowd wanted in the French Revolution of 1830', in J. Merriman (ed.), *1830 in France* (1975) p. 17.
10. Pinkney, *The French Revolution*, p. 258.
11. Ibid., pp. 252–73.
12. Newman, 'What the crowd wanted', pp. 17–22.
13. de Sauvigny, *La Révolution*, p. 73.
14. L. Girard, *La garde nationale, 1814–71* (1964) pp. 160–63.
15. Reprinted in de Sauvigny, *La Révolution*, p. 223. The proclamation was signed by Audry de Puyraveau, Mauguin, de Schonen and Odilon Barrot as secretary.
16. de Remusat (ed. Pouthas), *Mémoires*, pp. 350–51.
17. Cf., Pinkney, *The French Revolution* for an analytical revisionist approach. Much affected by the *événements* of May 1968 is Bory, *La Révolution de Juillet*, which is notable for a breath-taking recreation of the confusion of a revolutionary situation and a wealth of

18. P. M. Pilbeam, 'The "Three Glorious Days": the Revolution of 1830 in provincial France', *Historical Journal*, 26 (1983) 4, 831–44. A small number of centenary articles were published in *Revue d'histoire moderne*, VI (1931).
19. de Sauvigny, *La Révolution*.
20. The following diaries were helpful: Lebert's *Journal* (he was a designer for the textile manufacturer, Hartmann, who was a member of the liberal elite on Alsace); *Bibliothèque Municipale*, Colmar; Nicholas Louet, a *juge de paix* in Bar-sur-Aube, while primarily interested in meteorology, makes dry, humorous comments on the official world; *AD* Haute-Marne; J. Maillard de Chambure, a *juge* in the *Cour royale*, Dijon, was a Bourbon sympathiser who nonetheless took the oath to Louis-Philippe; *Journal des événements politiques en juillet 1830*; *BM* Dijon, Fonds Milsand; Charles Weiss, a literary, rather conservative and timid liberal, was librarian in Besançon; *Journal BM* Besançon – selections from his diary were published by E. Tavernier in a local publication *Les Gaudes* (1908–13).
21. Gendarmerie report, Jura, 30 July 1830, *AN* F7.4034.
22. Verronnais, *Annuaire du département de la Moselle* (1831) p. 93, *BM* Metz.
23. Diary of N. Louet.
24. Louet, 2 August 1830, 2J401.
25. Verronais, *Annuaire* p. 92, *BM* Metz.
26. Diary of Lebert, 28 July 1830, *BM* Colmar.
27. Louet, 2 August 1830.
28. Gendarmerie report, Rhône, 29 July 1830, *AN* F7.6771.
29. J. Maillard de Chambure, *Journal*, 28 July 1830, *BM* Dijon. *Journal de la Côte-d'Or*, 30 July 1830.
30. C. Weiss, *Journal*, 29 July 1830. *BM* Besançon.
31. 'Le préfet du Puy-de-Dôme aux habitants de Clermont', 1 August 1830, *AD* MO.147.
32. Prefect to mayor of Chaumont, 31 July 1830, *AD* 61M15.
33. Weiss, 5 August 1830.
34. *AD* 3M40.
35. Louet, 3 and 8 August 1830.
36. Order of Castex, the general commanding the fifth military division, 1 August 1830, *AD* Bas-Rhin 3M40.
37. Supplement to *Le Moniteur*, 31 July 1830.
38. *AM* Metz 2 I.148, *Affaire Terguem*. Report of *procureur-général*, Metz, to *garde des sceaux*, 31 August 1830, *AN* BB18.1187.
39. R. D. Price, 'The French army and the Revolution of 1830', *European Studies Review*, 3 (1973) 247.
40. Gendarmerie commander to provisional local committee, 5 August 1830, *AD* Puy-de-Dôme M.0147.
41. Bachelu, lieutenant-general commanding the nineteenth military division to minister of war, 6 August 1830, *AN* F7.6771.
42. *Moniteur*, 31 July 1830.
43. de Chambure, 1 August 1830.

(continuation from previous page:)
fascinating illustrations which go far beyond the over-used Delacroix masterpiece.

44. Lebert, 1 August 1830.
45. Gendarmerie report, July 1830, *AN* F7.3983. Charles Pichegru was murdered while under interrogation for his royalist activities in 1804. He was turned into a hero during the Restoration. *Biographie Universelle*, XXXIV (1823) 274–80.
46. Weiss, 2 and 7 August 1830.
47. Gendarmerie report, Jura, August 1830, *AN* F7.4034.
48. Prefect of Bas-Rhin to minister of interior, 28 August 1830, *AD* 3M40.
49. Police report, 29 July 1830, *AM* Metz 1D36; gendarmerie report, Moselle BB18.1186.
50. Lebert, 2 August 1830.
51. Prefectoral reports, Morbihan, *AD* 1M403.
52. Gendarmerie report, 6 August 1830, *AN* F7.4144.
53. Verronnais, *Annuaire*, p. 91.
54. *Archives de la Guerre*, E5.I.
55. Register of deliberations of municipal council, 24 August 1830, *AM* Nancy.
56. Gendarmerie report, Jura, August 1830, *AN* F7.4034.
57. *Commissaire de police* to prefect, 10 August 1830, *AD* Meurthe WM.2002.
58. *Spectateur*, 5 August 1830, *BM* Dijon. *Spectateur* was the most conservative of the local liberal papers.
59. *L'Impartial*, 2 August 1830, *AD* Doubs.
60. St-Amarin, Belfort, 19 August 1830, *AN* BB18.1186.
61. Haute-Marne Gendarmerie report, July 1830, *AN* F7.4080.
62. Deliberations, municipal council, Chaumont, 2 August 1830, *AM* Série D.
63. Gendarmerie report, 6 August 1830, *AN* F7.4144.
64. Lebert, 31 July and 2 August 1830.
65. *Commissaire de police* to prefect, *AD* Meurthe WM.2002.
66. Deliberations, municipal council, Nancy, 2 August 1830, *AM*.
67. M. Cohendy, *Mémoire historique sur les modes successifs de l'administration dans la province de l'Auvergne* (1856) p. 310.
68. *AD* M.0147.
69. *AD* M.0147.
70. Gendarmerie report, 6 August 1830, *AN* F7.4144.
71. Reports from delegates, 9 August 1830, *AD* Moselle 58M1.
72. Divisional military commander, Lyons, to minister of war, 6 August 1830, *AN* F7.6771.
73. *AD* Seine-Inférieure 1M179.
74. Rambervilliers, 7 August 1830, *AN* C.2110. Interestingly, the new regime thought the petitions of value and they still survive.
75. Petition from Langres, Haute-Marne, 26 August, *AN* F1cI.31; also Chaumont, 23 August, *AM* Chaumont Série D.

5 THE LIBERALISM OF THE ORLEANIST SETTLEMENT

1. An earlier version of this chapter was given as a paper to the Anglo-American Conference of Historians, Institute of Historical Research, London University, July 1989. 'The French Connection in British and American History', published in *Historical Research*, LXIII (1990) 151, 162–77.
2. Braun, *Nouvelle biographie des députés*. J. Dourille, *Biographie des députés de la nouvelle Chambre Septennale* (1829); *Biographie impartiale des 221 députés, précédée et suiuvie de quelques documents curieux* (1830). Numerous brief biographical dictionaries were produced, clearly catering to a political community that sought to classify its representatives.
3. A. Carrel, *Histoire de la contre-révolution en Angleterre sous Charles II et James II* (1827). This was one of a growing number of increasingly pointed comparisons. Their popularity can be gauged by the number of titles recorded in the *Bibliothèque Nationale* catalogue.
4. Pilbeam, 'The growth of liberalism', pp. 351–66.
5. Sauvigny, *La Restauration*, p. 449. Pinkney, *The French Revolution*, p. 121, gives a lower 'official' estimate.
6. Pinkney, *The French Revolution*, p. 294.
7. F. Guizot, *Mémoires*, vol. II (1858) pp. 16–17.
8. Ibid., p. 26.
9. de Broglie, *Souvenirs*, p. 393.
10. Duvergier de Hauranne, *Histoire du gouvernment parlementaire*, p. 705.
11. L. Blanc, *Revolution Française. Histoire de Dix Ans*, V (1841) 498.
12. Collingham, *The July Monarchy*, p. 12.
13. 'Séance royale du 9 août 1830', *Chambre des Députés. Procès-Verbaux des Séances de la Chambre des Députés. Session de 1830*, 1 (1830) 77. Charles X, on the other hand, when he opened his first parliament, after a solemn mass in Notre-Dame the previous day, promised to prostrate himself on the altar used by Clovis, and swore that he would preserve the constitution 'octroyée' by his brother, a phrase certain to antagonise all liberals.
14. 'Séance royale d'ouverture de la session du 22 décembre 1824', Mavidal and Laurent, *Archives Parlementaires*.
15. *Le Moniteur*, 8th August 1830.
16. L. Duguit and H. Monnier, *Les Constitutions et les principales lois politiques de la France depuis 1789* (1915, 3rd edn). Constitutions of 1814, pp. 183–90, and 1830, pp. 213–18.
17. *Manifeste de la Société des Amis du Peuple* (1830).
18. F. Ponteil, *Les Institutions de la France de 1814 à 1870* (1965) p. 146.
19. Ibid., pp. 219–30.
20. Ibid., pp. 231–2.
21. *Archives Départementales*, Côte-d'Or, Fonds Chaper 2J.
22. Church, *Europe in 1830*.
23. Pilbeam, 'Popular violence in provincial France'.
24. Girard, *La Garde Nationale*, pp. 165, 187.
25. Cf., AN BB18.1190.4545 for numerous examples from September 1830.

26. Weiss, 4 November 1830, *BM* Besançon.
27. *Bulletin des Lois, 9th series,* (1831) ii, 26.
28. *Procureur-général,* Dijon, June 1831, Archives Nationales BB3.1171.
29. Many incidents are recorded in reports. 'Esprit du clergé', *AN* F19.4258, F19.5728, et. seq.
30. Rader, *The Journalists,* p. 122.
31. *Loi sur les crimes, délits et contraventions de la presse, 9 séptembre 1835. Bulletin des Lois ix série I,6,247.* For an account of all the legislation and its impact see Collins, *The government and newspaper press.*
32. *AN* CC.575.
33. The extensive uproar is described at length and with decreasing sympathy by *procureurs* in *AN* BB18.1316.
34. Extensively recorded in *Documents Gasparin, Archives municipales de Lyon.* Thirteen bound volumes of the prefect's correspondence chart an intelligent Orleanist's reaction to these problems. See also *Archives Départmentales,* Rhône M257, and Bezucha, *The Lyon Uprising* for an efficient description.
35. D. H. Pinkney, *Decisive years in France 1840–47* (1986) pp. 23–49.
36. P. M. Pilbeam, 'The economic crisis of 1827–32 and the 1830 Revolution in Provincial France', *Historical Journal* (June 1989) pp. 319–38.
37. *Liste électorale,* Dijon, 1834, *AM* Dijon 4E.
38. L. A. Pagnerre, *Les hommes du mouvement et les hommes de la résistance. Biographie politique des ministres, de tous les membres de la Chambre des Députés* (1831) p. 163.
39. Dourille, *Biographie des députés,* p. 212. Rabbe, Vielle de Boisjolin, St Preuve, *Biographie universelle et portative de contemporains,* vol. III (1834) p. 524.
40. Guizot, *Mémoires,* p. 7.
41. *Biographie impartiale des 221 députés* (1831) p. 68.
42. J. Maitron, *Dictionnaire Biographique du Mouvement Ouvrier Français,* vol. I (1964) pp. 333–6.
43. G. Sarrut and B. St Edmé, *Biographie des hommes du jour,* vol. III (1834–43) p. 299.
44. *Les aventures de la fille d'un roi, racontées par elle-même* (1820) and *La nièce d'un roi* (1824).

6 RELIGION AND REVOLUTIONARY POLITICS

1. B. Fitzpatrick, *Catholic royalism in the department of the Gard, 1814–52* (1983) p. 188.
2. D. M. G. Sutherland, *France 1789–1815. Revolution and Counter-revolution* (1985) pp. 112–13.
3. G. de Bertier de Sauvigny, *Le comte Ferdinande de Bertier et l'enigme de la congrégation* (1948). Descriptions of the work of the missionaries can be found in E. Sévrin, *Les missions religieuses en France sous la Restauration* (1948, 1959).
4. Hartmann, 'The sacrilege law of 1825', pp. 21–37.

Notes 207

5. Ponteil, *Les Institutions de la France*, p. 108.
6. Fitzpatrick, *Catholic royalism*, op. cit.
7. See ch. 4, pp. 113–14.
8. Fitzpatrick, *Catholic royalism*, p. 100.
9. Lebert's diary, AD Haut-Rhin *Série J*.
10. Commissioner of police, Nancy, to prefect, 10 August 1830, AD Meurthe et Moselle WM.2002.
11. Sub-prefect to prefect, Haute-Marne, 4 Nov. 1830, AN F19.5732.
12. To minister of public instruction, 3 Dec. 1830, AN F19.5732.
13. Nogent, 10 August 1830, AD Haute-Marne, 61M15.
14. Prefect, Côte-d'Or, to minister of the interior, 12 September 1830, AD Côte-d'Or IV.418. Report of *procureur-général*, September 1830, AN BB18.1316.
15. Many incidents are recorded in reports. 'Esprit du clergé', AN F19.4258, F19.5728, *et. seq.*
16. Report of *procureur-général*, Dijon, April (second half) 1831, AN BB3.174. Most of the reports and their summaries are located here.
17. AN F.19.5601.
18. October 1830, AD Haute-Marne 20V.2.
19. 'Clergy who have been the object of complaints, both justified and groundless since the 1830 Revolution.' It was calculated that these had totalled 631 by the time of Périer's appointment as chief minister in March 1831. Report of January 1832, AN F19.5601.
20. A lecturer in philosophy at the seminary at Ornans, Doney was a follower of Lamennais for a time. He became bishop of Montauban in 1843. Bosson, *Notices biographiques*, vol. I (1889) pp. 303–15.
21. Prefect, Doubs, to minister of the interior, 2 Dec. 1830, AN F19.5721.
22. Report from *Cour Royale*, Besançon, to *Garde des Sceaux*, Feb. 1831, AN BB3.174. *Comptes d'Assise*, March 1831, AN BB20.54.
23. AN CC.
24. AN F7.9890, 'Service pour le mort du duc de Berri 11 fév. 1822' and subsequent years. AN O3.894, *Archives de la couronne*, 'Service solennel pour le repos de l'âme...', AN O3.520. The funeral costs ran to 450 000 francs, a bill no one wanted to pay.
25. J. P. Martin, *La nonciature de Paris et les affaires écclesiastiques de la France sous le règne de Louis-Philippe* (1949) p. 82, 85.
26. R. Limouzin-Lamothe, *Monseigneur de Quélen, archévêque de Paris*, vol. II (1957) pp. 47–9, 55.
27. 'Relation exacte de ce qui s'est passé le 14 fév. 1831 au service funèbre célébré pour le repos de l'âme de S. A. R. Mgr. le duc de Berri dans l'église de St Germain l'Auxerrois' (Paris, 1831).
28. R. Limouzin-Lamothe, 'L'émeute de St Germain l'Auxerrois d'après une relation inedite du chapitre metropolitain', *Etudes Franciscaines*, XIII (1963) 190.
29. Bulletin of the prefect of police, Paris, 17 Feb. 1831, AN F7.3885. There are no reports for the previous days.
30. Truchi, gendarmerie commander, to prefect (absent), 19 Feb. 1831, AD Côte-d'Or 20M756.
31. Commissioner of police, Nancy, 17 Feb. 1831, AD Meurthe-et-Moselle WM.755.

32. *AN* BB3.174.
33. 'Conspiration Carliste', *Constitutionnel*, 16 Feb. 1831, *BN*. J. J. Baude, 'Habitans de Paris', *Moniteur Universel*, 16 Feb. 1831. M. C. B. comte de Montalivet, *ministre de cultes* at time and subsequently *ministre de l'instruction publique*, 29 March 1831, in Mavidal and Laurent, *Archives parlementaires*, vol. LXVIII, p. 190.
34. 'Procès du service funèbre célébré le 14 fév. 1831 à St Germain l'Auxerrois', *BN* Lb51.690.
35. *AN* BB20.260, and personal dossier of de Quelen, F19.2556.
36. Circular to all mayors, 30 March 1831, *AD* Côte-d'Or IV9.
37. There were 267 complaints between March 1831 and January 1832, *AN* F19.5601.
38. Prefect, Vosges, to minister of the interior, 2 May 1834, *AN* 8M6bis.
39. D. C. Higgs, *Nobles in Nineteenth Century France. The practice of inegalitarianism* (1987).
40. Collingham, *The July Monarchy*, p. 117.
41. Fitzpatrick, *Catholic royalism*, p. 168.
42. Prefectoral reports, Ille-et-Vilaine, 1831, *AD* 1M.508; 1832 *AD* 1M.509.
43. June 1832, *AD* Morbihan 4M.444, 'Chouannerie'.
44. Prefectoral circular to mayors, 14 April 1832, *AD* Morbihan 4M.444.
45. *AD* Ille-et-Vilaine 1M.510, 1M.512.
46. Police commissioner, Loire-Inférieure, to prefect, Morbihan, 19 July 1833, *AD* Morbihan 4M.446.
47. 22 June 1833, *AD* Morbihan 1M.428.
48. G. de Bertier de Sauvigny, *Documents inédits sur la conspiration légitimiste de 1830–32* (1946) and 'La conspiration des légitimistes et de la duchesse de Berry contre Louis-Philippe, 1830–32', *Études d'histoire moderne et contemporaine*, 3 (1951) xvii–125.
49. Fitzpatrick, *Catholic royalism*, p. 124.
50. A. J. Tudesq, *Les Conseillers Généraux en France au temps de Guizot, 1840–48* (1967) pp. 221–30.
51. A. J. Tudesq, *Les Grands Notables*.
52. de Villeneuve-Bargemont, *Economie politique chrétienne*. See also K. A. Lynch, *Family, Class and Ideology in early Industrial France* (1988).
53. J. B. Duroselle, *Les débuts du catholicisme social en France (1822–70)* (1951) pp. 199–200, 236.
54. B. G. Smith, *Ladies of the Leisure Class* (1981).
55. *AD* Doubs M.271.
56. R. Anderson, *Education in France, 1848–70* (1975).

7 THE BOURGEOIS REVOLUTION

1. Pilbeam, *The Middle Classes*, ch. 1.
2. P. Higonnet, *Class, Ideology and the Rights of Nobles during the French Revolution* (1981) p. 152.
3. A. Cobban, 'The myth of the French Revolution'. An accessible

summary of recent trends appears in ch. 1 of W. Doyle, *Origins of the French Revolution* (1980).
4. Cobban, *Aspects*, pp. 90–111.
5. Furet, 'Le catechisme révolutionnaire', *Annales; Economies, Sociétés, Civilisations* (1971) 255–89.
6. R. Robin, *La société française en 1789. Semur-en-Auxois* (1970) pp. 342–3.
7. A. de Tocqueville, *The Old Regime and the French Revolution* (1955) pp. 91–2.
8. C. Church, *Revolution and Red Tape: the French Ministerial Bureaucracy 1770–1850* (1981) p. 278.
9. E. Beau de Lomenie, *Les responsabilités*, vol. I, p. 109.
10. L. Bergeron and G. Chaussinand-Nogaret, *Les masses de granit* (1979).
11. Innumerable examples can be found in the illuminating personnel dossiers preserved in the *AN* F1bI series.
12. G. Chaussinand-Nogaret, *Une histoire des élites 1700–1848* (1975) p. 14; Tudesq, *Les Grands Notables en France*.
13. G. V. Taylor, 'Types of capitalism in eighteenth century France', *English Historical Review*, LXXIX (1964) 478–97 and 'Non-capitalist wealth and the origins of the French Revolution', *American Historical Review*, LXXII (1967) 469–96.
14. Chaussinand-Nogaret, *Une histoire des élites*. G. Chaussinand-Nogaret, *La Noblesse* (1976).
15. Higgs, *Nobles in Nineteenth Century France* (1987).
16. Sutherland, *France 1789–1815*.
17. Cobban, 'The myth of the French Revolution'.
18. E. Faure, 'Prendre la Bastille', *Projet, septembre–octobre* (1988) pp. 5–9.
19. A. Daumard and F. Furet, 'Problèmes de méthode en histoire sociale', *Revue d'histoire moderne et contemporaine* (1964) 291–8.
20. A. Daumard, *La bourgeoisie parisienne 1815–48* (1963).
21. J. Lhomme, *La Grande Bourgeoisie au Pouvoir, 1830–80* (1960) quoted in G. Chaussinand-Nogaret, *Une Histoire des Elites*, p. 14.
22. A. B. Spitzer, 'The elections of 1824 and 1827 in the Department of the Doubs', *French History*, 3 (1989) 2, 153–77.
23. J. Oeschlin, *Le mouvement ultra-royaliste en France* (1960) p. 55.
24. Blanc, *Revolution Française*, vol. II, p. 33. Cabet, *La Révolution de 1830*, p. 108.
25. Cf., ch. 8.
26. K. Marx, *The Class Struggles in France 1848 to 1850* (trans. from German edn, 1895) p. 44.
27. Lhomme, *La Grande Bourgeoisie*, pp. 36–7, 42–3.
28. P. Bastid, *Les Institutions Politiques de la Monarchie Parlementaire Française 1814–48* (1954) p. 244 (n. 1).
29. Tudesq, *Les Grands Notables en France*, vol. I, pp. 211–36.
30. 'Rapport sur les circonstances electorales.' Prefect to minister of the interior, 21 November 1837, *AD* Haute-Marne 27M19.
31. P-B. Higonnet, 'La composition de la Chambre des Députés 1827 à 1831', *Revue Historique* (1968) 351–78. Pinkney, *The French Revolution,*

pp. 279–80. Figures for 1840 from Tudesq, *Les Grand Notables en France*, vol. I, pp. 364–8.
32. Beck, *French Legislators*.
33. Pinkney, *The French Revolution*, p. 294.
34. Provincial examples will mainly, but not exclusively, be drawn from the same departments as elsewhere in this study.
35. F. Ponteil, *Les Institutions de la France*, p. 43.
36. *Journal*, Louet, 29 August 1830, *AD* Haute-Marne 2J401, 4845.
37. *Annuaire du Doubs* (1835) p. 72. *AD* Doubs.
38. J. Balteau, *Dictionnaire Biographie Français*, vol. VII (1956) p. 79; E. Bourloton, G. Cogny and A. Robert, *Dictionnaire des Parlementaires Français*, vol. I (1889–91) p. 460.
39. R. Raban, *Petite Biographie des Députés* (1826) p. 28; Balteau, *Dictionnaire Biographie*, vol. VIII, pp. 1144–5; Dentu, *Biographie des Députés de la Chambre Septennale* (1826) pp. 143–4; O. Braun, *Nouvelle Biographie*, p. 147; M. A. Lagarde, *Nouvelle biographie pittoresque des députés de la Chambre Septennale* (1826) p. 45.
40. *Journal*, Weiss, 16 August 1830, *Bibliothèque Municipale*, Besançon.
41. Pinkney, *The French Revolution*, p. 276.
42. C. H. Pouthas, 'La réorganisation du ministère de l'intérieur et la reconstitution de l'administration préfectorale par Guizot en 1830', *Revue de l'histoire moderne et contemporaine*, X (1962) 244–56.
43. *Bibliothèque Nationale, Nouvelles Acquisitions Françaises*.
44. Pouthas, 'La réorganisation', p. 249.
45. *AD* Côte-d'Or, *Fonds Chaper* 2J3.
46. Careers are easily followed and reconstructed in personnel dossiers, *AN* F1bI. For example, Fargues appointed to Chaumont, F1bI160.2. See also H. Fauré, *Galérie administrative ou biographie des préfets depuis l'organisation jusqu'à nos jours* (1839).
47. Bourloton, et al., *Dictionnaire des Parlementaires*, vol. V, p. 319.
48. Armand Gabriel François Paperel Delaboissière was recommended for retention by the new prefect, 13 August 1830, *AD* Doubs M710.
49. *AN* F1bI158.14.
50. 3 October 1830, copy in several departmental archives, *AD* Haute-Marne 30M1, for example.
51. *AD* Côte-d'Or 1M2*.
52. *Conseils de département et d'arrondissement, confidentiel*, 30 July 1834, prefect to minister of interior, *AN* F1cIV7.
53. *AN* F1bII Vosges 6.
54. 6 June 1830, *AD* Vosges 8M13.
55. 13 August 1830, *AD* Doubs M710.
56. 'Hommes consciencieux et d'ailleurs propriétaires'. Prefect, Doubs, to minister of interior, 18 August 1830, *AN* F1bII Doubs 7.
57. *L'Impartial*, 19 May 1831, *AD* Doubs.
58. *Liste chronologique des maires de Dijon depuis 1789* (1888) *Bibliothèque Municipale*, Dijon.
59. Prefect, Vosges, to minister of interior, 29 August 1830, *AN* F1bII Vosges 6.
60. *Procureur du roi*, Chaumont, to *procureur-general*, Dijon, 30 November 1830, *AN* BB18.1190, 4545.

Notes 211

61. To prefect, Doubs, 17 September 1830, *AD* Doubs M710.
62. *AN* F1bII Vosges 6.
63. H. Lepage and C. Charton, *Le département des Vosges, statistique, historique et administrative*, vol. I, p. 752.
64. To minister of interior, 8 December 1833, *AD* Côte-d'Or 2.J3.
65. Prefect to minister of interior, 8 September 1837, *AD* Côte-d'Or 2.J4.
66. A. J. Tudesq, *Les conseillers généraux*.
67. Périer, first circular to all prefects, March 1831, *AD* Calvados M2312.
68. Périer to prefect, Haute-Marne, 24 March 1831, *AD* Haute-Marne 31M3.
69. See ch. 8, p. 195.
70. Bergeron and Chaussinand-Nogaret, *Les masses de granit*, p. 32.
71. N. Richardson, *The French Prefectoral Corps 1814–30* (1966) p. 15.
72. D. H. Pinkney, *Decisive years*, pp. 23–50. Pinkney holds that these were real 'take-off' years for the French economy.
73. M. Lyons, *Le Triomphe du Livre. Une Histoire Sociologique de la Lecture dans la France du XIXe Siècle* (1987) p. 86.

8 UNE RÉVOLUTION ESCAMOTÉE

1. *Code Pénal*, 12 fév 1810. *Les Cinq Codes de l'Empire* (1812), section 7, p. 636.
2. Minister of interior to prefect, 28 Jan. 1832, *AD* Vosges 8 M6bis.
3. Weiss, 5 Jan. 1831.
4. Prefect to minister of interior, 27 Dec. 1830, *AN* F1bI173.15 *Dossier personnel Sers*.
5. *Société constitutionnelle de Seurre*, 20 Dec. 1830, *AN* BB18.1337.
6. Church, *Europe in 1830*.
7. *Constitutionnel*, 14 Feb. 1831, *BN*.
8. The committee raised 35 000 francs for the Poles. *Indépendant de la Moselle*, 25 Feb. 1831.
9. Guizot, *Mémoires*, vol. II, p. 91.
10. *Constitutionnel*, 3 Mar. 1831.
11. Odilon Barrot, 31 Mar. 1831, Mavidal and Laurent, *Archives Parlementaires*, LXVIII, 273.
12. Maréchal Maison, 13 Nov. 1830, Mavidal and Laurent, *Archives Parlementaires*, LXIV, 384.
13. *L'Impartial*, 2 Dec. 1830.
14. To minister of war, *AG* Vincennes E5.8, E5.10.
15. *AN* BB3.174.
16. Paixhans and Semellé, 30 Mar. 1831, Mavidal and Laurent, *Archives Parlementaires*, LXVIII, 228.
17. F. Ponteil, *L'Opposition politique à Strasbourg sous la monarchie de juillet* (1932) p. 143.
18. *Procureur-général*, Besançon, to *garde des sceaux*, 25 Sept. 1830, *AN* BB18.1190.

19. 11 Feb. 1831, *AN* BB18. 1320.
20. *Indépendant de la Moselle*, 1 April 1831.
21. See ch. 6.
22. Military report, Metz, 8 March 1831, *AG* E5.8.
23. *Association Nationale pour assurer l'indépendance du pays et l'expulsion perpetuelle de la branche aînée des Bourbons*, *AN* BB18.1320.
24. Deputy of *procureur du roi*, Beaune, to *garde des sceaux*, 31 March 1831, *AN* BB6.178.
25. Prefect, Doubs, to minister of interior, 31 March 1831, *AD* M.1177.
26. Mavidal and Laurent, *Archives Parlementaires*, LXVIII, 212.
27. *National*, 15 April 1831.
28. *Journal de la Meurthe*, 13 March 1831, *BM* Nancy.
29. *L'Impartial*, 13 April 1831.
30. Minister of interior to minister of justice, 13 March 1831, *AN* BB18.1320.
31. Military reports, Metz, 8 and 14 March 1831, *AG* E5.8.
32. Prefect to minister of interior, 24 March 1831, *AD* M.0116.
33. *Association Patriotique de l'arrondissement de Limoux*, *BN*.
34. Prefect to minister of interior, 14 April 1831, *AD* 8M6. Deblaye had also figured on the Restoration *Aide-toi* committee, *AN* F7.6741.
35. The *Courrier* and the *Indicateur de l'Est* were for the society; the *Indépendant* was for the government.
36. To minister of interior, 28 March 1831, *AD* 8M6bis.
37. Departments where there was a local association, with the names of local deputies who were members, are as follows: Ain, Allier (Victor de Tracy), Aisne (Labbey de Pompières), Ardennes, Aube, Aude (Podenas), Calvados, Charente, Charente-Inférieure (Audry de Puyravault), Cher, Cors (Abatucci), Côte-d'Or (Hernoux, Mauguin), Côtes-du-Nord (Bernard), Creuse, Dordogne (Périn), Doubs (Gréa, Bouchot), Drôme, Eure (Dupont, Barrot, Legendre), Eure-et-Loir, Finistère (Las-Cases, Daunou, Kermorial), Gironde, Ille-et-Vilaine (Berthois, Dubois), Indre, Isère, Jura (Bachelu), Landes (Lamarque), Loire-Inférieure, Lot (Murat), Meurthe, Moselle (Semellé, Bouchot), Nord, Oise, Pas-de-Calais, Puy-de-Dôme (Baudet-Lafarge), Bas-Rhin, Haut-Rhin (Koechlin), Rhône (Conderc), Haute-Saône, Saônet-et-Loire (Thiard), Seine (Chardel, Corcelles, Delaborde, Demarçay, Ganneron, Salverte), Seine-et-Marne (Lafayette, general; Lafayette, G.), Seine-et-Oise, Seine-Inférieure, Deux- Sèvres, Vaucluse, Vendée (Duchafault), Vosges (Jacqueminot).
38. *BM Fonds Milsand* Dijon.
39. *Association Nationale*, Senlis, 20 March 1831, *BN*.
40. Périer to prefect, Doubs, 25 March 1831, *AD* M.1177.
41. F. Guizot, *Histoire parlementaire de la France* (1863) p. 240.
42. L. Blanc, *Révolution Française*, vol. II, p. 345.
43. Mayor to prefect, 20 July 1831, *AD* Rhône 4M152.
44. Sub-prefect to prefect, 10 July 1832, *AD* Jura M15.
45. *Globe*, 27 July 1830, *AN* CC547. *National*, 17 March 1831.
46. G. Perreux, *Aux temps des sociétés secrètes. La propagande républicain au début de la Monarchie de Juillet*, 183–35 (1931) p. 6.

47. *Association pour l'instruction libre et gratuite du peuple.*
48. *Procureur-général,* Dijon, to *Garde des Sceaux,* 20 Sept. 1833, *AN* BB18.1338.
49. Chaper to minister of interior, 25 Nov. 1832, *AD* Fonds Chaper 2J3.
50. Weill, *Histoire du parti républicain,* pp. 111–18.
51. J. Langeron, *Demontry, sa vie et sa mort* (1850) pp. 9–11.
52. *AN* BB18.1328.
53. *AD* 8M6bis.
54. *AN* F7.3983.
55. *AD* Fonds Chaper 2J10.
56. *AD* Bas-Rhin 3M52.
57. Mayor, Metz, to prefect, 25 Jan. 1834, *AM* Metz 1D37.
58. *AD* Bas-Rhin 3M39.
59. *AD* Jura M18.
60. *AD* Côte-d'Or FC.2J3.
61. Correspondence of prefect, Gasparin, *AM* Lyon; Bezucha, *The Lyon Uprising,* pp. 73–95.
62. *AM* Metz 1D37.
63. *AD, FC* 2J3, 24 Nov. 1833.
64. Prefect, Saône-et-Loire, to minister of interior, 17 March 1834, *AD* Saône-et-Loire 51M27.
65. *AN* BB20.18.
66. *Gazette de la Franche-Comté; Patriote Franc-Comtois, poursuites dirigés 5 août 1833, AD* Doubs 14U10 (no. 211) and *AN* BB20.72.
67. Prefect, Seine-Inférieure, to minister of interior, *confidentielle,* 1 Oct. 1833, *AD* 4M2703.
68. A number of these from August 1831 onwards can be consulted; *BN* Lb51.888.
69. 30 Nov. 1833, *AD* 8M6bis.
70. Lyons, *Le Triomphe du Livre,* p. 145.
71. D. Porch, *Army and Revolution. France 1815–48* (1974) pp. 47–60.
72. *Manifeste des Amis du Peuple,* 31 July 1830.
73. Gendarmerie commander Truchi to Chaper, 2 Dec. 1833, *AD* 8M29.
74. D. B. Weiner, *Raspail, Scientist and Reformer* (1968) pp. 135–63.
75. *Les justes alarmes de la classe ouvrière au sujet des mécaniques par un vieux typographe victime de l'arbitraire* (1830) pp. 3–5.
76. *Société des Droits de l'Homme. Association des Travailleurs* (n.d.).
77. *Société des Amis du Peuple* (Oct. 1831).
78. 18 Sept. 1833, *AN* BB18.1338.
79. 'Procès du journal républicain le Patriote de la Côte-d'Or', *BM* Dijon, *Fonds Milsand* B494.
80. Sub-prefect, Boulogne, to prefect, 14 Sept. 1830, *AD* M4603.
81. J. Merriman, 'The demoiselles of Ariège, 1829–31', in Merriman (ed.), *1830 in France.*
82. The phenomenon was not confined to France. See E. P. Thompson, *The making of the English Working Class* (1968) p. 529.
83. Agulhon, *La république au village.*
84. Corbin, *Archaisme et modernité.*
85. R. Aminzade, *Class, politics and early industrial capitalism. A study in mid-nineteenth century Toulouse* (1981).

86. Jones, *Politics and rural society*.
87. Pilbeam, 'Popular violence in provincial France', pp. 278–97.
88. *Procureur-général*, Besançon, to *garde des sceaux*, 25 Sept. 1830, *AN* BB18.1190.
89. Mayor of Lorient to prefect, *AD* Morbihan M501.
90. The wheat harvest of 1830 was only 53 million hectolitres, compared with 64 million in 1829 and 80 million in 1832. Ministry of agriculture and commerce, *Récoltes des céreales et des pommes de terres de 1815 à 1876* (1878) pp. 456–7.
91. In 1826 85 000 hectolitres of wheat were imported, mainly from Russia, Naples and Sicily. In 1830 this rose to 2 million and in 1832 to 4.3 million. *AN* F20.560.
92. *Procureur-général*, Dijon, to *garde des sceaux*, 21 Sept. and 8 Oct. 1830, *AN* BB18.1316.
93. *AN* F12.2713.
94. G. Bourgin, 'La crise ouvrière à Paris dans la seconde moitié de 1830', *Revue Historique* (1947) 203–14.
95. D. H. Pinkney, 'Les ateliers de secours à Paris (1830–31). Précurseurs des Ateliers Nationaux de 1848', *Revue d'histoire moderne et contemporaine* 12 (1965) 65–70.
96. *Procès-verbal conseil général*, Vosges, 16 May 1831, Vosges 2.
97. Prefect's speech to *conseil général*, 10 May 1831, *AN* F1CV Doubs 5.
98. Prefect's speech to *conseil général*, Haute-Marne, *AN* F1CV Haute-Marne 2.
99. *Conseil général*, Vosges, 16 May 1831, *AN* F1CV Vosges 2.
100. 6 Nov. 1831, *Bulletin des Lois* 9th series (1831) 31.
101. Mayor to sub-prefect of Wassy, 17 Feb. 1832, *AD* Haute-Marne 210M1.
102. To minister of interior, 2 June 1832, *AD* Côte-d'Or *FC* 2J1.
103. Prefect Haute-Marne to minister of interior, 31 May and 2 June 1832. *AD* Haute-Marne 61M16; *Citoyen de la Haute-Marne*, 3 June 1832, *BM* Chaumont.
104. 22 Nov. 1830, *AD* Morbihan 4M443.
105. *Correspondance du préfet*, Gasparin, vol. II. *Documents Gasparin AM* Lyons.
106. Guizot, *Mémoires*, vol. II.
107. Gendarmerie report, *AD* Eure 1M237.
108. Minister of interior to prefects, 22 March 1832, *AD* Vosges 8M6bis.
109. *Procureur-général*, Dijon, to *garde des sceaux*, 28 Feb. 1831, *AN* BB3.174.
110. Mavidal and Laurent, *Archives Parlementaires*, 1833.
111. *Documents Gasparin*, op. cit.
112. *AG* E5.46.
113. *Cour des Pairs. Affaire du mois d'avril 1834. Rapport fait à la cour par Girod de l'Ain*, vol. 3, p. 327.
114. *Archives de la Guerre*, Vincennes, E5.46.
115. *AD* Rhône M257.
116. Bezucha, *The Lyon Uprising*.
117. 'Recit de l'insurrection de Lyon en avril 1834, écrit en mai 1834' [Gasparin, prefect] in Guizot, *Mémoires*, vol. III, p. 425. Blanc, *Révolution Française*, vol. II, pp. 243.

Notes 215

118. *AN* CC575.
119. *AN* CC583; *AD* Jura M18.
120. Weill, Histoire du parti républicain, p. 130.
121. Ibid., p. 137.
122. Miran to president, *cour des pairs*, 28 Dec. 1835, *AN* CC582.
123. 23 March 1834.
124. *AN* CC576.
125. Chaper to minister of interior, 30 July 1834, *AD FC* 2J3.
126. Ibid., 27 Nov. and 26 Dec. 1834.
127. Ibid., prefectoral correspondence, 1835.
128. *AD* Bas-Rhin 3M53.
129. *AD* Saône-et-Loire 51M28.
130. *Loi sur les crimes, délits et contraventions de la presse*, 9 September 1835, *Bulletin des Lois*, 9th series, I, 6, 247.
131. Weill, *Histoire du parti républicain*, p. 147.
132. For instance, F. M. Fargues, appointed prefect in the Haute-Marne in August 1830, where he had been in office during the Hundred Days, was forcibly retired in March 1831. *Dossier personnel* Fargues *AN* F1bI160.2.
133. 2 July 1834, *AD* Bas-Rhin 3M5.
134. F. Guizot, *Archives Parlementaires* (1832).

9 CONCLUSION

1. Labrousse, 'Comment naissent les révolutions'.
2. L. Cahen, 'L'enrichissement de la France sous la Restauration', *Revue de l'histoire moderne et contemporaine*, V (1930) 178–207.

Bibliography

ARCHIVES CONSULTED

The following departments have been selected for examination, with evidence garnered, where appropriate, from both local and national sources:

Ain, Aisne, Ardennes, Aube, Calvados, Côte-d'Or, Doubs, Eure, Ille-et-Vilaine, Jura, Loire-Atlantique (Inférieure), Manche, Haute-Marne, Meurthe-et-Moselle, Meuse, Morbihan, Moselle, Nord, Oise, Pas-de-Calais, Puy-de-Dôme, Bas-Rhin, Haut-Rhin, Rhône, Haute-Saône, Saône-et-Loire, Seine-Maritime (Inférieure), Somme, Vendée, Vosges and Yonne.

National Archives

Archives de la Ministère de la Guerre, Vincennes.
Correspondance militaire générale et divers. 1830–48 E5.1–132.
This correspondence is organised chronologically. A large section in each *carton* is unclassified. Consulted up to E5.50 (1834). Also D3.130, 131, April–August 9 1830.

Archives Nationales (AN)

Série BB. Justice.

Information on the personnel of the judiciary and reports of *procureurs* on public opinion and elections.
BB1. *Justice; personnel.*
BB1.34, 227I.
BB2. *Justice. Affaires civiles.*
BB2.34–7, 82.
BB3. *Justice. Affaires criminelles.*
BB3.121, 122, 152, 167, 174, 195 (*délits forêstiers* 1828–30), 1171.
BB5. *Justice; demandes de places.*
BB5.243, 44, 49, 50, 51, 52, 73, 120, 357, 360, 361, 468.
BB6. *Cours et tribunaux. an VIII–1927.*
BB6.37, 81–91, II83, 178, 182, 187, 188, 189, 195, 198, 199A, 204, 208, 212A, 219, 220, 221, 262, 371–4, II376, 540, 542, 544, 545, 739.
BB17. *Bureau du cabinet du ministre.*
BB17.A.71–7, 84–7, 95, 146, 148–50.

BB18. *Correspondance générale de la division criminelle.* Correspondence of magistrates on public opinion.
BB18.1136, 1137, 1160, 1166, 1170, 1175, 1176, 1177, 1179, 1181, 1183, 1184, 1185, 1186, 1187, 1190, 1192, 1194–20, 1201–6, 1203, 1204, 1206, 1212, 1215, 1216, 1217, 1218, 1220, 1221, 1228, 1302, 1316, 1319, 1320, 1322, 1326, 1328, 1335, 1337, 1338, 1340, 1353–4, 1354b, 1355, 1361, 4545.
BB20. *Comptes d'Assises.*
BB20. In particular BB20.18, 45, 54, 55, 56, 59, 60, 61, 64, 65, 67, 72, 73, 74, 78.
BB21. Public opinion, reports of riots etc;
BB21.376, 382, 384, 390, 392–399.
BB24.100–15, 136–54.
BB30.194, 199, 207, 237, 240, 241 (elections 1822), 260, 276, 285 (1&2), 286A.

Série C.

C.210.
Enquiries into the state of industry; C.950, 951.
Elections, information on candidates and results (very formal *procès-verbaux*); C.1194, 1202, 1254, 1267, 1284, 1321.
Petitions and addresses to the government; C.2097, 2110, 2759, 2761, CC.450, 452.
Trial of Charles X's ministers; CC.546–551.
Trial of *Accusés d'Avril*; CC.574, 575, 576, 582, 583, 612, 664, 665.

Série F.

This series yielded valuable information on public opinion and politics, but little on economic affairs.
F1. *Administration générale.* Documents of the *administration générale* concerning departmental, communal and police matters.
F1A.58, 422.
F1bI. Personnel dossiers: Prefectoral etc.
Departmental affairs; F1bII.
F1cI. *Esprit Public.*
F1cI.31, 32, 33, 44–52.
F1cIII. Elections (organised departmentally).
F1cIV, F1cV, F1cVII, F1dIII; Departmental matters, organised alphabetically.
F2. *Administration départementale.*
Not very valuable but some information on industry in: F2. I.1217, 1218, 1220, 1221.
F7. *Police.* The gendarmerie reports in this series provided useful information on public opinion, sometimes offering a fascinating contrast with the views of the civil administration.
F7.3885, 3906, 3907, 3908, 3926–8, 3931, 3970, 3971, 3976, 3983, 4033, 4034, 4035, 4036, 4079, 4080, 4085, 4086, 4089–91, 4096, 4097, 4098, 4099, 4119, 4120, 4121, 4134, 4135, 4137, 4139, 4140, 4144, 4145, 4147–50, 4151–4, 4215, 4352A, 4915, 6680, 6684–9, 6690, 6691, 6694, 6695, 6697, 6698, 6702, 6703,

6706, 6719, 6740, 6741, 6742, 6746, 6754, 6767, 6768, 6770, 6771, 6772, 6776, 6777, 6778, 6779, 6780, 6782, 7031, 9338, 9451, 9633, 9682, 9685, 9731A, 9750, 9752, 9767, 9890.
F12. *Economic affairs. Trade and Industry.*
F12.193.3, 633–7, 2223, 2261, 2295, 2359, 2401, 2433, 2434, 2445, 2446, 2498, 2530 (enquiry into iron industry 1828–9), 2531 (as previous), 2532 (enquiry into iron industry 1833), 2711–15 (state of industry 1831), 3532, 4476A, 7590.
F19. *Cultes. Correspondence of government with bishops.*
F19.367A, 419–21, 2458, 2520, 2556, 2647, 4258, 5599, 5601, 5603, 5721, 5744, 5728–32, 5755.
F20. *Statistique.*
F20.498 (population of main towns 1789–1831), 560 (agricultural production 1804–55), 722 (bankruptcies 1820–35), 744 (wine industry 1821–38).
Archives de la couronne.
O3.894 O3.520.

Bibliothèque Nationale, Département des Manuscrits

Fonds Franc-Maçonnerie.
Nouvelles Acquisitions Françaises. 11909.
Lettres de Benjamin Constant à C. J. B. Hochet.

Bibliothèque Nationale (BN)

Large pamphlet collection relating to electoral propaganda and other political material.

Local Archives

Archives départementales were the most rewarding, but some interesting material was found in series D, F and K of municipal archives. Often these series lacked more specific numbers and are therefore not recorded separately below. In addition, local libraries occasionally owned private diaries of local notables or collections of pamphlets. Sustained 'runs' of local newspapers were sometimes found in departmental archives or libraries, never in municipal or national depositaries.

Archives Départementales (AD)

Archival material for the period after 1789 may be classified in a standardised manner, but common coding and cataloguing are far less rigorous for post-1789 documents than for the earlier period. The process of classification of the post-1789 series is on-going and numbers may change:

Série J includes diaries, family papers and occasionally a prefect's whole correspondence dossier, conventionally removed by him on leaving a department. This series, often enriched in recent years thanks to the assiduous pursuit of private archives by departmental archivists like Mlle Odile Colin (formerly *archiviste en chef* Haute-Marne), can prove the most rewarding source.

Série M is uniformly the most useful for projects involving mainly political and social questions. This group of documents includes material deposited by the prefecture concerning, consecutively (in principle), local officials, elections, police and gendarmerie reports and economic affairs.

Série Q, Administration de l'enregistrement des domaines, may supply information on the fortune of local notables, but in a far less wieldy form than the simple statement of direct tax paid afforded by electoral lists which often lurk in *série M*.

Série T, Presse, sounds promising, but habitually, where it exists, the series contains a paucity of mere formal information on local newspapers.

Série U, Justice includes the correspondence of magistrates, including the reports of *procureurs* on public opinion. Anything remotely controversial or vaguely informative was, presumably, never deposited. *Procureur* reports on public opinion during the early 1830s may be found in the *Archives Nationales*, both the full reports and numerous regional summaries. Also includes details of local *tribunaux de commerce*.

Série V, correspondence with the clergy.

Série Z, correspondance sous-préfets. Often non-existent; occasionally fascinating insights into local politics.

AISNE. All M series destroyed 1914–18 and 1944. Material in *Archives Nationales*.

ARDENNES. All M series destroyed 1914–18 and 1940. Material from *Archives Nationales*.

AUBE. *Archives départementales*.
M4c3.183–6 Police.

CALVADOS. *Archives départementales*.
There is a typed inventory of M in 6 volumes.
A few prefectoral reports survive.
M2312, M958, M16202, M16212.

CÔTE-D'OR. *Archives départementales* (some reclassification).
1M1, 1M2, 1M2*, 3/1, 4, 5/2, 5/3, 6/1, 7/1, 8/1, 9/1, 9/2.
Electoral lists 2M23, 24, 25, 27.
Elections, reports 2M53, 54; 3M38, 41, 42, 43, 45, 57, 52, M12.IIc1.
Local councils 4M4–9, 50–2.
5M4, 6M1–14, 62, 67.
Conseils généraux reports of meetings 1Na.2, 1Nc.5, 1Nd.3.
Police; gendarmerie reports.
7M6, 146, 147, 151, 152; 8M1, 3, 27–30. 20M.
Economic affairs.
M7f16, fII2, M8I.1, III.1, IV,15, M12.IIb2, M14.III, III1c, VIIIh.1.
Series Q, U and V were also consulted.

Série 2J. Fonds Chaper. Correspondence of Achille Chaper.
The entire, revealing and efficient correspondence of the prefect, including copies of outgoing and the incoming letters. Typical of bureaucrats, Chaper removed every letter of any conceivable interest when he moved to his next department. Fortunately for the historian the incoming letters and bound volumes of copies of his letters were discovered in a bookshop in Chaper's home town of Grenoble some years ago. The Dijon letters now form *série 2J* in the departmental archives and make up for an otherwise understandably bleak account of the period in the M series.
2J1–6 outgoing letters 1831–42.
2J7–16 letters received 1831–42.

Archives de la ville de Dijon.
Série D. Debates of the municipal council.
4E, 4F Agriculture, economic crisis. *Série K* electoral lists.
Bibliothèque Municipale, Dijon. Fonds Milsand.
Maillard de Chambure. *Journal des événements politiques en juillet 1830.*

DOUBS. *Archives départementales.*
Reorganised subsequent to publication of catalogues.
Administrative personnel.
M1, 4, 5, 7, 10, 11, 3048.
Elections.
M46, 47, 133, 134, 136, 137, 138, 139, 140, 141, 142, 143, 193–8.
Gendarmerie reports.
M708–14, 869, 950, 1061, 1171, 1175–7, 1251, 1226.
Série T. T9, 12.
Série U.
1U1, 14U8–12, 15U1, 17U2, 18U1, 23U1.
Série V. 4V2.
Bibliothèque Municipale, Besançon. Journal of C. Weiss.
E. Tavernier published selections from the diary of this librarian in *Les Gaudes* between 1908 and 1913.

EURE. *Archives départementales.*
Suau, B., Lucas, P. and Bachala, C., *Répértoire Numérique de la série M* (1977). This inventory is a model of order and clarity. There are no prefectoral or sub-prefectoral reports on public opinion as such, but there is useful material on industrial unrest in the early years of the July Monarchy.
1M168, 1M190;
Sureté Générale et Surveillance: 1M225 1823; 1M226 1824; 1M227 1825; 1M228 1826; 1M229 1827; 1M230–32 1830; 1M235 1830; 1M236 1831; 1M237 1832; 1M238 1833–5.
Also 1M347, 2M108, 3M138.

HAUTE-MARNE. *Archives départementales.*
Very well organised modern series.
Administrative personnel. 1M1–5M1.
Elections. 10M1–27M5.
Local councils. 29M1–36M2, 41M4–46M1, 48M1, 231N, 239N.

Bibliography   221

Gendarmerie reports. 61M14–16, 69M4, 72M13, 73M6, 96M1–3, 101M4, 102M1–8.
Economic affairs. 128M5, 146M1, 167M16, 172M5, 178M1, 179M1, 209M10, 210M1. Also série S (Mines).
Also consulted série Q and T.
Série U. 14U2, 15U2, 16U2.
Série V. 1V1, 2V1, 10V3, 20V1–5, 45V5, 46V1–2.
Série J.
2J. Collection Louet. *Journal des événements qui se sont déroulés à Paris, à Chaumont etc. du 15 séptembre 1791 jusqu'à 1847*, 11 volumes.
5J. Archives particulières du Château d'Ecot-la-Combe. The family papers of the Michel family, including both personal and business letters. The Michel brothers were important landowners and the richest iron-masters in the department. The deposited papers do not give much away, but convey a clear impression of attitudes to fairly public concerns.
6J. Archives de la famille Berthelin, maîtres de forges à Doulevant-le-Château. The family were significant in the industry.

ILLE-ET-VILAINE. Archives départementales.
Typed, reclassified inventory, following typical modern pattern.
1M90, 1M98 Esprit Public 1815–30, 1M508, 1M509, 1M510, 1M512.
Elections of 1827 3M43; 1828 3M44; Police reports 1820–7 4M32; 1830–33 4M33; 1834 4M34; 1833–45 4M35; 1830–1 4M35 d.

JURA. Archives départementales.
M15, 16, 17, 18, 19, 20, 98, 1177.

LOIRE-ATLANTIQUE (INFÉRIEURE). Archives départementales.
Série M is efficiently organised and presented in a card index catalogue.
1M100 Legislative Elections; 1M505, 1M507, 1M508 *Police Générale, situation politique 1823–31*; 1M509, 1M510, 1M511, 1M512 *Chouannerie de 1832*; 1M513 1833; 1M514 1834–8.
Correspondance du préfet A. Chaper. Série J.
55J1 Prefectoral correspondence (outgoing) 31 May 1842–22 Jan. 1847.
55J2 Prefectoral correspondence (outgoing), 23 Jan 1847–8 Aug. 1847.
Correspondence with minister of interior, June 1840–Apr. 1847.
Reports to *conseil général*, 1843, 1843–4.
1M512 contains interesting reports on the departmental situation and Chaper's observations of the 1840s were acute and wide ranging, referring back to the problems of the 1830s.

MANCHE. No material survived war-time destruction.

MEURTHE-ET-MOSELLE (Meurthe). Archives départementales.
WM.731, 732, 755, 1491, 1496, 2002.
Archives municipales. Nancy.
Deliberations municipal council Nancy, 2 August 1830.

MEUSE. Archives départementales.
Trizac, M., *Répértoire numérique de la série M* (1944).
1M–15M.
Elections. 33M1–3, 34M1–7.

Police politique. 71M4, 5, 6, 7, 8, 9, 10, 11, 73M4, 83M1–5, 84M1–5, 162M1–3, 163M1.
Subsistances. 391M1–2, 401M1–2, 451M1.
Industry. 553M1–2.
1U2.

MORBIHAN. *Archives départementales.*
Long-established typed and handwritten catalogue for M series, with some more recent internal reorganisation.
Police reports ranging from 1824 to 1848: 1M.428. 4M.444 'Chouannerie'. 4M.446, M501, M502, M517, M637, M638, M679.
Elections 3M.

MOSELLE. *Archives départementales.*
55M6, 58M1, 74M1, 1N30*,
Archives municipales. Metz.
1D36, 37; 2 I.137, 140–47, 148, *Affaire Terquem.*

NORD. *Archives départementales.*
Bruchet, *Répértoire numérique de la série M*, 4 vols (dactyl.).
Elections. M25, 26.
Police politique. M135, 136, 137, 199 (*mendicité*).
Subsistances. M433 (Crisis of 1830), 422, 445.
Trade and Industry. M547.

OISE. *Archives départementales.*
M series unclassified. Apparently very little material.
Administration Générale. Evénements politiques, 1820–40.
Corps municipaux, arrondissement de Beauvais, 1831.

PAS-DE-CALAIS. *Archives départementales.*
Bougard, *Archives départementales; Pas-de-Calais. Série M1–7810 1789–1953* (typed).
Elections 1830–47. Collection Delhomel.
Partial classification of M.
M49; M66–7; M1212, 1213, 1214, 1217, 1254, 1256, 1303, 1304.
M4610; M4612A *Affaires politiques 1814–* ; M4592 Police 1824–67.
M4593 Police and prefectoral reports 1830–33.
M4594 Police 1821–9; M4603 *Police générale 1830–31*; M4604.
Affaires politiques 1830–69.

PUY DE DÔME. *Archives départementales.*
M62, M094, M.0116, M0143, M.0147, 0265,

BAS-RHIN. *Archives départementales*
Catalogue of series M (1968).
3M28, 3M29, 3M30, 3M39, 3M40, 3M41, 3M43, 3M47, 3M48, 3M49, 3M50, 3M51, 3M52, 3M53.

HAUT-RHIN. *Archives départementales.*
Non-standard classification.
1M10.1, 1M10A, 1M50.4, 1M50.12, 1M54.14, 1M124.1, 1M126.9.1, 1M127.8, 1M128.1, 1M11757, 1M11760.

Bibliothèque Municipale, Colmar.
Journal de Nicholas Lebert.

RHÔNE. *Archives départementales.*
2M32, 4M152, M257.
Archives Municipales Lyon.
Documents Gasparin, 13 bound volumes. Correspondence of prefect.

SAÔNE-ET-LOIRE. *Archives départementales.*
51M27, 51M28.

SEINE-MARITIME (INFÉRIEURE). *Archives départementales.*
M series reclassified.
1M162 *Situation morale et politique* 1816–99.
1M179 *Opposition* 1815–29.
1M175, 1M176, 1M177 *Affaires séditieuses 1815–30.*
1M179 *Esprit et ordre public* 1830–48.
3M159 *Elections* 1824.
4M2703 *Associations politiques* 1824–88.

SOMME. *Archives départementales.*
Non-standard, embryonic and very incomplete classification of M.
Mfd97151, Mfd80896, Mb95147, Mb95019 Elections 1827–8; Mb95001, Mb95002, Mb95006, MBb107492, MBb107533.

VENDÉE. *Archives départementales.*
Excellent catalogue of M series published in 1983 by J. Joquet and R. Giraud.
1M402 Prefectoral correspondence 1815; 1M403 Prefectoral reports 1815–30; 1M426 Reports 1831–47; 1M427 1835–46; 1M428 *Troubles de 1832;* 1M517 1815–16.
3M26–34 Elections 1815–30; 3M35, 3M36, 3M52–62.
4M23 an VII–1828; 4M393; 4M394 *Agitation légitimiste* 1836–40.
3M395 *Agitation républicaine* 1836–46; 4M434–42.
4M443 *Chouannerie* 1830–39 prefectoral reports; 4M446 *Chouans et refractaires;* 4M447 *Etat de poursuites* 1830–35; 4M456.

VOSGES. *Archives départementales.*
Reclassified; a series Z discovered by the archivist in the 1960s, which provides interesting sidelights on the July Days. Unfortunately a nineteenth-century archivist eliminated all information on economic matters (reason unknown).
Administrative personnel. 1M1.
Elections. 4M1–49, 5M1–5.
Local councils. 6M2, 4–7, 10. 1N2.1, 1N3, 4, 2N3, 4, 4N2.
Gendarmerie reports. 8M5, 8M6, 8M6bis, 7–8, 12–15, 10M1, 1Z26.
Série U. 2U7, 7U1, 7, 8U1, 10U1.
Série V. 1V5, 2V12, 14V1, 2V3, 10V2, 15V1.
Also consulted *Archives de la papeterie de Lana*. Used with the generous permission of J. N. Janot.

NEWSPAPERS CONSULTED

L'Ami de la Charte: founded 1820 (from March 1829, *Journal de Puy de Dôme, de la Haute-Loire et du Cantal*). Liberal before 1830, *résistance* subsequently. Circulation c. 1000 in 1831. AD Puy de Dôme.
Citoyen de la Haute-Marne: 7 Aug. 1830–32 Nov. 1833. Orleanist. Bibliothèque Municipal (BM) Chaumont.
Constitutionnel: founded in the Hundred Days, liberal in Restoration; powerful in 1830 with circulation of 22 000, but by 1837 reduced to 3700.
Courrier de la Haute-Marne: 1819–31. BM Chaumont 1819–22.
Courrier de l'Ain: founded in 1830, increasingly pro-government. BM Bourg-en-Bresse.
Courrier de la Moselle: founded in 1829, *mouvement*.
Courrier Français: founded 21 June 1819. Liberal, then *mouvement* after 1830.
Echo de la Haute-Marne: took over from the *Citoyen* in Oct. 1833; run by prefectoral employees. BM Chaumont.
Le Franc Parleur: July 1828–July 1829. Liberal. AD Pas-de-Calais.
La Gazette d'Auvergne: 1831–43. Clone of *Gazette de France*. AD Puy de Dôme.
Gazette de Bourgogne: June 1831–Sept. 1835. Also legitimist. BM Dijon.
Gazette de la Franche-Comté: Aug. 1831–April 1834. BM Besançon.
Gazette de Strasbourg: 5 June–30 July 1830.
Globe: influential liberal paper founded in 1824; a daily from Feb. 1830.
L'Impartial: started March 1829. Liberal, Orleanist; *mouvement* Oct. 1830–32, subsequently conservative. AD Doubs.
Indépendant de l'Est: Orleanist.
L'Indicateur de Calais: 1829–32; at first nonpolitical, later *mouvement*. BM Calais.
L'Indicateur de l'Est: *mouvement*.
Journal de Dijon et la Côte-d'Or, sometimes *Journal de Carion* after its editor, later *Journal de la Côte-d'Or*: 1794–1863. BM Dijon.
Journal de la Haute-Marne: founded 1807. BM Chaumont Bibliothèque Barotte.
Journal de l'Ain: Literary preferences. BM Bourg-en-Bresse (incomplete).
Journal de Saone-et-Loire: Restoration to Second Republic. AD (incomplete).
Journal de Commerce: (national) *an* III–1848.
Journal des Vosges: Nov. 1832–March 1853; moderate *mouvement*. Very few copies survive either in Paris or Epinal.
Journal du Puy de Dôme; 1805–31. 'Vive le roi longtemps! Bourbons regnez toujours!' BM Clermont-Ferrand.
Le National: Jan. 1830–Dec. 1851. Liberal Orleanist; from 1832 republican.
Le Patriote de la Côte-d'Or: Feb. 1831–Sept. 1835. *Mouvement*, later republican. BM Dijon.
Patriote de la Saone-et-Loire: 1830–46. As Dijon *Patriote* in politics.
Patriote Franc-Comtois: Feb. 1832–April 1834. Similar to others in politics. AD Doubs and BM Besançon.
Patriote. Journal politique, littéraire et d'annonces du Puy-de-Dôme, Allier, Cantal et Haute-Loire: June 1831–Aug. 1835. Politics as above. BM Clermont-Ferrand.

La Semaine Vosgienne: Feb. 1831–March 1832. Orleanist. No copies extant.
La Sentinelle des Vosges: Feb. 1831–June 1833. *Mouvement*, later republican. BM Epinal incomplete. Consulted in the private collection of J. P. Janot (complete).
La Sentinelle du Jura: founded 1831. AD Jura.
Le Spectateur de Dijon: April 1830–1853. Conservative Orleanist. BM Dijon.

PRINTED WORKS

Aguet, J. P., *Contribution à l'histoire du mouvement ouvrier français: les grèves sous la Monarchie de Juillet, 1830–47* (Geneva, 1954).
Agulhon, M., '1830 dans l'histoire du XIXe siècle', *Romanticisme* 28–9 (1980) 15–27. Reprinted in M. Agulhon, *Histoire vagabonde II. Ideologies et politique dans la France du XIXe siècle* (Paris, 1988) 31–48.
Agulhon, M., *La république au village*. Translated as *The republic in the village* (Cambridge, 1970).
Alazard, J., 'La population ouvrière sous la Monarchie de Juillet', *Revue du Mois* (10 Nov. 1911).
Alazard, J., 'Le mouvement politique et social à Lyon entre les deux insurrections de novembre 1831 et d'avril 1834', *Revue d'histoire moderne* (1911).
Alazard, J. 'Les causes de l'insurrection lyonnaise de novembre 1831', *Revue historique*, CXI (1912).
Alexander, R. *Re-writing the French Revolutionary Tradition. Liberal opposition and the Fall of the Bourbon Monarchy* (Cambridge, 2003).
Ame, L., *Etude sur les droits de douanes et les traités de commerce* (Paris, 1867).
Aminzade, R., *Class, politics and early industrial capitalism. A study in mid-nineteenth century Toulouse* (Albany, New York: State University of New York Press, 1981).
Anderson, R., *Education in France, 1848–70* (Oxford, 1975).
Annuaire du Doubs (Besançon, 1835).
Aprile, S., Caron J-C and Fureix E. (sous la direction de) *La liberté guidant les peuples. Les révolutions de 1830 en Europe* (Seyssel, 2013).
Archives Parlementaires (2nd series). See Mavidal and Laurent.
Bagge, D., *Les idées politiques sous la Restauration* (Paris, 1952).
Balteau, J., *Dictionnaire Biographie Français* (Paris, 1933–)
Barbier, H., *Biographie du clergé contemporain*, 10 vols (Paris, 1840–51).
Barral, P., 'La franc-maçonnerie en Lorraine aux XIXe et XXème siècles', *Annales de l'Est* (1970) 3–39.
Barral, P., *Les Périer dans l'Isère au XIXe siècle, d'après leur correspondance familiale* (Paris, 1964).
Barrot, O., *Mémoires posthumes d'Odilon Barrot*, I (Paris, 1875).
Bastid, P., *Les Institutions Politiques de la Monarchie Parlementaire Française 1814–48* (Paris, 1954).
Baude, J. J., *De l'enquête sur les fers* (Paris, 1829).
Beck, T. D., *French Legislators 1800–34. A study in quantitative history* (Berkeley, California: University of California Press, 1974).
Bergeron, L. and Chaussinand-Nogaret, G., *Les masses de granit* (Paris, 1979).
Bezucha, R. J., *The Lyon Uprising of 1834* (Harvard, 1974).
Bezucha, R. J., *Modern European Social History* (Lexington, Massachusetts, 1972).

Biographie des députés de la chambre septennale de 1824–30 (Paris, 1826).
Biographie des députés, session de 1828 (Paris, 1828).
Biographie des préfets depuis l'organisation des préfectures jusqu'à ce jour (Paris, 1826).
Biographie impartiale des 221 députés (Paris, 1831).
Biographie impartiale des 221 députés, précedée et suivie de quelques documents curieux (Paris, 1830).
Biographie nouvelle et complète de la Chambre des Députés, contenant les députés nouvellement élus (Paris, 1829).
Biographie politique des députés, session de 1831 (Paris, 1831).
Biographie spéciale des pairs et députés du royaume, session 1818–19 (Beauce, 1819).
Biographie Universelle (Paris, 1823).
Blanc, L., 'Organisation du Travail' in J. A. R. Marriot, *The French Revolution of 1848 in its economic aspect*, vol. I (Oxford, 1913).
Blanc, L., *Révolution Française. Histoire de Dix Ans*, 5 vols (Paris, 1841–4).
Blanning, T. C. W., *The French Revolution. Aristocrats v. Bourgeois* (London, 1987).
Blanqui, A., 'Extrait de la relation d'un voyage au midi de la France pendant août et septembre 1828', *Archives historiques, statistiques et littéraires du département du Rhône*, IX (Lyon, 1828–9).
Bory, J. L., *La Révolution de Juillet* (Paris, 1972).
Bosson, *Notices biographiques* (Paris, 1889).
Bourgin, G., 'La crise ouvrière à Paris dans la seconde moitié de 1830', *Revue Historique* (1947) pp. 203–14.
Bourgin, G. and H., *Le régime de l'industrie en France, 1815–30*, 3 vols (Paris, 1912–41).
Bourloton, E., Cogny, G. and Robert, A., *Dictionnaire des Parlementaires Français*, 5 vols (Paris, 1889–91).
Brandt, A., 'Quelques aspects de la vie politique à Mulhouse sous la Restauration', *Bulletin de la société industrielle de Mulhouse*, 101 (1935) 341–66.
Braun, J. B. M., *Nouvelle biographie des députés ou Statistique de la Chambre de 1814 à 1829* (Paris, 1830).
Broglie, A. L. V. C. duc de, *Souvenirs*, 3 vols (Paris, 1886).
Bron, J., *Histoire du mouvement ouvrier français* (Paris, 1970).
Bulletin des Lois du Royaume de France, 9 série.
Buonarroti, P., *Conspiration des égaux, dite de Babeuf* (Brussels, 1828).
Cabet, E., *Histoire populaire de la Révolution française 1789–1830* (Paris, 1840).
Cabet, E., *La Révolution de 1830 et la situation présente* (Paris, 1831).
Cabet, E., *Ma ligne droite, ou le vrai chemin du peuple* (Paris, 1841).
Cahen, L., 'L'enrichissement de la France sous la Restauration', *Revue de l'histoire moderne et contemporaine*, V (1930) 178–207.
Calmette, A., 'Les carbonaris en France sous la Restauration', *La Révolution de 1848*, IX (1912–13); X (1913–14).
de Carné, L., *Des intérêts nouveaux en Europe depuis la Révolution de 1830*, 2 vols (Paris, 1838).
Caron, J.-C. *Trois jours qui ébranlèrent la monarchie* (Paris, 2010).

Bibliography 227

Carrel, A., *Histoire de la contre-révolution en Angleterre sous Charles II et James II* (Paris, 1827).
Chalmin, P., *L'officier français de 1815 à 1870* (Paris, 1957).
Chambre des Députés, Procès-verbaux des Séances de la Chambres des Députés.
Chaptal, J. A. C., *De l'industrie française* (Paris, 1819).
Charléty, S., *La Restauration* (Paris, 1921).
Charton, C., 'Souvenirs de 1814 à 1848', *Annales de la Société d'Emulation des Vosges*, XIV (1872).
Chaussinand-Nogaret, G., *La Noblesse* (Paris, 1976).
Chaussinand-Nogaret, G., *Une histoire des élites 1700–1848* (Paris, 1975).
Chernov, I. A., *Le parti républicain dous la Monarchie de Juillet* (Paris, 1901).
Chevalier, L., Classes laborieuses et classes dangereuses à Paris pendant la première moitié du XIXe siècle (Paris, 1958). Also in translation.
Church, C. H., *Europe in 1830* (London, 1983).
Church, C. H., *Revolution and Red Tape: the French Ministerial Bureaucracy 1770–1850* (Oxford, 1981).
Cobban, A., 'The myth of the French Revolution', inaugural lecture, University College, London, 1955; reprinted in A. Cobban, *Aspects of the French Revolution* (London, 1968).
Code Pénal, 12 fév. 1810. Les Cinq Codes de l'Empire (Paris, 1812).
Cohendy, M., *Mémoire historique sur les modes successifs de l'administration dans la province de l'Auvergne* (Clermont-Ferrand, 1856).
Collingham, H. A. C., *The July Monarchy. A Political History of France 1830–48* (London, 1988).
Collins, I., *The government and newspaper press in France, 1814–81* (Oxford, 1959).
Contamine, H., 'La Révolution de 1830 à Metz', *Revue d'histoire moderne*, IV (1931) 115–23.
Contamine, H., *Metz et Moselle de 1815–70*, 2 vols (Nancy, 1932).
Corbin, A., *Archaisme et Modernité en Limousin 1845–80*, 2 vols (Paris, 1975).
Cours des Pairs. Affaire du mois d'avril 1834. Rapport 1835, 4 vols (Paris, 1835).
Crook, M. (ed) *Revolutionary France 1780–1880*, OUP 2001.
Daumard, A., 'L'evolution des structures sociales en France à l'époque de l'industrialisation', *Revue Historique* (1972).
Daumard, A., *La bourgeoisie parisienne de 1815–48* (Paris, 1963).
Daumard, A. and Furet, F., 'Problèmes de méthode en histoire sociale', *Revue d'histoire moderne et contemporaine* (1964) 291–8.
Delabrousse, L., 'Les députés de l'Alsace sous la Restauration', *Revue Alsacienne* (1883–4).
Dentu, J. G. and Massy, P. F. M., *Biographie des Députés de la Chambre Septennale* (Paris, 1826).
Dolléans, E., *Histoire du mouvement ouvrier*, 3 vols (Paris, 1936–53).
Dollfus, E., 'Rapport sur les métiers à tisser à la mécanique, 30 oct. 1829', *Bulletin de la Société Industrielle de Mulhouse*, III (1830).
Dourille, J., *Biographie des députés de la nouvelle Chambre Septennale* (Paris, 1829).
Doyle, W., *Origins of the French Revolution* (Oxford, 1980).

Drumont, C., *La France Juive* (Paris, 1888).
Duguit, L. and Monnier, H., *Les Constitutions et les principales lois politiques de la France depuis 1789* (Paris, 3rd edn, 1915).
Dupeux, G., *Aspects de l'histoire sociale et politique du département de Loir-et-Cher, 1848–1914* (Paris, 1962).
Dupin, C., *Académie de Lyon, Archives historiques, statistiques et littéraires du département du Rhône*, X (Lyon, 1829).
Dupin, C., *Forces productives et forces commerciales de la France* (Paris, 1827).
Duroselle, J. B., *Les débuts du catholicisme social en France (1822–70)* (Paris, 1951).
Dutacq, F. and Latreille, A., *Histoire de Lyon de 1814 à 1940* in A. Kleinclausz, *Histoire de Lyon*, III (1952).
Dutens, J. M., *Essai comparatif sur la formation et la distribution du revenu de la France en 1815 et 1835* (Paris, 1842).
Duvergier de Hauranne, P. L., *Histoire du gouvernement parlementaire*, 10 vols (Paris, 1857–72).
Ellis, G., 'The Marxist interpretation of the French Revolution', *English Historical Review*, XCIII (1978) 353–76.
Ellis, G., *Napoleon's continental blockade: the case of Alsace* (Oxford, 1981).
Esler, A., '"Youth in revolt": the French generation of 1830', in R. Bezucha (ed.), *Modern European Social History* (1972).
Faiseau Lavanne, J. B. F., *Recherches statistiques sur les forêts de la France* (Paris, 1829).
Faucher, J. A. and Ricker, A., *Histoire de la franc-maçonnerie en France* (Paris, 1967).
Faure, E., 'Prendre la Bastille', *Projet, septembre–octobre* (1988) 5–9.
Fauré, H., *Galérie administrative ou biographie des préfets depuis l'organisation jusqu'à nos jours* (Paris, 1839).
Fitzpatrick, B., *Catholic royalism in the department of the Gard, 1814–52* (Cambridge, 1983).
Furet, F., *Interpreting the French Revolution* (trans) (Cambridge, 1984).
Furet, F., 'Le catechisme révolutionnaire', *Annales; Economies, Sociétés, Civilisations* (1971) 255–89.
Girard, L., *La Garde Nationale, 1814–71* (Paris, 1964).
Giraud-Mangin, M., 'Nantes en 1830 et les journées de juillet', *Revue d'histoire moderne*, VI (1931).
Gonnet, J. P., 'Esquisse de la crise économique en France de 1827–32', *Revue d'histoire économique et sociale*, XXXIII (1955) 249–92.
Gonnet, J. P., *Un grand préfet de la Côte-d'Or sous Louis-Philippe, 1831–40*. Dijon, *Société de Analecta Burgundica*, 1970.
Goujon, B. *Monarchies postrévolutionnaires 1814–1848* (*Histoire de la France contemporaine*, vol.2. Paris, 2012).
Guillon, P., *Les complots militaires sous la Restauration* (Paris, 1905).
Guizot, F. P. G., *Des moyens de gouvernement et des moyens d'opposition dans l'état actuel de la France* (Paris, 1821).
Guizot, F. P. G., *Histoire parlementaire de la France, recueil complet des discours prononcés par M. Guizot dans les Chambers de 1819 à 1848* (Paris, 1863–4).
Guizot, F. P. G., *Mémoires pour servir à l'histoire de mon temps*, 8 vols (Paris, 1856–64).
Harsin J. *Barricades. The War of the Streets in Revolutionary Paris, 1830–48* (Basingstoke, 2002).
Hartmann, M., 'The sacrilege law of 1825 in France: a study in anti-clericalism and myth-making', *Journal of Modern History* (1972) 21–37.

Haussez, C., baron de, *Mémoires du Baron d'Haussez, dernier ministre de la Marine sous la Restauration* (Paris, 1896–7).
Heron de Villefosse, A. M., 'Des métaux en France', *Annales des Mines* (1827) 401–620.
Heron de Villefosse, A. M., 'Mémoire sur l'état actuel des usines de fer de la France 1826', in J. G. V. de Moléon (ed.), *Recueil Industriel* (1827).
Higgs, D. C., *Nobles in Nineteenth Century France. The Practice of inegalitarianism* (Baltimore: Johns Hopkins University Press, 1987).
Higgs, D. C., *Ultraroyalism in Toulouse from its origins to the Revolution of 1830* (Baltimore: Johns Hopkins Press, 1973).
Higonnet, P-B., *Class, Ideology and the Rights of Nobles during the French Revolution* (Oxford, 1981).
Higonnet, P-B., 'La composition de la Chambre des Députés 1827 à 1831', *Revue Historique* (1968) 351–78.
de la Hodde, L., *Histoire des sociétés secrètes et du parti républicain de 1830 à 1848* (Paris, 1850).
Holyrood, R., 'The Bourbon army 1815–30', *Historical Journal*, *XIV* (1971), 3, 529–52.
Hopkin, D. *Voices of the People in Nineteenth-Century France* (Cambridge, 2012).
J. A. F. O., 'Mémoire dur l'état actuel des soieries en France', in J. G. V. de Moléon, *Annales de l'industrie manufacturière, l'agriculture et commerce*, vol. I (1827).
Johnson, C. H., 'The Revolution of 1830 in French Economic History' in Merriman, J. (ed.), *1830 in France* (New York, 1975) pp. 139–89.
Johnson, D. W. (ed.), *French society and the Revolution* (Cambridge, 1976).
Johnson, D. W., *Guizot. Aspects of French History 1787–1874* (London, 1963).
Jones, P. M., *Politics and rural society. The southern Massif Central c. 1750–1880* (Cambridge, 1985).
Kahan-Rabecq, M. M., *L'Alsace économique et sociale sous le règne de Louis-Philippe*, 2 vols (Paris, 1939).
Kent, S., *The Election of 1827 in France* (Massachusetts, 1975).
Kent, S., *Electoral procedure under Louis-Philippe* (New Haven, 1937).
Kerr, D. *Caricature and French Political Culture 1830–1848* (Oxford, 2000).
Koechlin, N., *Enquête Commerciale. Interrogation du Président du Chambre de Commerce de Mulhouse* (Mulhouse/Paris, 1835).
Labrousse, E., 'Comment naissent les révolutions', *Actes du congrès historique de centénaire de la Révolution de 1848* (1948). Reprinted in F. Crouzet, W. H. Chaloner and W. M. Stern, *Essays in European Economic History 1789–1914* (London, 1969).
Labrousse, E., Romano, R. and Dreyfus, F. G., *Le prix de froment en France au temps de monnaie stable 1726–1913* (Paris, 1970).
Lagarde, M. A., *Nouvelle biographie pittoresque des députés de la Chambre Septennale* (Paris, 1826).
de Lamartine de Prat, M. L. A., *Histoire de la Restauration*, 28 volumes (Paris, 1851–2).
Langeron, H., *J. Demontry, sa vie et sa mort* (Paris, 1850).
Lepage, H. and Charton, C., *Le département des Vosges, statistique, historique et administrative*, 2 vols (Nancy, 1845).
Leroux, P., *De la ploutocratie, ou gouvernement des riches* (Boussac, 1848).
Les justes alarmes de la classe ouvrière au sujet des mécaniques par un vieux typographe victime de l'arbitraire (Paris, 1830).

Leuilliot, P., *L'Alsace au début du XIXe siècle. Essai d'histoire politique, économique et religieuse, 1815–30*, 3 vols (Paris, 1959–60).
Levasseur, E., *Histoire des classes ouvrières et de l'industrie en France de 1789 à 1870*, 2 vols (Paris, 1867).
Levy-Leboyer, M., 'Innovation and business strategies in nineteenth and twentieth century France', in E. Carter (ed.), *Enterprise and Entrepreneurs in Nineteenth and Twentieth Century France* (Baltimore, 1976).
Lhomme, J., *La Grande Bourgeoisie au pouvoir 1830–80* (Paris, 1960).
Limouzin-Lamothe, R., 'L'émeute de St Germain l'Auxerrois d'après une relation inedite du chapitre metropolitain', *Etudes Franciscaines*, XIII (1963).
Limouzin-Lamothe, R., *Monseigneur de Quélen, archévêque de Paris son rôle dans l'église de France de 1815 à 1839 d'après les archives privées*, 2 vols (Paris, 1957).
Liste chronologique des maires de Dijon depuis 1789 (Dijon, 1888).
de Lomenie, E. Beau, *Les responsabilités des dynasties bourgeoises*, 4 vols (Paris, 1964).
Lullin de Chateauvieux, J. F., *Voyages agronomiques en France* (Paris, 1843).
Lynch, K. A., *Family, Class and Ideology in early Industrial France* (Madison, Wisconsin, 1988).
Lyons, M., *Le Triomphe du Livre. Une Histoire Sociologique de la Lecture dans la France du XIXe Siècle* (Paris, 1987).
Maitron, J., *Dictionnaire Biographique du Mouvement Ouvrier Français* (Paris, 1964–).
Manifeste de la Société des Amis du Peuple (Paris, 1830).
vicomte de Martignac, J. B. S. G., *Défense de M. le Prince Jules de Polignac* (Paris, 1831).
Martin, J. P., *La nonciature de Paris et les affaires écclesiastiques de la France sous le règne de Louis-Philippe* (Paris, 1949).
Marx, K., *The Class Struggles in France 1848 to 1850* (Moscow, n.d., translated from German edn, 1895).
Marx, K., *The Eighteenth Brumaire of Louis Bonaparte* (London, 1852, 1926).
Mater, A., 'Le groupement régional des partis politiques à la fin de la Restauration, 1824–30', *La Révolution Française*, XLIII (1902) 406–63.
Mavidal, M. J. and Laurent, M. E., *Archives Parlementaires de 1787 à 1860* (2nd series), 127 vols (Paris, 1888).
Maza, S. *The Myth of the French Bourgeoisie* (Camb. Mass., 2003).
Merriman, J., 'The demoiselles of Ariège, 1829–31', in J. Merriman (ed.), *1830 in France* (Franklin Watts: New York, 1975).
Mieg, M., *Relation historique des progrès de l'industrie commerciale Mülhausen et ses environs* (Mulhouse, 1823).
Ministère de l'Agriculture et du Commerce. Direction de l'Agriculture. Bureau des Subsistances. Récoltes des céreales et de pommes de terres de 1815 à 1876 (Paris, 1878).
Moniteur Universel.
Mounier, L., *De l'agriculture en France d'après les documents officiels* (Paris, 1846).
Newman, N., 'What the crowd wanted in the French Revolution of 1830', in J. Merriman (ed.), *1830 in France* (1975).
Oeschlin, J., *Le mouvement ultra-royaliste en France* (Paris, 1960).

Pagnerre, L. A., *Les hommes du mouvement et les hommes de la résistance. Biographie politique des ministres, de tous les membres de la Chambre des Députés* (Paris, 1831).
Parent, F., 'Les cabinets de lecture dans Paris; practiques culturelles et espace social sous la Restauration', *Annales*, 34 (1979) 1016–38.
Penot, A., *Recherches statistiques sur Mulhouse* (Mulhouse, 1843).
Perreux, G., *Aux temps des sociétés secrètes. La propagande républicain au début de la Monarchie de Juillet, 1830–35* (Paris, 1931).
comte de Peyronnet, P. D., *Discours de M. le comte de Peyronnet prononcé devant la cour des pairs, 19 décembre 1830* (Paris, 1830).
Pilbeam, P. *Saint-Simonians in Nineteenth-Century France: from Free Love to Algeria*. (Palgrave, 2014).
Pilbeam, P. M., 'The economic crisis of 1827–32 and the 1830 Revolution in Provincial France', *Historical Journal* (June, 1989) 319–38.
Pilbeam, P. *French Socialists before Marx. Workers, Women and the Social Question in France* (Teddington, 2000).
Pilbeam, P. M., 'The growth of liberalism and the crisis of the Bourbon Restoration', *Historical Journal*, XXV (1982) 2, 351–66.
Pilbeam, P. M., 'The "liberal" revolution of 1830', *Historical Research*, LXIII (1990) 151, 162–77.
Pilbeam, P. M., *The Middle Classes in Europe 1789–1914; France, Germany, Italy and Russia* (London, 1990).
Pilbeam, P. M., 'Popular violence in provincial France after the 1830 Revolution', *English Historical Review*, XCI (1976) 278–97.
Pilbeam, P. M., 'The "Three Glorious Days": the Revolution of 1830 in provincial France', *Historical Journal*, 26 (1983) 4, 831–44.
Pinkney, D. H., *Decisive years in France 1840–47* (Princeton, 1986).
Pinkney, D. H., *The French Revolution of 1830* (Princeton, 1972). Also translated into French as *La Révolution de 1830 en France* (Paris, 1988).
Pinkney, D. H., 'Les ateliers de secours à Paris (1830–31). Précurseurs des Ateliers Nationaux de 1848', *Revue d'histoire moderne et contemporaine*, 12 (1965) 65–70.
prince de Polignac, A. J-A. M., *Etudes historiques, politiques et morales* (Paris, 1845).
Ponteil, F., *Les Institutions de la France de 1814 à 1870* (Paris, 1965).
Ponteil, F., *L'Opposition politique à Strasbourg sous la monarchie de juillet* (Paris, 1932).
Porch, D., *Army and Revolution. France 1815–48* (London, 1974).
Pouthas, C. H., 'La reorganisation du ministère de l'intérieur et la reconstitution de l'administration préfectorale par Guizot en 1830', *Revue d'histoire moderne et contemporaine*, IX (1962) 241–63.
Price, M. *The Perilous Crown. France between Revolutions 1814–1848* (Basingstoke, 2007).
Price, R. D., 'The French army and the Revolution of 1830', *European Studies Review*, 3 (1973).
Raban, R., *Petite Biographie des Députés* (Paris, 1826).
Rabbe, Vielle de Boisjolin, St Preuve, *Biographie universelle et portative de contemporains*, 5 vols (Paris, 1834).
Rader, D. L., *The Journalists and the July Revolution in France* (The Hague, 1973).
de Remusat, C. F. M. (ed. C. H. Pouthas), *Mémoires de ma vie*, 3 vols (Paris, 1959).
Richardson, N., *The French Prefectoral Corps 1814–30* (Cambridge, 1966).
Robin, R., *La société française en 1789. Semur-en-Auxois* (Paris, 1970).
Rule, J. and Tilly, C., '1830 and the Unnatural history of Revolution',

Journal of Social Issues, 28 (1972) 49–76.
Sarrut, G. and St Edmé, B., *Biographie des hommes du jour*, 6 vols (Paris, 1834–43).
de Sauvigny, G. de Bertier, *Documents inédits sur la conspiration légitimiste de 1830–32* (Paris, 1946).
de Sauvigny, G. de Bertier, 'La conspiration des légitimistes et de la duchesse de Berry contre Louis-Philippe, 1830–32', *Études d'histoire moderne et contemporaine*, 3 (1951) xvii–125.
de Sauvigny, G. de Bertier, *La Restauration* (Paris, 1955).
de Sauvigny, G. de Bertier, *La Révolution de 1830 en France* (Paris, 1970).
de Sauvigny, G. de Bertier, *Le comte Ferdinande de Bertier et l'enigme de la congrégation* (Paris, 1948).
de Sauvigny, G. de Bertier, 'Quarante ans d'historiographie 1940–1980', 'Mille-huit-cent-trente', *Romanticisme: Revue du XIXe siècle*, 28–9 (1980) 69–84.
Sevrin, Abbé, *Les missions religieuses en France sous la Restauration 1815–30*, 2 vols (Paris, 1948, 1959).
Smith, B. G., *Ladies of the Leisure Class. The Bourgeoises of Northern France in the Nineteenth Century* (Princeton, New Jersey, 1981).
Spitzer, A. B., 'The elections of 1824 and 1827 in the Department of the Doubs', *French History*, 3 (1989) 2, 153–77.
Statistique Générale, Commerce Extérieure de 1787 à 1837 (Paris, 1838).
Sutherland, D. M. G., *France 1789–1815. Revolution and Counter-revolution* (London, 1985).
Taylor, G. V., 'Non-capitalist wealth and the origins of the French Revolution', *American Historical Review*, LXXII (1967) 469–96.
Taylor, G. V., 'Types of capitalism in eighteenth century France', *English Historical Review*, LXXIX (1964) 478–97.
Thiers, A., *La monarchie de 1830* (Paris, 1831).
Thompson, E. P., *The making of the English Working Class* (London, 1968).
Thureau-Dangin, P., *Histoire de la Monarchie de Juillet*, 7 vols (Paris, 1884–92).
Thureau-Dangin, P., *Royalistes et Républicains* (Paris, 1874).
Tilly, L., 'La récolte frumentaire, forme de conflit politique en France', *Annales: Economies, Sociétés, Civilisations*, 27 (1972) I.
de Tocqueville, A., *Recollections* (trans. G. Lawrence) (New York, 1971).
de Tocqueville, A., *The Old Regime and the French Revolution* (New York, 1955).
Trélat, U., 'La Charbonnerie', *Paris Révolutionnaire*, II (1838) 275–341.
Truchon, D., 'La vie économqiue à Lyon 1814–30', *Revue d'histoire de Lyon*, XI (1912).
Tudesq, A. J., *Les conseillers généraux en France au temps de Guizot 1840–48* (Paris, 1967).
Tudesq, A. J., *Les Grands Notables en France 1840–49. Etude Historique d'une Psychologie Sociale*, 2 vols (Paris, 1964).
Vatout, J., *Les aventures de la fille d'un roi, racontées par elle-même* (Paris, 1820).
Vatout, J., *La nièce d'un roi* (Paris, 1824).
Verronnais, F., *Annuaire du département de la Moselle* (Metz, 1831).

Vidalenc, J., *Le département de l'Eure sous la Monarchie Constitutionnelle 1814–48* (Paris, 1952).
Vigier, P., *La séconde république dans la région alpine, 1845–52* (Paris, 1963).
Villeneuve-Bargemont, J. P. A., *Economie politique chrétienne*, 2 vols (Paris, 1834).
Villermé, L. R., *Tableau de l'état physique et moral des ouvriers employés dans les manufactures* (Paris, 1840).
Vivier, R., 'Esprit d'opposition à Strasbourg sous la Monarchie de Juillet', *La Révolution Française* (1924) 230–47, 313–32 and (1925) 48–57.
Weill, G., *Histoire du parti républicain en France de 1814 à 1870* (Paris, 1900).
Weill, G., 'La Révolution de 1830 dans les départements', *Revue d'histoire moderne*, VI (1931) 289–94.
Weiner, D. B., *Raspail. Scientist and Reformer* (Columbia, 1968).

Index

Action Française 3
adresse of 221 deputies 33
Affre, archbishop of Paris 118
Aide-toi, le ciel t'aidera 2, 28–35, 72, 93, 96, 150–51, 152
Ain, department of 26
Alsace 15, 43, 71–2, 74
Amis de la Liberté de la Presse 28, 31, 94
Amis du Peuple 161–3
Angoulême, duc de 15, 114
Angoulême, duchesse de 71
anti-clericalism 23–5, 73–5, 92, 99, 103–7, 110–12, 119–20
arable land, price of 43
Arbois, commune of 71, 73, 74, 160, 164, 165, 167, 182
Ardennes, department of 51–2
Argenson, Voyer see Voyer d'Argenson
army 3, 17–18, 64, 69–70, 136, 167
article fourteen of constitution 86
artisans 8, 61–4, 74–5, 105–6
associations, laws on 92, 179–80
attroupements, law against 93, 158–9

Babeuf 20
bankruptcies 45–6
banquet campaign 90
Barrot, O. 31, 62, 112, 160
Bar-sur-Aube 69, 78, 137
Bas-Rhin, department of 68
Beaune, Côte-d'Or 154–5
Beck, T. 11
beggars 41
Belfort conspiracy 21–3
Belmas, bishop of Cambrai 118
Berri, duc de 16, 109–10
Berri, duchesse de 115–16
Besançon 67, 69, 71, 73, 74, 76, 137–8, 164
biens nationaux 24, 92
bishops 33–4, 73–4
Blanc, L. 8–9, 22, 63, 84, 132
Blanqui 9, 22
'*blessés de juillet*' 62
Bonapartism 18–22, 71, 83, 135–6, 147
Bordeaux, Henri duc de 110, 114
Bouchotte, E. 155, 164
Bourbon-Vendée 72
Broglie, duc de 31, 84

Buchez, P. 22
Buonarotti 20
bureaucracy 127–9, 147
bureaux de bienfaisance 42

Cabet, E. 8–9, 22, 62–3, 88, 97, 132, 167, 183
cabinets de lecture 32, 166
Calvados, department of 42
carbonari, see *charbonnerie*
Carrel, A. 31, 156, 158
Catholic Church 23–4, 73, 92, 99–100, 101–3, 107–9, 117–19
cereals 39
Chalons 165, 183
Chamber of Deputies 58, 134–5
Chamber of Peers 2, 88–9, 133
chambre introuvable 16
Chaper, A. 117, 140, 144, 185
charbonnerie 21–3
charcoal 47–8
Charles X 1, 15, 28–30, 34, 60–61, 102–3, 131, 188–9
Chateaubriand, F. 30–32
Chaumont, Haute-Marne 67, 74, 137
chevaliers de la liberté 23
children 41, 62
chouans 116
Clermont-Ferrand 70, 77
clock-making 55
coal 47
Cobban, A. 10, 126
commercial policy 39–40, 46–7
communal institutions 55–6, 167
compagnonnages 54
concordat 103
congrégation 101, 102
Constant, B. 13, 31
constitution, 1814 13
constitution, 1830 85–7, 89–90
Constitutionnel 30, 156
Côte-d'Or 142, 144, 176
cotton industry 49–53
councils, local 141–4
Courrier Français 31, 156
Cousin, V. 31
crieurs publics 166–7, 179

Daumier, H. 134

234

Index

Decazes, E. 15, 22
Delacroix, E. 62, 84
Devoir Mutuel, Lyon 54
Dijon 14, 67, 69, 71, 74, 106, 110–11, 137, 155, 163, 164, 165, 185
Doney, abbé 109
double vote, law of 16, 25
Doubs, department of 27, 68, 141–3, 151, 155, 176
Drapeau Blanc 31
Droits de l'Homme 162
droits réunis 44–5, 175
Dupont de l'Eure 22, 31
Duvergier de Hauranne, P. 31, 84

Ecole Polytechnique 62
education 102, 120
education law, 1833 119
Elbeuf 77
elections 25–7, 28–9, 34–5, 75–9, 87–8, 134–5
emigration à l'intérieur 112–17
Epinal 156

fabricant 53
Flaubert, G. 134
Fourier, C. 9
Forbes-Jansen, bishop of Nancy 105
Forest Code 172
franchise 13, 16
Fraysinnous, Mgr de 101
Frères des Écoles Chretiennes 100–1

Gallicanism 102
Gard, department of 74, 102, 105, 115, 172
Garnier-Pagès, E. 151, 168
Gazette de France 31, 114, 118
Gazette des Tribunaux 31
Genoude, abbé de 31, 114
Girod de l'Ain 104
Globe 6, 31, 61
grain trade 39–42
Guizot, F. 4–5, 20, 30–31, 142, 162, 179

Hartmann, F. 23, 105
harvest failure 40
Haute-Marne, department of 47, 69, 106, 176
Haut-Rhin, department of 26, 27, 67
Hernoux, E. 14, 32, 96, 143, 155
Hundred Days 14

Impartial 79
indemnification, law of 24–5
industry, rural 52–5

iron industry 47–9

Jesuits 31, 101–3
Jouffroy, T. 31
Journal de Commerce 31, 156
Journal de la Côte-d'Or 78
Journal des Débats 30
journalists, see press
judiciary 69, 136–9

Kent, S. 10
Koechlin, J. 21
Koechlin, N. 23

Labrousse, E. 37
Lafayette, marquis de 19, 22, 31, 65, 84, 91, 152, 155
Laffitte, J. 31, 64–5, 121–2, 153
Lamarque, general 152, 156, 160, 169
Lamennais, abbé de 118
land, subdivision of 39
leather industry 55
Lebert, N. 72, 105
legitimism 2–4, 109–18, 126
Leroux, P. 9–10, 22
liberals 14–15, 20, 24–30, 30–32, 34–5, 56–8, 64–5, 75–9, 80–83, 93–8, 148–9, 159–60
Lons-le-Saulnier 67
Lorient, Morbihan 174–5
Louis-Bazile, J. 96
Louis-Napoleon 20
Louis-Philippe 5–6, 65–6, 78–9, 83–6, 149
Louis XVIII 15
Lyons, Rhône 67, 72–3, 75, 77, 155, 165, 177–8, 180–81

Maistre, J. de 4
Marmont, duc de 64
Marrast 31
Martignac, vicomte de 2, 28–93, 48–50, 103
Marx, K. 1, 10, 37, 121, 125, 132–3
Marxists 125–6
masons 22
Mathieu (of Epinal) 156, 166, 180
Mauguin, F. 22, 61, 65, 71, 96, 152
Merville, V. de 14, 155
Metz 42, 67, 69, 71, 72, 140, 151–7, 160, 165
Meurthe 43, 140
Meuse, department of 27
Mirecourt, Vosges 46
missionary crosses 73, 105–7

236   Index

Missions de la France   23–4, 101
Montalivet, comte de   22
Moselle, department of   40, 77, 145
mouvement   5–8, 82, 89–90, 97, 145, 150–1
Mulhouse   49–53, 75

Nancy   73–4, 75, 105–6, 111, 181
Nantes   69
Napoleon   13–14
National   5, 31, 152, 156, 161, 166, 184
National Associations   90, 154–61
National Guard   17–18, 61–2, 72–3, 77, 91, 105–6, 110, 113–14, 155, 175, 178, 185
nationalism   90–91
newspapers, see press
Nord, department of   32, 39, 43, 56
notables   3, 88, 128–9, 133–5, 141–2

oath, loyalty   84–5
oath, allegiance   87
occupation, military   17
octroyée   85
ordinances, four   60–61
Organic Articles   100
Orleanists   1, 4–8, 66, 90–91, 94–8, 108–9, 112–14

papacy   102–3
paper-making   55
Paris   58–9, 63–4, 175–6
Pas-de-Calais, department of   42
Patriote Franc-Comtois   166, 184
patriotism, see nationalism
Périer, C.   5, 64–5, 113–14, 145, 154–5, 158–60, 178
petits seminaires   101, 103
Pichegru, general   71
Pinkney, D.   1, 11
Pire, de, general   160
Polignac, J. de   2
Populaire   166
population statistics   39
potato harvests   40–41
prefects   25–7, 60–79, 139–41, 147
press   30–33, 61, 78–9, 93–4, 158–9, 183–4
Protestants   23, 74, 92, 102, 105
Proudhon, P.   9
Puy-de-Dôme, department of   68, 75, 155

Quatretaillons   115–16
Quotidienne   31
Quelen, Mgr de   33–4, 92, 102

Raspail, F.   162, 169
Rémusat, C. de   6–7, 31
Republicans   8–11, 18–23, 71, 163–73, 183
résistance   5–8, 82, 94–8, 145
La Revue du Progrès Social   91
Revue Française   31
Rohan-Chabot, cardinal   102
Rouen   49–53
Royer-Collard   20, 29, 31
Rugles, Eure   178

sacrilege, law against   101
St Germain l'Auxerrois, sacking of   109–11
Saint Vincent de Paul   115
Salvandy, N. de   31
Saunac, G. de   97
Schonen, baron de   65
Scott, W.   149
Sémonville, marquis de   21
septennale   17, 25
Sentinelle des Vosges   156, 166, 184
Sieyès, abbé   122
silk industry   53–4, see also Lyons
Siméon   141
socialists   8–10
Spectateur   78
Stendhal   68, 124
Strasbourg   69, 71, 76, 164, 183

tariffs   41, 44–5, 46–7, 48–9, 52–3
Temps   31
Terror, White   14–16
textile industry   46–7
Thiers, A.   5, 31, 65, 112
Thionville   70
Thureau-Dangin, P.   8
timber prices   47–9
tobacco industry   43
Tocqueville, A. de   7, 16
Toupot de Bévaux, H.   108
trees of liberty   177
Trélat, U.   162, 167, 182
Tressé, abbé   108
Tribune des Départements   31, 166, 184
tricolore   61, 72

ultras   15–17, 30–31, 35–6, 101–3, 130–31, 188–9

Vatout, J.   97
Vendée   74
Vichy regime   3–4
Villèle government   24, 31

Villeneuve-Bargemont 118
Vosges, department of 26, 68, 142, 143, 164
Voyer d'Argenson 21

Weiss, C. 76

wheat, price of 40
wine industry 43–5
women 41, 51–2, 62, 119, 174–5
wood-stealing 74
wool industry 55
workers 50, 51, 53

The manufacturer's authorised representative in the EU is Springer
Nature Customer Service Centre GmbH, Europaplatz 3, 69115 Heidelberg,
Germany. If you have any concerns regarding our products, please
contact ProductSafety@springernature.com

Printed and bound by CPI Group (UK) Ltd, Croydon, CR0 4YY

23/03/2026

02076673-0017